WORLD
OF THE
UNEXPLAINED

WORLD
OF THE
UNEXPLAINED

CONTENTS

PSYCHIC
WORLDS

Share the secrets of those with astonishing
paranormal powers

Contents

Introduction

Do you sometimes feel you are psychic? Or do you know someone who definitely is? Psychics are capable of many different types of amazing mental feat, among them precognition (awareness that something will happen before it actually does); mind-reading (insight into what someone else is thinking); telepathy (making mental contact with another or others); the materialisation of objects or even the deceased, in ghostly form; and other seemingly paranormal phenomena.

A degree of psychic ability probably exists in most of us. But researchers have discovered that the most skilled of psychics often share similar physical characteristics – they tend to be hairy, bruise and bleed easily, and usually have a Rhesus negative blood group, for instance.

Such talents are sometimes presented purely for entertainment. Some clairvoyants, however, are able to put their powers to more positive use – perhaps as psychic sleuths, helping the police to detect missing persons when more 'normal' methods of investigations have proved unsuccessful.

Throughout this enthralling volume you will find numerous examples of the achievement and potential of the psychically gifted. It may also come as a surprise to you to learn that the views of a considerable number of scientists are no longer a million miles apart from the experiences of psychics. Indeed, the ability of some mystics to move backward and forward in time at will may not be that strange after all. It may even fit in quite neatly with the prevalent theory that our Universe is one without any past, present or future as such, except for that introduced by the observer.

Your journey into the spell-binding world of the psychic is about to begin. We trust you will enjoy it and find much to be marvelled at.

BORN TO BE PSYCHIC?

Are some people more likely to be psychic than others, simply because of their race or even their blood group? One theory suggests that being psychic could well be a matter of heredity.

A psychic is someone in whom extrasensory perception – telepathy, clairvoyance or precognition, for instance – shows itself at an unusually high level. A degree of *psi* (another term for psychic abilities) probably exists at some level in all humans, and is known to surface more easily when we are young. Indeed, small children often have a telepathic link with a brother or sister, and almost always have such a bond with at least one parent until, that is, more precise communication, through use of words, begins to develop.

Psychiatrist Dr Berthold Schwarz even recorded as many as 1,520 instances of *psi* among his own children, up to the time they were 15 years old. Schwarz concluded that telepathy among family members is much more frequent than has often been supposed; but, because telepathic communication is rarely of a significant nature, it passes unrecorded and without comment.

Another reason why this form of *psi* may go unnoticed is that we are often unaware that we are actually receiving information telepathically. Some years ago, researchers at Newark College of Engineering in New Jersey, USA, set out to prove this in the laboratory. Two volunteers were seated in different rooms: one was given a list of names, some but not all of which were relevant to the other sitter, who was wired to a machine that plotted changes in blood pressure.

Subconscious telepathy

When the experiment began, the one with the list was told to concentrate on the names in random order. It was shown that whenever a name came up that was known to the other sitter, the machinery to which he was connected registered a slight change in blood pressure. Importantly, he must have been receiving information at a subliminal level: at no point did the sender announce that he was thinking of a specific name; rather, the telepathic interaction was played out subconsciously.

Psychic awareness probably diminishes as a child learns how to speak and concentrate on a task in hand. As he grows older, he no longer allows himself to be distracted by a ticking clock or passing traffic; and, in the process of blocking out such irrelevant data, he may also unwittingly shut out information that he is receiving telepathically.

There are, however, various possible reasons why certain children seem able to retain psychic abilities into later life. A child who feels neglected or left out may, for instance, seek, cultivate and publicise *psi* as a way of attracting attention. He may also find that knowledge of some totally unexpected event can put him in the limelight in a most gratifying way. Certain factors, meanwhile, may influence the rate at which psychic awareness fades: its original intensity; the attitude towards psychic phenomena in the society to which the individual belongs; and the effects of climate, diet and day-to-day activity. Individual experiences may have a part to play, too. For example, someone who foresees an event in a dream may, thereafter, pay much more attention to all of his dreams, finding that nocturnal visions do indeed tally with subsequent events in the waking world.

Intriguingly, *psi* does occur much more often in some groups than in others – notably gypsies, Celts and Basques, among whom, oddly and perhaps significantly, Rhesus negative blood is found with unusual frequency.

An attempt to link *psi* with physiological characteristics was made by French researchers in the 1960s. They suggested that mediums tend to have a good deal of hair, to bruise and bleed easily, and to suffer from weak ligaments. American psychologist Dr W. H. Sheldon also investigated a possible link between physique and the psychic personality.

Sheldon studied the physique of a vast number of subjects, and found that human body types can be described in terms of three main somatotypes – the endomorph, the mesomorph and the ectomorph. Some people, however, do not fall neatly into any of these categories but are a mixture of the three, to some degree.

The typical endomorph is physically plump and emotionally a good mixer; he enjoys comfort, food, drink and social events, and needs company when he is unhappy. Most significantly, the endomorph is predominantly extrovert, and extroverts tend to be more successful than introverts in parapsychological experiments. Other traits that appear to be associated with the high scorer in ESP tests include warmth, sociability, cheerfulness and enthusiasm. (Interestingly, this evidence seems to contradict that presented by mystics who claim that isolation and fasting heighten *psi*.)

The mesomorph, according to Sheldon, also tends to be extroverted, has an athletic, muscular build, and is tough, quick, alert and adventurous. Parapsychologists have discovered that people with these characteristics also seem to do remarkably well in ESP tests.

At the other end of the Sheldon scale are the ectomorphs – those with thin, bony physiques who tend to be tense, excitable, timid, withdrawn and prone to depression. They frequently do badly in laboratory tests of ESP. What remains unclear, however, is whether or not introverts have more spontaneous experiences of ESP.

Electrical disturbances

Another characteristic of the psychic in both primitive and civilised cultures may possibly be disturbances in the electrical functioning of the brain, notably those brought about by epilepsy, once regarded as a 'sacred disease'. It is a belief that continues among certain peoples of the world. When anthropologist Adrian Boshier went to live among the primitive tribes of South Africa, for example, he was accepted by them largely because he had epileptic seizures. Interestingly, too, the well-known medium Leonora Piper (1857-1950) was also seen to be afflicted by what were called 'small epileptiform seizures' just before going into a trance. Further evidence comes from a paper by the American parapsychologist William G. Roll that appeared in the *European Journal of Parapsychology* in 1978. Entitled *Towards a Theory of the Poltergeist,* it suggests that epilepsy may be connected with poltergeist activity, and that a particularly lively example of the phenomenon may be equivalent to a *grand mal* fit.

The ideas, customs, beliefs and assumptions of the particular social group into which a child is born and brought up will undoubtedly affect his development in every way. A marked degree of paranormal cognition may also be accepted and rationalised. In ancient Greece, for example, in Japan at one time (where there was an official Ministry of Divination until the mid-19th century), and in Africa even today, a child's curious gift may be respected and cultivated. In a pre-eminently industrial civilisation, meanwhile, it may be rejected as fraud or lunacy. Elsewhere, opinion may be uncomfortably divided, especially where no distinction is made between psychical and spiritual activities, or the paranormal and the supernatural.

Free spirits

The part played by the physical environment in determining *psi* is difficult to pin-point. But psychic ability does seem to emerge more often in nomads than among settled peoples, perhaps because the former tend to lead unstructured lives, free from bounds of order and routine, which makes them more relaxed and receptive. Certainly, studies since the turn of the century give the impression that *psi* is more likely to occur in subjects who are relaxed, conscious attempts to induce it seemingly self-defeating.

This could be why certain subjects tend to perform badly under laboratory conditions. The controlled environment obviously puts a strain on the person under investigation, whether or not he is known to have psychic abilities, and may influence results. For example, subjects tend to perform best when they are in a happy mood. A good relationship with the parapsychologist, when a feeling of mutual trust exists, is also productive. In telepathy experiments, the relationship between the sender and the receiver would appear to be influential, too. Studies also suggest that subjects who go into the laboratory expecting to produce negative results usually do badly, while those with a positive attitude to *psi* tend to score more highly. One study has even concluded that telepathy may occur most frequently on nights of the full moon.

Spontaneous psychic experiences, as opposed to those that occur under laboratory conditions, are also influenced by state of mind, though since most accounts are anecdotal, the exact conditions that precipitate the phenomenon are more difficult to pin down. Someone who is rather tired, resigned, with low blood pressure and in the stage between waking and sleeping seems more prone to extrasensory impressions than someone who is awake, alert and concentrating on a particular matter. We also seem more likely to experience *psi* when we have just emerged from meditation – a fact that tallies both with clinical studies and personal experiences.

Those who both recognise and value extrasensory perception can, and often do, stimulate it by using meditation and other psychophysical techniques such as yoga and deep breathing. Rhythmic singing, drumming, chanting and dancing may also be used, as they frequently were by those who were anxious to increase their psychic powers in ancient times.

Diet, too, may have a part to play. Vegetarianism is allegedly valuable in the cultivation of psychic powers, yet many groups in which *psi* seems to be unusually common – Eskimos, Bushmen, and Australian Aborigines – are hearty carnivores. In the 1950s, too, researchers discovered that a marked absence of calcium (and possibly of sugar) in a diet may cause the subject to become prone to visions.

Virgin talents

Sex and sexuality may also influence psychic powers. Traditionally, the scryer – the young person employed to see visions in water or a crystal ball – had to be a virgin who had not yet reached puberty. In the same way, it was popularly believed that mediums lost their powers after marriage. However, this was certainly not the case with the great Victorian medium D. D. Home.

Another theory, put forward in 1914 by Edward Carpenter in his book *Intermediate Types Among Primitive Folk,* suggests that a homosexual temperament may be conducive to psychic development. It could indeed be that this kind of personality, sensitive to the feelings and problems of both sexes, experiences a profound uncertainty about his or her own orientation, which in turn makes him or her more sensitive and receptive to *psi.*

Different motives will, of course, fuel the desire to develop paranormal powers: scientific curiosity, a sense of vocation, a craving for fame, reverence, money or power. Some people, though, do not actively seek *psi;* they have it thrust upon them. Thus, the fasting hermit, seeking silence and solitude for prayer, may find himself distracted by telepathic impressions which he may not be able to ignore.

Whether a psychic experience is welcome or unwelcome, whether it is cultivated or repressed, and whatever are the many factors that may influence it, a lot more research needs to be carried out before firm conclusions can be drawn concerning either its nature or its source. But perhaps one of the most significant possibilities to have emerged so far is that, to varying degrees, we may all be capable of *psi.*

THE GREATEST MEDIUM OF THEM ALL

The extraordinary phenomena produced by the medium Daniel Dunglas Home suggest that he was endowed with the most amazing psychic powers.

If the paranormal feats attributed to the medium Daniel Dunglas Home were genuine, then they immediately raise questions about the true potential of Man and his interaction with others. For, more than any other medium, D.D. Home furnished the most remarkable proof of bizarre abilities – such as bodily elongation, psychokinesis and incombustibility. Impossible though they sound, these phenomena were so well-attested by impeccable witnesses that surely only the most hidebound sceptic would refuse to consider what their implications might be, both for science and for society.

One such phenomenon was touched upon by E. B. Tylor, later to become the first professor of anthropology at the University of Oxford, in his book *Primitive Culture*. He was struck by the similarities between the phenomena that Home and other 19th-century mediums were producing and those that were being reported by travellers and missionaries to be occurring among 'savages' (as people of primitive cultures were then described), and asked:

'Do the Red Indian Medicine Man, the Tartar necromancer, the Highland ghost-seer and the Boston medium share the possession of a belief and knowledge of the highest truth and import which, nevertheless, the great intellectual movement of the last two centuries has simply thrown aside as worthless?'

Savage accusations

Wherever tribal communities were studied, the same kind of phenomena as those witnessed at Spiritualist seances were being reported. Tylor could hardly believe it; but he had to admit that what scientists had regarded as bringing enlightenment, through the purging of old superstitions, just might have entailed the *loss* of important faculties. If so, Tylor concluded, 'savages' who had been dismissed as degenerate may 'turn on their accusers and charge them with having fallen from the high level of savage knowledge'.

Home appeared repeatedly to demonstrate that he had somehow rediscovered the ancient abilities that shamans and witch doctors possessed, such as incombustibility. Firewalking had often been reported by travellers: the shaman, followed by members of the tribe, would be seen progressing unscathed across white-hot stones or glowing ashes.

But Home's feats were even more remarkable than that. When the eminent Victorian scientist William Crookes invited him to be the subject of a series of experiments, Home began by showing how he could influence a spring balance from a distance, and then went on literally to play with fire. He first stirred the burning coals in the grate with his hand; then, taking up a red-hot piece of coal that was nearly as big as an orange, and covering it with his other hand, he blew on it until it was nearly white hot.

On a less alarming level, Home used to hold a finger in a candle flame to demonstrate that it would not scorch as long as he remained in his entranced state. Significantly, this was a trick often performed by stage hypnotists at the time. Volunteers from the audience would be called for; and those who were susceptible to hypnotism would be put into a trance and made to behave in eccentric ways for general amusement. But such shows raised some serious points, and the protection that hypnosis could give from both burns and the accompanying pain was one of them.

Later, when hypnotism became recognised by the academic world as a reality – instead of an occult superstition, traded upon by rogues – psychologists found that a degree of incombustibility could be provided, so long as a deep enough trance state was entered into by the subject. Thus it seemed that Tylor's 'savages' had indeed possessed knowledge of great importance, but which had been brushed aside by the outside world as so much 'mumbo-jumbo'.

Home also demonstrated a range of phenomena that tied in with miracles frequently reported in connection with the lives of saints. As the young Lord Adare reported after a seance in 1867: 'Standing there beside me, Home grew, I should say, at least six inches [15 centimetres].' Elongations of this kind were quite often reported by witnesses at Home's seances – just as they had been commonly reported of holy men in their trance states throughout history.

Tongues of flame

On another occasion, Adare's friends, Charles Wynne and the Master of Lindsay – Lindsay, a notable scientist, was soon to be made a fellow of the Royal Society – saw tongues of flame projecting from Home's head. 'We all then distinctly heard, as it were, a bird flying round the room, whistling and chirping,' Adare noted. 'There then came the sound of a great wind rushing through the room; we also felt the wind strongly.' In his trance, Home spoke to them in a strange language, before explaining that the manifestations had been designed to show them a repeat performance of the phenomena associated with the first Pentecost (when the Holy Spirit entered the Apostles in the form of tongues of flame).

At the time of Home's greatest fame, not only had paranormal phenomena of all kinds been rejected by orthodox scientists, but the miracles of the saints had been singled out for particular derision. It was assumed they were the product of fallacious memory, coupled with superstitious awe, worked upon craftily by the clergy who would benefit if their nominee were canonised, for then their church or monastery would become a shrine.

Home's career, therefore, provided a link between the reports of phenomena witnessed by explorers and anthropologists, and the descriptions of the feats of the saints. Certain aspects of his career also accorded with the reports of the early mesmerists – some of whom had subjects who, in their trance states, developed psychic powers. Other aspects tied in with the reports of poltergeist cases, which presented many similar features – including apports (objects that seem to materialise out of nowhere, sometimes to dematerialise again, only to reappear elsewhere).

It is worth recalling the astonishing range of phenomena that Crookes encountered in his five years of research with mediums – most of them with Home, whom he greatly admired and trusted. Crookes listed: movement of heavy bodies with contact, but without physical pressure; currents of air; changes of temperature [these were not subjective: but registered on a thermometer]; percussive noises [sometimes raps, sometimes faint scratchings, sometimes detonations]; alteration in the weight of objects; movement of furniture with no contact;

levitation of furniture with no contact; levitation of Home himself; movement of articles at a distance; tunes on musical instruments which nobody was playing; luminescences; materialisations [in Home's case, often of hands]; direct writing [hands, visible or invisible, taking up pens to write messages]; phantoms; demonstrations of intelligence that could not be attributed to the medium; and apports.

Curiously, Crookes forgot to include incombustibility in his list, although he had been present when Home exhibited this extraordinary gift on more than one occasion.

Crookes had also witnessed some of these strange abilities under trial conditions. Alteration of the weight of objects, for example, had been accomplished while investigators used a gadget that made it impossible for Home to exert any physical pressure. This test and its successful outcome were also witnessed by William Huggins, a fellow of the Royal Society (who was later to become its president), and a lawyer, Serjeant Cox.

Crookes designed another entertaining test specifically to find if Home could play an accordion by psychic force in circumstances that ruled out any possibility of physical contact. A cage was insulated with copper wire, and the accordion put into it. Home was permitted to hold it by the end furthest from the keys; and as it was possible to see through the mesh of the cage, he could not have reached down to touch the keys without the witnesses noticing. Thus, if the accordion were to play, it would play paranormally.

Amazingly, the accordion did soon begin to play; and Crookes' assistant reported that its bellows were expanding and contracting, although Home's hands could be seen to be perfectly still. Crookes said: 'The sequel was still more striking, for Mr Home then removed his hand altogether from the accordion, taking it [his hand] quite out of the cage, and placed it in the hand of the person next to him. The instrument then continued to play, no person touching it, and no hand being near it.'

Crookes was not the first scientist to investigate Home. On one of his visits to Russia in the mid 19th century, Home met Julie de Gloumeline at the court of the Tsar. It was love at first sight for both, and she was soon to become his second wife. Her brother-in-law was Alexander von Boutlerow, a celebrated Russian scientist, and he took the opportunity to make what may reasonably be considered the first truly scientific trial of a medium.

One of the little games that Home used to play with sitters was to ask them to try to move a table when they had ordered it not to move: their united efforts would fail to cause it to budge – though seconds later, when they told the table it could now float, they found they were able to lift it with ease. Might this be an illusion? Boutlerow proceeded to investigate, using specially constructed scales. The table weighed in at 100 pounds (45 kilograms), but with Home's fingertips lightly touching the tabletop – in good light – the scales recorded that the table dropped to 30 pounds (14 kilograms) whenever it was instructed to be 'light', and showed a gain of up to 150 pounds (68 kilograms) when it was instructed to be 'heavy'.

Reliable witnesses

In almost every respect, the evidence that Home demonstrated remarkable psychic powers is clear. Indeed, if the testimony of scores of men and women of intelligence and standing counts for anything, we must accept that he not only actually performed the feats they described, but performed them week after week, year after year. Nobody has even attempted to replicate them and show how they could have been done by sleight of hand – or, as Home did them, in good light, unfamiliar surroundings and unaided.

The famous stage magician Maskelyne toured with a 'D. D. Home act'; but according to Thomas Augustus Trollope – in those days, better known as an author than his brother Anthony – it was a travesty. Trollope had not liked Home when he had met him as a young man, but he had never doubted that his feats were genuine. Maskelyne's, he insisted, bore no resemblance to them.

But could Home have in some mysterious way hypnotised his sitters, thus providing them with the illusion of levitation and other extraordinary phenomena? This was often suggested, no doubt in desperation, by people who did not want to accept him as a genuine psychic, but who realised that the charge of conjuring could not be made to stick. In fact, there is no hard evidence that this type of group illusion works.

Hard-line sceptics still maintain that what Home allegedly did was contrary to the laws of nature, and therefore impossible. However, much of what scientists once regarded as laws have since proved to be mutable: at the atomic level, they are endlessly being broken.

We do not yet know why psychic forces should operate through a medium such as Daniel Dunglas Home. But the evidence is surely far too strong for their reality – and potential significance – to allow the timidity of academics or the rancour of sceptics to block research in this area any longer.

This illustration shows Edward Kelley raising the dead in the churchyard of Walton-le-Dale in Lancashire. Kelley won the confidence of John Dee with his psychic skills, which are recounted on page 77.

Daniel Dunglas Home, right, as you will discover on page 20, was a notorious Victorian medium who claimed all kinds of supernatural powers. On one occasion, under test conditions, he even 'played' the accordion, top, whilst it was placed in a copper cage.

In this detail from a work by El Greco, both St Francis and St Andrew seem to demonstrate the curious phenomenon of bodily elongation. D. D. Home, too, is said to have been able to produce this phenomenon. Indeed, in 1867, Lord Adare reported that Home once grew six inches (15cm) in front of him.

On page 103, we ask if it is really possible for the human mind somehow to travel back and forth in time. The disastrous voyage of The Titanic, above, for example, is known to have been the subject of many premonitions.

OBEYING THE INNER VOICE

Many of the world's great leaders – Abraham Lincoln, Winston Churchill and Franklin Roosevelt, among them – all believed in psychic power. So to what extent might international politics have been influenced by ESP?

Winston Churchill was entertaining three of his ministers at 10 Downing Street during World War II, when he suddenly had a strong premonition. An air-raid had begun, but the dinner party continued without interruption, as the British Prime Minister suddenly rose and went into the kitchen where the cook and a maid were both working next to a high plate-glass window.

'Put dinner on a hot-plate in the dining room,' Churchill instructed the butler. Then he ordered everyone in the kitchen to go to the bomb shelter. The Prime Minister returned to his guests and his dinner. Three minutes later, a bomb fell at the back of the house, totally destroying the kitchen.

Churchill's intuitive powers were evident throughout his life and he learned to obey them. But it was during wartime that their influence was at its most dramatic.

In 1941, for instance, Churchill made a habit of visiting anti-aircraft batteries during night raids. Once, having watched a gun crew in action for some time, he went back to his staff car to depart. The near-side door was opened for him because it was on that side that he always sat. But for some reason, he ignored the open door, walked round the car, opened the far-side door himself, and climbed in.

Minutes later, as the car was speeding through the darkened London streets, a bomb exploded close by. The force of the blast lifted the Prime Minister's vehicle on to two wheels, and it was on the verge of rolling over when it righted itself. 'It must have been my beef on that side that pulled it down,' Churchill is said to have remarked.

Later, when his wife questioned him about the incident, Churchill at first said he did not know why he had sat on that side of the car that night. But then he added: 'Of course I know. Something said "Stop!" before I reached the car door held open for me. It then appeared to me that I was told I was meant to open the door on the other side and get in and sit there – and that is what I did'.

What the British prime minister had done was to listen to the 'inner voice' that we usually refer to as intuition or a hunch, and heed its advice. He knew from experience that he could trust it, just as many top executives have learned to be guided by ESP in making business decisions.

Other statesmen, too, have at times been guided by intuition, or have allowed the psychic talents of others to guide them. Indeed, the influence of the paranormal may well have shaped the destinies of several of the world's nations.

Spiritual messages

Many believe, for instance, that American slaves owe their emancipation to the intervention of a teenager, Nettie Colburn Maynard, who gave spirit messages to Abraham Lincoln. While in trance, young Nettie is said to have lectured the President for an hour on the importance of freeing the slaves. Lincoln also attended other seances, at one of which he and his bodyguard are reported to have climbed on to a piano. Despite its load, it then lifted off the ground, until the tune being played by a medium, Mrs Miller, was finished.

When a newspaper, the Cleveland *Plain-dealer*, published a fascinating story about some of Lincoln's alleged psychic experiences, he was asked if it was true. 'The only falsehood in the statement', said the President, 'is that the half of it has not been told. This article does not begin to tell the wonderful things I have witnessed.'

No one knows how much the paranormal influenced the great Canadian statesman, William Lyon Mackenzie King, but his diaries certainly show that he had very distinct beliefs and was convinced that the spirits of dead politicians were regularly in touch with him. Whenever he visited England, he always consulted top mediums – among them Geraldine Cummins who was particularly well-known for her automatic writings. Franklin D. Roosevelt also consulted the psychic Jeane Dixon, known as the 'Washington seer'.

Star-struck first lady

But, while some world leaders have based decisions purely on hunches, others in the corridors of power believe they are guided by higher forces. Nancy Reagan, wife of the former US President, Ronald Reagan, is among those who believe fervently in the value of astrology. In her early days as a Hollywood film actress, she often consulted astrologers, even attending evening astrology classes.

Later, she found support for her occultish interests in her actor-husband, Ronald. Taking advice from an astrologer on the most propitious time for his installation as governor of California in 1967, Reagan insisted on taking the oath of office in the middle of the night – at 12.16 a.m. to be exact – while facing west.

Governor Reagan continued to show an interest in all things astrological. Whenever he flew to Washington, DC, for example, he met with the well-known astrologer Jeane Dixon who repeatedly promised him that he would eventually get to occupy the White House. (The Reagans dropped Dixon when she – correctly – refused to predict Ronald as President in 1976.)

Nancy Reagan's reliance on the stars reached its zenith during her husband's presidency (1980-1988). As America's First Lady, she would secretly spend hours each week on a three-way telephone link-up with San Francisco astrologer Joan Quigley and a presidential assistant, coordinating the President's movements in and out of the White House according to a zodiac chart.

If the stars predicted a good day, Reagan's appointments could be kept; if a bad day was in store, and there was a chance the President could be harmed, an alternative date would be proposed.

Sometimes, however, much to Nancy's fury, Reagan's advisers could not deter him from going out spontaneously – say, to a baseball game – when the stars advised against it. So great a trust did she have in astrology that she even had President Gorbachev's chart drawn up during the 1985 Geneva summit.

In 1987, the stars were again brought in to direct the President's schedule. After he had undergone prostate surgery in January, astrologers told Nancy that her husband should stay out of the public eye for 120 days. Said Joan Quigley: it was the 'malevolent movements of Uranus and Saturn' which 'were in Sagittarius' that kept Reagan hidden in the White House.

There are times, too, when ordinary citizens have premonitions about what presidents are going to do. In 1971, for example, a Brooklyn, USA, toy manufacturer, Herbert Raiffe, had a hunch that toy pandas were going to be good-sellers. There was no logic behind the decision he made. Nevertheless, he ordered that panda production should be increased severalfold at his factory.

In February of the following year, President Nixon visited China, toured the Forbidden City, and returned to America with a gift of two much-publicised pandas. No one was better placed to meet the sudden and unexpected demand for cuddly replicas than Raiffe, whose intuition seems to have tuned into an aspect of the President's China mission, long before the visit had even been arranged.

In America and Europe, the police use psychics at times to help them solve serious crimes or find missing people. Psychics have even been able to guide archaeologists to the sites of long-buried ancient remains. And around the world, the ability of dowsers to locate subterranean water supplies and other resources is well documented. So why should we find it so odd that eminent men in the political arena are also prepared to open their minds to information which comes to them in a way that by-passes normal sensory channels?

Not that it is always helpful to know what the future holds. Abraham Lincoln, for example, awoke one day, having had a vivid dream. In it, he had heard the sound of sobbing and had followed it, through the White House, until he reached a room where he found a coffin that was draped with the American flag. Lincoln, in his dream, asked a soldier who had died. 'It's the President,' came the reply. 'He has been assassinated'.

Days later, Lincoln was dead... killed by an assassin's bullet. The President's dream, it seems, had been a truly prophetic one.

A GREAT RUSSIAN MYSTIC

One of the giants of 19th-century occultism was undoubtedly Madame Blavatsky, whose 'paranormal' feats were, however, often regarded with suspicion.

In 1850, the American painter A.L. Rawson, who was engaged in leisurely journeyings through the more picturesque countries of the Mediterranean, arrived in Cairo. He recorded that he was fascinated by the city, its permanent inhabitants and most of all, the floating population of Bohemian cosmopolitans who had made it their temporary home. He was particularly intrigued by a certain Madame Blavatsky, who claimed to be a Russian princess, habitually dressed as an Arab, regularly smoked hashish, and took an active interest in the occult.

On one occasion, claimed Rawson, together with a friend, she visited Paulos Metamon, a Coptic (Egyptian Christian) magician, and asked him for instruction, saying: 'We are students who have heard of your great learning and skill in magic and wish to learn from you.' Paulos Metamon replied: 'I perceive that you are two Feringhees [Europeans] in disguise and I have no doubt that you are in search of knowledge. I look for money.' At this point, the interview came to an abrupt end.

There can be no certainty that Rawson's story was not invented. The 20-year-old Madame Blavatsky may indeed have been studying magic in Cairo, but she was undoubtedly a woman whose character was such that improbable stories were widely told about her.

Tall stories

Blavatsky herself complained about such legends in a letter dated March 1875: 'There is not a day that some new story about me does not come out in the papers. Blavatsky was in Africa and went up with Livingstone in a balloon. Blavatsky was in the Sandwich Islands and dined with the cannibal King. Blavatsky converted the Pope of Rome to Spiritualism; she predicted to the Emperor Napoleon his forthcoming death; she cured the Queen of Spain's facial warts by means of Spiritualism – and so on... They say that I have spent several days at Salt Lake City, and have induced Brigham Young to renounce polygamy.'

It is symptomatic of the utter confusion and controversy that always surrounded Madame Blavatsky that more than one person believed that she herself was responsible for the dissemination of such remarkable stories. Nevertheless, it has to be admitted that the plain facts about Madame Blavatsky's life

41

were quite as extraordinary as any invented legends about her.

She was born in the Ukraine in 1831, Helena Petrovna von Hahn, the daughter of a Russian army officer of German extraction. In 1849, she married General Blavatsky, the Vice-Governor of Erivan, but soon ran away to lead a wandering life – at first, according to her cousin Count Witte, as a bareback rider in a circus. Subsequently, she contracted a bigamous marriage with the opera singer Metrovitch, and there is reason to believe that she bore him a child. Her life with Metrovitch was interrupted by many quarrels and temporary estrangements.

On one occasion, she left him to become an assistant to D.D. Home, undoubtedly the most remarkable Spiritualist medium of his time; and later, she contracted a trigamous marriage, this time to an anonymous Englishman, whom she rapidly deserted. But the marriage of Madame Blavatsky and Metrovitch ended in July 1871, when they were passengers on the steamship *Eumonia* which suffered a boiler explosion and then sank. Metrovitch perished; but Madame Blavatsky survived, having been picked up by a passing freighter and landing in Egypt.

Now a wandering medium, always poor, and continually hoping for the patronage of the wealthy, in 1873 she made her way to New York – wearing a red shirt, chainsmoking the cigarettes that she dextrously hand-rolled, sleeping in a hostel for 'working girls' and earning a precarious living by making artificial flowers.

Escape from this dreary existence came about through her acquaintance with Colonel Henry Olcott, a Spiritualist lawyer and journalist whom she first met at the Vermont farm of the Eddy brothers, the most famous of the many mediums who were active at the time. The occult wonders that took place at the farm were (if the accounts given by Madame Blavatsky, Colonel Olcott and many others can be believed) truly remarkable.

Here, for example, Madame Blavatsky not only saw the spirit of her dead father materialise in a form so solid that she could actually touch him, but had a conversation with him in Russian, and was presented by him with a medal that she claimed had been buried with him in his grave. But the account she published of this was to lead to great controversy, for it was asserted that it was not in fact Russian practice to bury medals with a soldier's body and that Madame Blavatsky had invented the whole story as a way of publicising her own supposed mediumistic abilities.

Olcott, however, was greatly impressed by what he referred to as 'the spiritual miracles' he saw at the Vermont farm, and noted that they increased in number and dramatic appeal whenever Madame Blavatsky was present. He attributed this to what he believed were her mediumistic powers. She was, he considered, an altogether remarkable person; and he listened with fascination to tales of her occult adventures in Russia and Mongolia, hypnotised by what he described as her 'mystical blue eyes'. She, in turn, was attracted by his undoubted kindliness and generosity. He certainly gave her a good deal of financial support in the early years of their friendship, her exact needs being indicated to him by the spirit world, which regularly materialised instructional letters on to his desk or into his pocket. Somehow, the Russian seeress was always about on these occasions; but Olcott's faith in his friend never wavered at all.

An evil spirit weds

There followed another illegal marriage, this time to a young Armenian named Michael Bettanelly. Fortunately, the couple soon parted. Her husband's sexual habits, claimed the unhappy Madame Blavatsky, were quite insufferable – she had agreed to marry him, so she said, only after he had promised that there would be no physical relationship.

In any case, she claimed, it was not really she who had entered into the marriage, but an evil spirit that had temporarily possessed her.

On 7 September 1875, Olcott and Madame Blavatsky – or H.P.B. as her friends now called her – attended a lecture on the subject of the occult significance of the Egyptian pyramids. Olcott was fascinated, particularly by the lecturer's claims that spirits could be evoked to physical appearance by the use of geometrical formulae, and scribbled a note to his friend: 'Should not a society be established for the study of these things?' Only 13 days later, Madame Blavatsky was describing the new society to a correspondent:

'Olcott is now organising the Theosophical Society in New York. [The noun 'theosophy', literally meaning 'divine wisdom', was a 17th-century synonym for mystical religion. Blavatsky and Olcott's adoption of it for the Spiritualistic system they taught was totally unjustified and has led to much confusion.] It will be composed of learned occultists ... and of passionate antiquaries and Egyptologists generally. We want to make an experimental comparison between Spiritualism and the magic of the ancients by following literally the instructions of the old Cabbalahs... I have for many years been studying Hermetic philosophy in theory and practice, and am every day coming to the conclusion that Spiritualism in its physical manifestations is nothing but... the astral, or starry, light of Paracelsus... '

The 'experimental comparisons' were somewhat odd, to say the least. On one occasion, the early Theosophists applied a mild electric current to a cat, causing it to rise some way into the air. They decided that this proved that levitation was an electrical phenomenon and increased the power of the current, hoping that the animal would achieve weightlessness, but it suddenly expired.

With members engaging in such tomfoolery, it is not surprising that the infant Theosophical Society failed to attract new members and that, two years after its foundation, it had almost expired. It was restored to life, however, by the publication in 1877 of Madame Blavatsky's *Isis Unveiled*, a study of the occult that, so Olcott claimed, was inspired by astral visions. He wrote: 'Her pen would be flying... when she would suddenly stop, look into space with the vacant eye of the clairvoyant seer... and begin copying on her paper what she saw.'

Blavatsky unveiled

Whatever the source of the text of *Isis Unveiled*, there is no doubt that it is, at first sight, impressive. It gives the impression that its author was a woman of immense learning and wisdom, and the possessor of a secret knowledge known only to a few. But in reality, Madame Blavatsky's learning was not as profound as it sounds. W.E. Coleman, an American scholar, pointed out that no less than 2,000 passages in *Isis Unveiled* were plagiarised from other books, and he argued that readers of the book had been misled into thinking its author was: '... possessed of vast erudition; while the fact is her reading was very limited, and her ignorance was profound in all branches of knowledge.'

In spite of the extent and verbosity of *Isis Unveiled* – Madame Blavatsky never used one word when she could use six, never wrote a sentence when she could write a paragraph – the basic doctrines taught in the book are simple enough.

First, it was asserted that the physical and mental phenomena of the Spiritualists' seance rooms – everything from table turning to raps and the materialisation of departed spirits – had all been known to the great philosophers and religious teachers of the ancient world. Many of these, so it was claimed, had themselves been powerful mediums, in touch with far more 'advanced spirits' than those contacted by modern Spiritualists. Through studying the lives and teachings of these ancient seers, it would become possible for 19th-century mediums to receive 'spiritual communications' of a higher nature than were normally available to them.

Secondly, it was stated that the old alchemical and magical treatises, seeming gibberish to modern readers, revealed under a veil of symbolism many scientific and spiritual truths of tremendous significance. Those possessing the 'keys' of initiated understanding – and the pages of *Isis Unveiled* strongly hinted that Madame Blavatsky was among them – could unlock the doors that would lead to a treasure house of wisdom, beauty and truth.

Thirdly, it was strongly suggested, although never openly stated, that Madame Blavatsky had been entrusted by some secret organisation of spiritual 'supermen' with the task of reviving the old spiritual truths and introducing them to the industrial world of the 19th century.

Isis Unveiled was a modest success and there was a revival of public interest in Madame Blavatsky and her Theosophical Society. Then, in the following year, D.D. Home published a book in which he told a number of hostile and unpleasant stories about her. These proved so upsetting that Olcott and Madame Blavatsky decided to go to India: 'I want to go,' she wrote, 'where no one will know my name.'

Teatime apport

In India, the Theosophical Society also met with considerable success, making many converts among both English expatriates and native Indians. The most important of the former was A.P. Sinnett, a well-known journalist, who was converted to Theosophy by a number of supposedly miraculous, but very probably fraudulent, phenomena produced by Madame Blavatsky – among them, the apport of a missing cup and saucer at a picnic. Supposedly, this had been magically precipitated by the Mahatmas (or Masters), immortal 'supermen', living in the Himalayas, whose pupil and servant Madame Blavatsky claimed to be.

Not surprisingly, some of the new Theosophists desired to be put in touch with the Mahatmas and to be accepted as their pupils. Sinnett decided to write them a letter, did so, and asked Madame Blavatsky to pass it on to them. A week or so later, he received a reply, which mysteriously appeared on his desk, from someone who claimed to be 'the Mahatma Koot Hoomi'. A lengthy exchange of letters followed. Sinnett would write out his questions on a wide variety of occult subjects – the occult nature of the Moon, spiritual evolution, the nature of the Masters themselves, the lost continent of Atlantis, and so on – and send them (always via Blavatsky) to the Mahatmas. In due course, he would receive detailed replies.

On the basis of the information that was given in these letters, Sinnett wrote *Esoteric Buddhism,* a lengthy book outlining a complex occult system that involved spiritual evolution through reincarnation, a hierarchy of Masters, 'the secret government of the world', and a hidden wisdom available only to a few.

Occult wonders

Esoteric Buddhism and *The Occult World,* another book by Sinnett that was largely concerned with 'miraculous' phenomena of the teacup variety, sold well and soon several branches of the Theosophical Society came into existence in England, France and other European countries.

Then, in 1884, Blavatsky and Olcott journeyed to Europe to visit their new disciples. In London, they called upon the Society for Psychical Research (SPR) and, along with Indian Theosophists, gave evidence of the occult wonders they had witnessed. As a result, the SPR decided to send out an investigator to India and prepare a report about the nature of the miracles.

The report, when it came, was devastating. The 'miracles', it was asserted, were fraudulent, the product of clever conjuring tricks performed by Madame Blavatsky and some of her closest associates; and the Mahatma letters were said to have been forged by Blavatsky, their mysterious 'precipitation' due to having been dropped through gaps in the ceiling rafters. As for Blavatsky herself, the report was damning: 'We regard her neither as the mouthpiece of hidden seers, nor as a mere vulgar adventuress; we think she has achieved a title to permanent remembrance as one of the most accomplished, ingenious and interesting impostors of history.'

Madame Blavatsky spent most of the few remaining years of her life in England, lecturing to her still numerous followers, writing copious occult articles, essays, explanations and an enormous book, *The Secret Doctrine,* which is a treatise on, and elaboration of, the system outlined in Sinnett's *Esoteric Buddhism.* Her practices were criticised by many; yet, the society she founded has survived, and still flourishes. Indeed, there have been, and are, many thousands who have sought to come to a better understanding of the mysteries of existence through a study of Madame Blavatsky's extensive later writings.

WAS HOUDINI
PSYCHIC?

*To his audiences, Houdini was a superman; to
mediums, a scourge; and to Sir Arthur Conan
Doyle, a man who went out of his way to deny
his strange gifts. What was the real nature of the
Houdini enigma?*

The notion that Houdini worked real magic, rather
than sleight-of-hand, seemed preposterous to most of
those who knew him, especially in view of his frequent
and savage attacks on mediums who purported to be
able to create materializations, or to move objects at a
distance by their powers. But circumstantial evidence
may often be very strong, and Sir Arthur Conan
Doyle proceeded to present it in order to prove his
theories about Houdini, believing him to be one of
the greatest physical mediums of all time.

   Doyle did not, however, dispute that Houdini was
'a very skilful conjurer'. What marked him out from
his fellow conjurers were not his remarkable feats as
an escapologist – extricating himself from ropes,
chains and padlocks while in a sealed coffin
suspended in the air or dunked in the sea, for instance
– but the sheer speed with which he was able to
perform them and, even more, the fact that he was

able to repeat them, time and again, when the slightest slip would almost certainly have meant injury or even death. Many conjurers have since sought to explain Houdini's tricks; but although many have claimed to repeat the more dangerous feats of the legendary Houdini, not a single one has actually done so.

Some of the alleged evidence that Houdini *was* indeed a medium came from mediums; some from people who knew him; and some from incidents in his life that can be explained away as chance, but may actually have been psychic.

The first category, perhaps the weakest, largely consists of stories, such as that told by Hewart Mackenzie in his *Spirit Intercourse.* Mackenzie claimed that Houdini actually dematerialized himself during one of his performances: Houdini had been submerged under water in a locked container on stage, but reappeared, dripping, a mere minute-and-a-half later from a different part of the stage. Mackenzie elaborated: 'While the author stood near the tank during the dematerialization process, a great loss of physical energy was felt by him, such as is usually felt by sitters in materializing seances who have a good stock of vital energy, as in such phenomena, a large amount of energy is required.'

Perhaps Houdini had indeed drawn upon psychic energy, but almost certainly he did not do this in order to dematerialize: he may simply have been concentrating all his faculties on the accomplishment of his trick. And there is evidence that he was aware of this. Indeed, an English journalist, H.L. Adam, described how, 'before a trance, while Houdini was waiting at the side of stage ready for his "turn", he sat in his chair, threw his head back, closed his eyes, and appeared plunged in the profoundest meditations.' Houdini had been talking to Adam, when he suddenly broke off and sank into this state. Then, after about 10 minutes, Adams claimed, 'he continued his conversation with me as though nothing had intervened.'

Houdini himself made no secret of his skilful breath control. In 1926, a few months before his death, he took up a challenge to remain under water in a sealed container for over an hour, with no air intake – and he succeeded. His method, he told the press, was to take deep breaths before the box was closed, and then to relax, while continuing to breathe rhythmically.

His fellow conjurers simply did not believe him. One of them, Joseph Rinn, was sure that there must be a false bottom to the container, or that Houdini had somehow managed to extract air from the emergency line that was attached to it. Irritated, Houdini insisted that he had given the true explanation, and that there was no gimmick.

Houdini also insisted that he had not been 'in a cataleptic state' – a sly reference to the 'Egyptian miracle man', Rahman Bey, who also allowed himself to be sealed up in a container, as well as lying on beds of nails and performing other feats that are generally associated with Indian fakirs. What Houdini did not know, however, was that the deep breathing exercises he indulged in are, in fact, one of the traditional methods of inducing a trance state. They are also widely used in yoga; but because yoga, in those days, was classified as an 'occult' practice, he could not risk his reputation by admitting that he employed it.

Lucky breaks

Nevertheless, Houdini admitted that he had an 'inner voice'. This, he explained to Doyle, was 'independent of his own reason or judgment', and told him what he could and could not do, adding that 'so long as he obeyed the voice, he was assured of safety'. To Doyle, the voice was a psychic manifestation, but not to Houdini, who simply regarded its promptings as 'lucky breaks'.

Houdini was occasionally involved in seances at which inexplicable phenomena occurred; and he did not even attempt to deny the fact, though he usually claimed that there must have been some 'natural explanation'. At a table-turning seance in a Long Island country house, the home of the New York lawyer Bernard Ernst, for example, a table levitated. Ernst at first assumed that this was Houdini rising to the occasion, but he later realized, after due consideration, that Houdini could not have used trickery; and Houdini himself repudiated the charge. This was not as improbable as it may sound, in view of Houdini's detestation of Spiritualism: he did not care to be associated with it in any way. Even the great conjurer Maskelyne (who, like Houdini, rejected Spiritualism and endlessly satirized mediumship in his act) made an exception for 'table-turning' because he happened to have had first-hand experience that it was genuine.

Conan Doyle himself was given one or two intimations of Houdini's psychic powers, much to the magician's embarrassment. On one occasion, following a demonstration of automatic writing, Houdini offered to try his hand at it. He took up a pencil and, without conscious effort, wrote one word. 'Then he looked up at me, and I was amazed, for I saw in his eyes that look, impossible to imitate, which comes to the medium who is under the [psychic] influence.' Doyle looked at the paper: the word was 'Powell' – and Doyle's friend Ellis Powell had just died. 'Why, Houdini, Saul is among the prophets!' Doyle cried. 'You are a medium!' Houdini, disconcerted, muttered under his breath only that he knew somebody called Powell who lived in Texas.

There was also the celebrated occasion when Houdini gave what he claimed was a bogus seance for President Theodore Roosevelt on board ship. Roosevelt wrote down the question: 'Where was I last

Christmas?': the answer was to be written by 'psychic' means on a slate. Houdini obtained the correct reply that the President had been in South America (a fact not generally known).

At the time – as usual – Houdini declined to give an explanation, beyond insisting that it was a trick. But later, according to his biographer Harold Kellock, he did offer an explanation. He had, he said, collected information in advance – not just for the President, but for other people he knew would be on board. It was his own suggestion, Houdini asserted, that the 'seance' should be held; he had also written the answers on prepared slates, and had merely substituted them for the slates upon which the sitters thought the 'spirits' were writing.

So far, so good; but even Conan Doyle – though his detective work at seances was notoriously poor – realized that one question remained unanswered: how did Houdini know in advance that the President was going to ask that particular question, so that he would be prepared with the answer?

By themselves, Doyle's stories about Houdini's psychic powers are suggestive rather than convincing. Some simply indicate that Houdini was skilled at tricks that, though actually simple to perform, would be regarded as 'miraculous' – until, that is, the explanation was divulged. Thus, Houdini was not particularly impressed when he heard about the game that Gilbert Murray, Regius professor of Greek at

Oxford University and President of the League of Nations Union, used to play together with his family and friends.

Murray would go out of the room while they chose a subject, and then come back and tell them what they had chosen. His record was astonishing: over a period of years, one out of three of his guesses would be 'hits' and another third near-misses, though the subjects he was set ranged from episodes in novels to events he had never even heard of.

Houdini claimed he could do the same trick, and invited a distinguished audience – the publisher Ralph Pulitzer, financier Bernard Baruch and newspaperman Walter Lippmann, among others – to test him.

While they chose a subject in one room of Houdini's New York home, Houdini was shut up in a crate in a room two floors above, and the door guarded. Yet he, too, got three out of four of the subjects more or less right. This prompted Doyle to cite it as one of many indications that 'Houdini possessed that psychic sensibility which is the ground work of mediumship.' Not so: Houdini had instructed his brother always to repeat whatever subject was chosen, aloud – and the room was 'bugged'. He had simply listened in his upstairs confinement. But 'bugging' was new; so new, in fact, that, even five years later, it had not crossed Doyle's mind as a possible explanation for Houdini's 'hits'.

Yet some of the evidence that Houdini may have had psychic powers comes from sceptics. In *Houdini: The Untold Story,* Milbourne Christopher, himself a magician and one of the founder members of the notoriously sceptical Committee for the Scientific Investigation of Claims for the Paranormal (CSICOP), described an incident that took place during Houdini's tour of Britain in 1920, with Houdini in the unaccustomed role of the sorcerer's apprentice.

Request for a sign

One of Houdini's first British engagements was at the Empire Theatre in Edinburgh. It was here, in the 1900s, that his old friend the Great Lafayette had been burned to death, shortly after his beloved dog, which had been a gift from Houdini, had died. Houdini and his wife Bess went to visit the cemetery where Lafayette and the dog were buried, taking pots of flowers to put on the grave; and by Houdini's own account, he was prompted to say 'Lafayette: give us a sign you are here!'

Apparently, Lafayette did just that. According to Christopher, the pots overturned, 'as if a spirit hand swept them to the ground'; and when Houdini set them upright, they crashed again. 'This time they fell with such force that the pots broke,' Houdini wrote: 'it was all very strange.' However, he recovered himself, attributing the phenomenon to the high wind at the time. A photograph of the Houdinis at the graveside clearly shows Bess' coat being tugged open by the wind.

Joseph Rinn, who collaborated with Houdini in his campaign against mediums in the 1920s, was also to recall in his book, *Sixty Years of Psychical Research*, that Houdini had described one occasion in his career when he was – apparently – beaten by a European locksmith, who had trapped him in a device that he was unable to open. But, just as he despaired, 'the lock, without any help from me, sprung open.'

But if Houdini had so many intimations of his psychic powers – no matter how vague – why would he so vehemently have denounced those mediums who were trying to demonstrate them?

Partly it was for the very reason that he himself advanced: he loathed the way in which bogus mediums exploited grief by purporting to provide communication from deceased loved ones. But there was, perhaps, a simpler reason. To admit to having psychic powers would have destroyed his chance of achieving his life's ambition: to become recognized as the greatest magician the world had ever known. It was an ambition that he succeeded in achieving. And although he died in 1926, Houdini's name remains a household word. He is still the greatest escapologist of them all.

PSYCHIC DETECTION

Clairvoyants are sometimes called upon to help detect missing persons, as described in the following account.

Pat McAdam, a Scottish teenager, went missing while on a journey home on 19 February 1967. She was one of the 3,000 or so people who disappear in Great Britain every year. Most of these are found again – either dead or alive; but Pat was one of the five per cent who are not. The search for this particular missing girl had one remarkable feature – detective work by the renowned Dutch clairvoyant and psychic sleuth Gerard Croiset.

Croiset was introduced to the case by a Dumfries journalist, Frank Ryan of the *Daily Record*, who had covered Pat's mysterious disappearance and the police investigation right from the beginning. When, by chance, he was in Holland, he decided to visit Gerard Croiset in Utrecht. This meeting, in 1970, and Croiset's subsequent work with Ryan, form the basis of one of the psychic's most striking cases.

The Dumfries CID had been able to reconstruct Pat McAdam's last recorded movements fairly easily. Pat was 17 years old and worked in a local knitwear factory. She and a friend, Hazel Campbell from nearby Annan, had decided to go to Glasgow on Saturday, 18 February. They took the bus to Gretna and then hitched a lift into Glasgow. The two girls then spent the day shopping. Hazel bought clothes and shoes, and they both bought black patent leather handbags.

Pat and Hazel also met some young people over a drink and went to the Flamingo dance hall. Just before midnight, the girls went to a boy's house where there was a party going on; and they stayed on there after the party was over.

Early the next day – Sunday, 19 February – the girls set off for Central Station, where they washed before catching the bus to London Road. There, they did not have to wait long before a lorry stopped to offer them a lift. At about 11.30, the driver pulled into a café at the Star service station at Lesmahagow, 20 miles (32 kilometres) from Glasgow on the A74 road. The girls were hungry and Pat ate a hearty meal, consisting of a hamburger, eggs and beans.

Hazel was tired and left to grab some sleep in the cab of the lorry, while the driver and Pat drank whiskies in the café. Later, the three continued their journey south. Hazel dozed, while Pat and the driver chatted together. At Kirkpatrick Fleming, the lorry swung off the A74 towards Annan, and the girls realised that the driver was leaving his route to take them home. Hazel was dropped outside the

Cooperative Stores in Annan just as the town clock showed 2 p.m. From that moment, no one has heard a word from Pat McAdam.

Police description

On Tuesday, 21 February, Pat's parents, Mary and Matthew McAdam of Lochside Road, Dumfries, went to the police station to report their daughter's disappearance. Pat's description was issued: it read 'Patricia Mary McAdam, born 25.6.49, medium build, fresh complexion, brown eyes, dark hair cut in a "Mia Farrow" style'.

The police learned that she had been wearing a purple coat over a black and silver woollen dress that was low-cut and sleeveless. She had black suede shoes, a yellow cardigan, and a green and red headscarf. Mrs McAdam said Hazel had assumed that the lorry had dropped Pat at home before continuing south to Hull, the driver's destination.

The police suspected that Pat may have intended to leave home and would get in touch, sooner or later, with her family. But as time passed, it became clear that Pat had not run away. She was very interested in clothes – yet she left a complete wardrobe behind. She enjoyed a good time – yet she left £47 in cash at home. She did not take her national insurance card and has never applied for a replacement.

The police enquiry hinged on tracing the lorry driver. Despite a nationwide appeal, it took three weeks to find him. He claimed that he had dropped Pat on the outskirts of Dumfries, but had no idea what had become of her. Since the driver was the last person known to have seen Pat alive, efforts were concentrated on establishing the lorry's movements after it left Annan.

Witnesses came forward, and eventually its route was reconstructed. After setting out on the A75 to Dumfries, the lorry turned off and took the narrow B7020 towards the village of Dalton. The lorry was large – a 26-tonne articulated vehicle. It blocked the narrow lanes, and local people remembered seeing just such a lorry manoeuvring north of Dalton, near Williamwath Bridge. It could have been on its way to the Birkshaw Forest and the A74, leading towards the south. The police continued to appeal for witnesses: 'Will any person who saw a motor lorry on 19th February anywhere in Dumfriesshire or the adjoining areas, in any unusual circumstances – for instance, stationary in a lay-by or on a quiet country road – please communicate immediately with the police.'

The same day, 17 March, police with tracker dogs combed the undergrowth in the Dalton area but found no clues.

The Regional Crime Squad in Glasgow joined the hunt on 20 March. The *Daily Record* distributed posters and leaflets throughout the country, and the lorry driver faced more interviews with the police. Pat's father expressed fears that something terrible had happened to his daughter, and the police were prepared to accept that it had. The rest of the month saw increased digging in the lonely woodlands and river banks of the search area.

During April, there were responses to the posters but they produced no leads; and despite television appeals by Mrs McAdam, nothing was heard from Pat. Detective-Inspector Cullinan, in charge of the investigation, said he believed the secret of Pat's disappearance lay hidden in the Dalton area. He begged the villagers to rack their brains to recall any odd happenings on that fateful Sunday in February. The Dumfries police force held regular press conferences, an unusual event in missing persons cases, and they dug regularly for Pat's body between Annan and Dumfries.

Frank Ryan, the journalist, had all this in the back of his mind when he happened to find himself in Holland in 1970, three years later. Ryan knew that the Dutch clairvoyant Gerard Croiset had been involved in the hunt for Muriel McKay, a Fleet Street newspaperman's wife who had been kidnapped in 1969. Her body was never found, and it was conjectured that her corpse had possibly been cut up and fed to pigs. Croiset was involved in the case only to the extent that relatives of the missing woman had asked him to help.

On 16 February 1970, Frank Ryan arrived in the town of Utrecht to talk to Gerard Croiset at his home at 21 Willem Zwigerstraat, where he had small consulting rooms and an office. Ryan explained that he was interested in a missing girl. He showed Croiset the poster bearing Pat's picture and said she had gone missing three years earlier. Croiset interrupted, not wishing to be told any more. Just two questions, he said, needed answering. Was the girl happy at home? And where was she last seen?

Ryan answered and indicated the general area of south-west Scotland on a map that he had brought along. Croiset paused and then said he 'saw' a transport café. This, he explained, had significance in the story. Next, Ryan indicated, with the map, the area between Annan and Dumfries where Hazel had last seen Pat. Concentrating on the area in more detail, Croiset said that he 'saw' a place where there were fir trees and exposed tree roots on the banks of a river. He described vividly how water had undermined the banks. Near there, he said, was a flat bridge over the river, with grey tubular railings. Ryan would find this bridge, he was told, at the foot of a hill. If he crossed the bridge, Croiset continued, he would come to a cottage. The building was now being used for some other purpose than as a residence, for it had advertising signs on it. Round the cottage would be found a white paling fence, Croiset added.

He now rapidly sketched the hilly setting on large sheets of notepaper, which he gave to Ryan, and then instructed Ryan not to publish anything until he had found the site and photographed it. Ryan returned to Dumfries in a state of some excitement and set off with a local photographer, Jack Johnstone, to the search area.

Hair-raising sight

Croiset seemed to have been describing the Williamwath Bridge, near Dalton. But to Ryan's dismay, the bridge, though flat, was not in the setting the Dutchman had described. However, Jack Johnstone recalled that there was a bridge in Middleshaw, about 3 miles (5 kilometres) away. Ryan had not been aware of this, as there had been no reports of the lorry there. However, as they drove towards it, Frank Ryan's hair stood on end.

It was exactly as Croiset had described. The bridge, lying at the foot of a hill, had grey tubular railings. Ryan searched for a particular detail that Croiset had predicted and sketched – bent railings, with a kink in the handrail. In fact, none of the rails was bent, but Johnstone photographed a wire fence attached to the bridge that drooped in exactly the way that the Dutchman had pictured.

Could this have been the bridge in Croiset's vision? They looked for other details, and soon found that the river bank was indeed undermined, and that tree roots were exposed.

There was also a building, carrying advertising signs and surrounded by a white fence, a short distance up the road from the bridge. As Croiset had described, the hills were covered in fir trees.

Ryan decided to tell Mrs McAdam what he was doing. He also explained that Croiset needed to make contact with something belonging to Pat and, borrowing the girl's Bible, set off for Utrecht.

Croiset was delighted when shown the photographs. 'This is what I saw!' he exclaimed. He was very impressed with the accuracy of his vision and was now even more determined to help Ryan.

When handed Pat McAdam's Bible, however, Croiset said bluntly: 'She's dead.' With no hesitation, he told Ryan she had been buried in the area he had 'seen'. The body lay hidden, he said, in a sort of cave made by the tree roots in the river bank. Ryan pressed for more details and Croiset said he would try to 'see' clothing belonging to the girl. Ryan's large-scale map was produced, and Croiset showed him where to look. At a point marked 'Broom Cottage', Ryan would find a car with a wheelbarrow beside it. Later, the interpreter clarified this: he told Ryan that it was, in fact, only part of a car – a wreck with a wheelbarrow leaning against it.

After this detailed briefing, Ryan returned to Dumfries, determined to collect witnesses before his next visit to the area. The bridge that figured so clearly in Croiset's first vision crosses a river called the Water of Milk, west of Middleshaw; and the car in the second vision was predicted to be three-quarters-of-a-mile

(1 kilometre) downstream. Ryan told his wife and another journalist just what he was hoping to find, and the party set off for Broom Cottage.

Accurate prediction

There, in the garden of Broom Cottage, exactly as Croiset had described it, was an old green Ford Popular with no wheels, being used as a henhouse. An old wheelbarrow was leaning against the boot. It was an electrifying experience for the search party. Later, Frank Ryan emphasized that he had never been near Broom Cottage in his life and therefore could not be persuaded that he had managed to transfer, unconsciously, an image of the scene to Croiset. He also felt he now had proof that Gerard Croiset was using some form of power quite beyond the normal .

Ryan wrote up the story for the *Daily Record* and told his friend Detective-Inspector Cullinan exactly what had happened. That night, Sunday, 15 February 1970, Ryan and two detectives returned to the spot to search for clothing. Croiset had been right. The remains of a black dress, parts of a handbag, and a stocking were found, caught in the undergrowth on the river bank.

These discoveries made front page news, and local people waited impatiently for the police to announce developments. When these came, however, they were disappointing. No trace of Pat's body had come to light, and the clothing had been eliminated from the enquiry. The long-sleeved dress was apparently not Pat's, and the other articles, along with a quantity of rubbish, were merely debris deposited by floodwater. It seemed that three years after Pat's disappearance, there was to be no dramatic discovery.

Ryan now returned again to Utrecht to explain the setbacks. Croiset was a trifle disappointed but explained that, when he was focusing on a scene, he could not be sure that the details he 'saw' would help the police. He was pleased, however, with the new photographs and saw them as encouraging proof that he had indeed received a vision of a place he could never have seen with his own eyes.

Far from being discouraged, Croiset proceeded to give Ryan a description of the man that the police should question. He was, he said, aged between 32 and 34, about 5 feet 4 inches (1.63 metres) tall and dark-haired, with one ear larger than the other. Croiset claimed to have a mental image of Pat taking a walk with this man before she died. They strolled near an area where trees had been felled, and her body was nearby, he said.

On 19 February, Ryan conducted seven interviews with Croiset, each one adding a little to the picture that the clairvoyant was painting of Pat's last hours. Forestry workers confirmed that there had been felling in recent years, and Mrs McAdam recalled giving Pat £5 to buy a new dress. Croiset was still convinced that the dress found by Ryan *was* Pat's –

not the one she had been wearing but one she had bought. The police, however, had no evidence of Pat having bought a dress in Glasgow: Hazel had bought clothes but, she insisted, Pat had bought only the handbag.

Lost at sea?

Hopes of finding more clues in the area were dashed by a heavy snowfall, and there were no developments until the end of the month. The *Daily Record* realised that they had a strong story on their hands, and flew Gerard Croiset to Scotland to visit the scenes he had described. Accompanied by the head of the local CID, he spent a day touring the area.

Croiset had never been to Scotland before, but was sure of everything he had told Ryan. He was also convinced that Pat had been murdered, and claimed that her body had been dumped in the Water of Milk. After being lodged in tree roots, he said, it had been swept away to sea. If this is true, her body will probably never be found.

Five years later, in 1975, a BBC Television team carried out its own investigation into the Pat McAdam case. Interviewed in Utrecht, Croiset was able to recall the case clearly from the notes he had made at the time. He believed there had been a complete triumph for his clairvoyance, as a friend had told him, misleadingly, that the police search had produced a body.

A corpse had indeed been found in the area, but it was not identified as Pat's. In a routine search, the remains of a woman had been found in a pond. She was in her forties, wore a wedding ring and had coins in her possession dating from after Pat's disappearance.

The person who, as far as is known, saw Pat last – the lorry driver – did not shed any more light on it. Subsequently, he was sent to prison to serve two concurrent life sentences for offences involving other people: one sentence was for murder, the other for crimes including rape and attempted murder. The judge recommended that he be detained in prison for at least 30 years.

Despite the fact that his visions did not lead to Pat McAdam being found, either alive or dead, Gerard Croiset maintained that this case stood as one of his most successful, and he clung to this belief until his death in 1980, at the age of 71.

How, then, did Croiset score his 'hits'? Could Frank Ryan unwittingly have transmitted images of the search area to him? All the pertinent facts of the case were in Ryan's mind and Croiset may have 'read' them somehow.

Typical Croiset cases are full of images of drowning. In the Netherlands, the canals claim as many victims as the roads, and most missing persons are eventually found there. Similarly bridges, white-painted wooden fences and tubular railings are to be seen everywhere in the Netherlands. The timber house with the advertising signs at Middleshaw has a Dutch look about it. So could it be that Croiset, using Ryan as a link, seized on these familiar images?

If Pat McAdam's body had been found, the case would have become a classic work of psychic detection. But before rejecting the clairvoyant's successes as pure coincidence, one must pause and calculate the odds against finding a cottage with a particular garden containing an old car with a wheelbarrow leaning against it. That car and barrow are testimony to the accuracy of the strange vision that came to Gerard Croiset, hundreds of miles away in Utrecht.

Winston Churchill, seen above during the Second World War, claimed that he often listened to a mysterious 'inner voice'. By heeding its advice, he managed both to escape serious injury himself and to help others do the same. There is more about the 'inner voice' on page 33.

Madame Blavatsky – the great Russian mystic whose psychic abilities we investigate on page 40 – is seen above *with Colonel Henry S. Olcott. Both founded the Theosophical Society in New York for the propagation of occult studies.*

A Victorian lantern slide satire, at the expense of the Theosophical Society, is shown above. Most of the allusions refer to alleged 'miracles' performed either by Madame Blavatsky, or through her by one of her 'Masters', known as Koot Hoomi. 'Glass and china matched and riveted,' for example, refers to a broken cup that she seemed to mend paranormally. There is some reason to believe, however, that the 'repaired' cup was merely a substitution.

Many respected figures – including the writer Sir Arthur Conan Doyle – believed that Harry Houdini's prodigious feats of escapology were impossible to achieve merely by sleight of hand and muscle control. Even when Houdini explained how he performed his tricks – such as an escape fom this milk churn – they claimed that some sort of psychic power must be involved. Houdini's extraordinary abilities are examined on page 51.

TALKING WITH
THE ANGELS

*A highly respected Elizabethan mathematician
had more than a scholarly interest in the occult
and developed his own school of magic.*

John Dee rates an entry in most standard reference
works for his contribution to 16th-century
mathematical and navigational knowledge. Yet this
same man believed he had also learned the secrets of
the angels – what goes on in heaven and which angels
control various parts of the world, for example. So did
he actually communicate with angelic spirits? Or was
he perhaps the victim of self-delusion and the
deception of a cunning medium?

The majority of those who have studied Dee's life
and opinions have come to the latter conclusion. The
Biographica Britannica, for instance, describes him as
having been 'extremely credulous, extravagantly vain
and a most deluded enthusiast'.

But occultists tend to take a very different view –
particularly those inclined to what has been called the
'Western Esoteric Tradition'. This is a synthesis of
European astrology, ritual magic, alchemy and other
techniques of practical occultism, as developed in the
late 19th century by S.L. MacGregor Mathers and his

associates of the Hermetic Order of the Golden Dawn. It also incorporates some of the principles of Dee's system of 'Enochian magic', based on his presumed mastery of the language of the angels, 'Enochian'. Some believe that Dee did indeed learn the angels' tongue, and therefore argue that Enochian magic is of great significance and value. Unlike other systems, it is not concerned with demons or devils, however; and, because the language is of heavenly origin, it is supposed to enable the magician to control the spirits more successfully.

Whether Dee was wise or foolish, an obsessed eccentric or a magus, there can be no doubt of his dedication to scholarship. His library, the printed and manuscript contents of which cost him more than £3,000 (a huge amount at the time), was a very large one for the period, and it included works on every subject with which 16th-century scholars concerned themselves. Theology, mathematics, geography, navigation, alchemy, astronomy, astrology and ritual magic – all these areas of study were duly represented.

Dee was born on 13 July 1527 at Mortlake, now a suburb of London. In view of the importance he always attached to astrology, it is interesting to note that, at the hour of his birth, the Sun was in Cancer and the zodiacal sign of Sagittarius was on the horizon. This combination, according to astrological devotees, is favourable for a career based on scholarship and the study of secret sciences.

Such astrological indications were certainly confirmed when, at the age of 15, Dee became an undergraduate at Cambridge and commenced his studies with great intensity. As he himself recorded: 'I was so vehemently bent to studie, that for those years I did inviolably keep this order; only to sleepe four houres every night; to allow to meate and drinke (and some refreshing after) two houres every day; and of the other 18 houres all (except the times of going to and being at divine service) was spent in my studies and learning.'

Creature from hell

Dee's efforts received their due reward: in 1546, he was appointed Greek under-reader, a sort of junior professor. He was also made a fellow of the newly founded Trinity College. But even at this early stage of his career, there were whispers that he dabbled in black magic. Some even suspected that an ingenious mechanical beetle, devised by him for use as a special effect in a Greek play, was a creature from hell.

The next 30 years or so of Dee's life were eventful, exciting, and sometimes perilous. He travelled widely in Europe, lecturing at universities and making friends among the scholars. He also became interested in the 'angelic magic', expounded by Abbot Trithemius in his manuscript *Steganographia;* and, in addition, he cast the horoscopes of many of the great men and women of his time.

It was this last activity that, in 1553, during the reign of 'Bloody Mary', brought Dee into danger.

At the time, Queen Mary's half-sister, the Princess Elizabeth, was being held in semi-confinement, since she was suspected of plotting with Protestant malcontents to overthrow the Queen and place herself on the throne. Through one of her ladies-in-waiting, Blanche Parry, the Princess entered into a correspondence with Dee, which eventually resulted in the astrologer showing her Queen Mary's horoscope.

Through the agency of two informers, the links between Dee and Elizabeth were conveyed to the Queen's council. Immediately, the unfortunate astrologer was arrested and thrown into prison. Not only were his astrological researches into the probable duration of Mary's life regarded as near treason, but it was believed likely that he was attempting to murder her by black magic.

Eventually, Dee was cleared of the charge of treason, but he was immediately rearrested on the charge of being a suspected heretic. He gained his final release in 1555.

In 1558, Mary died and Elizabeth came to the throne. Dee enjoyed Elizabeth's favour as her astrological adviser. Indeed, it was he who selected a propitious date for her coronation; and it was he who was called upon for advice when it was suspected that sorcery was being employed against the throne.

Nevertheless, Dee's life was not entirely happy. He was perpetually short of money, spending most of his income on his library and alchemical experiments; and he was distressed by the continued suspicions of many that he was, to quote his own words, 'a companion of hellhounds, and a caller and conjuror of damned and wicked spirits.'

Crystal visions

It is likely that those who regarded Dee in this light would have thought their worst suspicions confirmed if they had known of Dee's experiments in communication with the angels, which he is believed to have begun in October 1581.

The six months before this were troubled ones for Dee. His sleep was much disturbed, his dreams were peculiar, and there were mysterious knockings in his house. But as the Australian philologist and writer on Enochian magic, Dr Donald Laycock, remarked, it would seem that the spirits wished to contact Dee, rather than the other way round.

Dee worked through mediums, the first being Barnabas Saul who claimed to see angels and other spirits in a magic crystal. But Dee was not satisfied with Saul and dismissed the seer after a few months.

On 8 March 1582, a new medium approached Dee – a certain Edward Kelley, a strange young man whose antecedents were obscure. He was only 27 years old, but his short life seems to have been full of mystery, danger and questionable deeds. He had been a student but had not taken a degree, becoming a notary instead. Accused of forgery in the course of his work, he was said to have had his ears cropped for his offence. He had also supposedly employed ritual magic in the search for buried treasure, had studied alchemy and was in possession of strange elixirs, powders and coded manuscripts. Most sinister of all, he was reputed to practise necromancy, the rite of raising the dead for the purposes of prediction and divination. At first, Dee was suspicious of Kelley, but not for long – for Kelley saw the angel Uriel in Dee's 'shewstone' and was given instructions for the manufacture of a powerful talisman. This convinced Dee of his magical powers.

The association between Dee and Kelley lasted seven years, and the two held hundreds of seances, the first at Mortlake, the last at Cracow in Poland. On the instructions of the angels who spoke through Kelley, the men and their families had wandered thousands of miles up and down Europe.

Records of many of their experiments, carefully compiled by Dee, have survived to the present day, but they are often virtually meaningless to the modern reader who has not made a specialised study of Elizabethan magic and alchemy. They do, however, contain passages that seem to be precognitive.

Take, for example, the following exchange that is said to have taken place between Dee and the angel

Uriel on 5 May 1583:

Dee: As concerning the vision which was presented yesternight (unlooked for) to the sight of Edward Kelley as he sat at supper with me, in my hall, I mean the appearing of the very sea, and many ships thereon, and the cutting of the head of a woman, by a tall black man, what are we to imagine thereof?

Uriel: The one did signify the provision of foreign powers against the welfare of this land: which they shall shortly put into practice. The other, the death of the Queen of Scots: it is not long unto it.

In other words, Uriel – speaking through Kelley in the year 1583 – was specifically prophesying an attempt at the invasion of England by some large fleet, and the execution of Mary Stuart, Queen of Scots. The reference to the executioner as a 'black man', meanwhile, may well have been an indication of his black hood.

As it turned out, Mary was executed in 1587 and the attempted invasion by the Spanish Armada came in 1588. But little of the information supplied by the angels was as specific as this. Much of it consisted of obscure magical, mathematical and, particularly, linguistic teaching. The language of Enochian was, according to Uriel and his fellows, that originally spoken in the Garden of Eden. Lengthy discourses were dictated to Dee in this tongue – at first sight, gibberish. For instance, *micaolz olprt* means 'mighty light' and *bliors ds odo* means 'comfort which openest'.

But sometimes, translations were obligingly provided by the angels. From these, it is clear that Enochian is more than mere strings of syllables. It exhibits traces of syntax and grammar, and has the rudiments of a structured language.

Dr Laycock carried out a detailed study of Enochian and; in the introduction to his *Complete Enochian Dictionary*, he concludes that its structure and grammar are remarkably similar to those of English. In spite of his scepticism about the language, Dr Laycock is prepared to admit that there may be something in Enochian magic. Indeed, he has remarked: 'I have known well people who have pursued the study of Enochian from the point of view of practical occultism, and who claim that, whatever the origin of the system, it works as practical magic.'

The seance held on 17 April 1587 was the beginning of the end for the Dee-Kelley association. On that day, an angel, calling herself Madimi, gave instructions that the two men should sleep with each other's wives. Dee was deeply disturbed by this prospect, wondering whether it could be devils who were impersonating angels; but the spirits emphatically urged him on: '... In hesitating, you sin... All these things... are permitted to you.' Dee still hesitated; but, on 22 May, he gave in and the wife-swapping actually took place.

This event finally placed too much of a strain on the Dee-Kelley relationship, however, and Dee returned to England, giving up all practice of magic. He died in abject poverty in 1608. Kelley preceded him in death, killed abroad in unknown circumstances, in 1595.

What then, of the value of the Enochian magic, the Enochian language, and the other occult teachings conveyed to Dee and Kelley by their supposed angels? No one can be quite sure. But there is a lot to be said for the point of view expressed by Laycock: 'If the true voice of God comes through the shewstone at all, it is certainly as through a glass darkly'.

FASHIONS IN PHENOMENA

Gone are apports and ectoplasm as subjects of paranormal investigations. In, instead, are such areas as telepathy and poltergeists. Why should there be such fads in the psychic's world?

The early history of Spiritualism produced floods of ectoplasm, hosts of full-bodied materialisations, and enough apports to stock a department store. Yet, before and after a period bridging the late 19th and early 20th centuries, such phenomena of physical mediumship were almost unheard of. Fashions in phenomena have changed, and with them fashions in psychical research. Indeed, the investigators of today have all but deserted the seance for laboratory tests of metal-bending, ESP and the like.

Could it actually be that, as Charles Fort observed in the early 20th century: 'There are phenomena that exist relatively to one age, that do not, or do not so pronouncedly, exist in another age'?

One example of a phenomenon no longer in vogue is that of certain birds hibernating over the winter in dark, dry places, usually underground. Although this idea is not taken seriously by 20th-century naturalists, it was not dismissed by such eminent founders of the natural sciences as Linnaeus and Baron Cuvier. A number of cases were reported in 18th- and 19th-century scientific accounts and discussed in professional journals. Gradually, however, such reports ceased and the phenomenon was forgotten. This fact was noticed by Philip Gosse, the populariser of science, who included a not entirely sceptical review of the subject in the second volume of his celebrated *Romance of Natural History* (1861). Gosse wondered why the discoveries of hibernating birds 'instead of increasing in frequency with the increase of scientific research and communication, strangely become more rare'.

There are a number of possible reasons for this. Scientific literature has become more rigorous and academic, and the anecdotal and circumstantial nature of the evidence for bird hibernation is regarded as weak. In such a climate of scepticism, few scientists would risk their careers by opposing the almost universally accepted doctrine of bird migration. Then again, the adoption of explosives and heavy machines for demolition and earth removal could have destroyed evidence that might have been uncovered in the days of the spade and shovel. Finally, there may have been a change in the instinctive behaviour of the birds – something that is not unknown to happen in animals as the environment changes.

Of course, a distinction has to be made as to whether the appearance, or disappearance, of certain kinds of phenomenon are the result of increased knowledge or the product of social processes. The pioneering ufologist John Keel has shown, for example, that only a fraction of the UFOs seen ever get reported, and only a fraction of those reported ever get publicized. Consequently, he and other ufologists have warned of the shock to society if the true proportion of the phenomenon were ever disclosed.

Vanishing serpents

Similarly, it would seem that the once ubiquitous sea serpent has suffered virtual extinction – but not so, according to the world's greatest expert on these creatures, Dr Bernard Heuvelmans. After compiling a chronology of sightings between the years 1639 and 1964 for his book *In the Wake of the Sea Serpents*, Heuvelmans remained convinced that they still averaged about two a year. The apparent decline, he said, was a product of the shyness of the creatures, the fact that modern shipping keeps largely to well-defined routes, and fear of ridicule. As he put it: 'The sound of laughter has driven away as many sea serpents as that of ships' engines.'

But nothing has driven away lake monsters, which have been regularly sighted for centuries. Indeed, since the Loch Ness monster first surfaced in 1933, sightings of huge, long-necked serpent-like creatures have proliferated in lakes all over the world.

Another long-lived phenomenon is that of stigmata, although the first instance did not occur until nearly 1,200 years after the crucifixion. Since St Francis of Assisi was stigmatised in 1224, however, there has hardly been a year without a report of a stigmata case.

Stage management

To most of us, the things we perceive around us in our everyday lives are solid and real. They are the tangible proof of that state of existence we agree, by consensus, to call reality. It therefore seems preposterous that the furniture of reality could be subject to the whims of something as ephemeral as fashion. But there can be, of course, as many definitions of reality as there are people to perceive it.

Research into the nature of coincidence has established strong links between the unconscious mind, of both individuals and the collective, and the phenomena of reality. The familiar story of how a lost or stolen item finds its way back to its owner, for example, often through a revealing dream, recurs consistently.

The German psychologist Wilhelm von Scholz thought that the coincidences in such cases were so outrageous to the view of conventional physical causality that he was moved to believe they must be 'stage-managed... as if they were the dreams of a greater and more comprehensive consciousness... '

The theory towards which von Scholz was groping in 1924 is surely close to what many Forteans and others subscribe to today: that powerful projections from the unconscious of archetypal forms or behaviour are able to manifest themselves in what we call reality, or to alter that reality by influencing related events. This semi-mystical view is related to three converging streams of thought. One explores the world of meaningful coincidence, which C. G. Jung termed 'synchronicity'. Another is the hypothesis of 'formative causation' proposed by Dr Rupert Sheldrake, which describes a mechanism for the communication, beyond normal restrictions of space and time, of form and behaviour in nature. The third concerns 'tulpas' or thought forms and the way a consensus can influence reality by creating its own separate 'bubble' of reality.

Magic wand

The crazes or obsessions that can grip a community, as well as an individual, exemplify this. In Gustave Le Bon's neglected study, *The Crowd* (1897), he showed how a community can be galvanised in such a way that a particular set of ideas or imagery – sublime or even trivial – may come to dominate their perceptions, actions and rationalisations of their resulting unusual behaviour. The 'magic wand' that turns a group of individuals into a crowd or mob is simply a shared state of heightened suggestibility. Le

Bon thought that this was brought about when any group of people in physical proximity become suddenly aligned psychologically by any unusual form of stimulus.

This type of phenomenon is characterized in the title to Charles Mackay's pioneering historical study, *Memoirs of Extraordinary Popular Delusions and the Madness of Crowds*. In this book, he discusses the medieval craze for relics, the South Sea Bubble swindle, the frenzied witch-hunts, and the wild and wasteful Crusades, among other topics. The medieval dancing manias are another example of some kind of unconscious collective behaviour. Dancing could be set off instantly by the sight of a pointed shoe, a snatch of music, the colour red, the rant of a preacher, the sight of someone already dancing, or the imagined bite of a tarantula.

On the basis of the 'projections' theory, and by extension of Le Bon's idea, one might reach the conclusion that a 'crowd' need not be together physically. Its constituents could be spread widely apart – even over a whole country – and become aligned through individual contact with the collective unconscious, so that an idea arising out of this unconscious would occur to them all.

An excellent example of this curious form of collective hysteria occurred in France in 1789, and is called the 'Great Fear' by historians. It began immediately after the fall of the Bastille in Paris.

Entire villages were abandoned as rumours reached them of a huge army of brigands killing and looting their way towards them. Terrified people babbled of seeing the flames of burning houses in the sky, of being captured and of seeing friends killed by brutal bandits, and so on. But the whole affair had been hallucinated. The panic had not even spread out from Paris in the ordinary way, as rumours carried by travellers. Instead, it seems to have sprung up independently in several locations across France, and to have spread out like a forest fire from each of these.

Historians are at a loss to explain how such panic could grow faster than anyone could travel at the time, but the populace was in a state of suggestibility due to general anxiety about the political crisis. The initial outbreaks needed only a simple stimulus, such as a flash of lightning – unusual natural phenomena were indeed recorded in association with the Great Fear – and rumour and panic did the rest.

Elementals, witches or aliens?

Some phenomena have not varied much throughout history, however – among them pathological and mental illness, strange falls from the sky and ball lightning. But explanations for them have been subject to changing fashions in belief and, consequently, were attributed to a succession of gods, devils, elementals, ghosts, fairies, witches, psychic powers or even aliens.

Consider the huge flying machines, with powerful searchlights and 'foreign-looking crews', seen in the skies across North America in 1896 and 1897 by reliable witnesses – at a time when there were thought to be no such craft in existence. These sightings cannot all have been misidentifications of natural phenomena; and, indeed, there is another possibility.

The late 19th century was the heyday of the hero-inventor, such as Thomas Edison and Nikola Tesla; and whereas today's mysteries of the skies are attributed to UFOs, that era attributed them to unidentified great inventors. It was only when Andrew Rothovius compared some of the 1897 incidents with the Great Fear (in *Pursuit* magazine, 1978) that the airship sightings were seen to have originated spontaneously, from apparently unconnected initial incidents in several different locations throughout the country, and then by rumour.

Jung thought that the UFO was a sign of changes in the constellation of archetypes in the human unconscious, and that such antigravity, dream-like discs of light were omens of the need for psychic unity at a time when the split between people's rational, scientific side and their instinctive, mystical side had never been greater. Jung could not have known of the later developments in UFO manifestations, bringing the frightening abductions and sinister behaviour of fantastic entities. But perhaps he would have agreed with ufologist John Rimmer that the UFO has become 'the antiscience symbol par excellence'.

Projections from the unconscious have the power of archetypes, and address themselves to our main personal and collective anxieties. They can possess us and direct our actions, sweeping through a community like a rumour. Indeed, Jung likened the UFO to a 'visual rumour'. The same might be said of today's frequent sightings of monsters. These appear in strikingly archaic forms, as though somehow attempting to remind us that we are eroding our psychic landscape as surely as we are spoiling the world's last wildernesses. Such weird phenomena, clearly 'fashionable' today, are in many ways like collective dreams, and there is surely much to be learned from them.

A NEW VIEW OF REALITY

As physicists study the sub-atomic world, their views about the nature of reality have begun to coincide with the observations of both mystics and psychics.

The strange and beautiful sub-atomic Universe that has been discovered as a result of the brilliant research of 20th-century physicists lies hidden from our senses, more suited as these are to interpreting the far larger world of everyday reality. But we do now know a considerable amount about that minute Universe, in which the laws of relativity and quantum physics (study of the flow of energy particles) rule.

Following such scientific advancement, what has also become strikingly obvious is that statements from physicists about the nature of reality and the immediate sensory world resemble more and more those of mystics, both eastern and western, as well as others who seem to be blessed with psychic faculties. Indeed, the medium, the mystic and the physicist – in descriptions of the complex nature of reality – have suddenly begun to find themselves in unexpected accord. The odd man out, meanwhile, is the one who still firmly believes that the simplistic, 19th-century picture of the Universe is adequate to explain the whole of reality.

In the world of the paranormal, everyday concepts of space and time are inadmissible. Indeed, the ability of a sensitive to acquire information seems totally independent of distance or time intervals.

Detailed predictions

The Dutch clairvoyant Gerard Croiset, for instance, could predict detailed events in the lives of people he had never met. In one case, he correctly predicted, on 6 January, the events that a woman, 'Mrs M', would experience on 1 February. The idea of a brain-to-brain 'mental radio' breaks down here if one supposes that Croiset's brain could somehow have been reading the physical memory traces that were to be laid down in Mrs M's brain a month later. For, on 1 February, Mrs M was not only a month ahead of the point at which Croiset made his prediction, but also 42 million miles (67 million kilometres) away from Croiset's physical position on 6 January, because of the Earth's motion around the Sun. Thus, it seems that the mind cannot be localised in time or space.

What, then, corresponds in the 'psychic mechanics' of clairvoyant reality to the non-material fields of quantum mechanics? Strangely enough, the first steps along the road to such a concept may have been taken by certain researchers in the very period when demolition of 19th-century scientific theory was underway. At that time, eminent psychologists, such as the American William James (1842-1910), the Austrian Sigmund Freud (1856-1939) and the Swiss Carl Gustav Jung (1875-1961), were all exploring another world invisible to the senses – that of the unconscious mind, the strange, often paradoxical operations of which covertly influence human thoughts and actions.

All three were interested in the paranormal – James and Jung intensely so – for the light it might shed on the dark continent of the psyche. In his attempts to understand psychic phenomena, James, the founding father of American psychology, used the idea of the 'block Universe'. In this, the Universe is represented as having four dimensions – length, breadth, width and time – through which human consciousness travels like a point of light. Although this Universe is static, humans are under the illusion that 'things happen' – as in the illusion experienced by a driver at night, when trees that are actually stationary seem to appear in the headlamps' beams, rush past and disappear.

Jung, who later collaborated with the Swiss physicist Wolfgang Pauli in an attempt to come to grips with synchronicities – that is, coincidences – was well aware of the amazing revolution in physics going on throughout his long life, and introduced the concept of the 'collective unconscious', which in some ways related to James's own idea of a psychic repository or record of all human experience. A major feature of the Jungian collective unconscious, however, was that it was not merely a passive record, but a dynamic, creative one, giving rise to dreams, myths, religion and artistic creation.

Racial memory

The existence of the collective unconscious – the racial memory of mankind – is supported by dream analysis, the universality of myths and paranormal phenomena. It looks, too, as if this great submerged continent of the psyche exists outside space and time. Like an island in the ocean, each human mind lies separated from all others above the threshold of consciousness. But just as all islands join below the ocean surface – connected by the ocean floor – so Jungian teaching suggests that below conscious level, at greater and greater depths of the psyche, there is a merging of each personal subconscious.

The pioneers of quantum mechanics focused on non-material fields (regions where entities, such as atomic nuclei and orbiting electrons, exert influence on each other), rather than on gross matter. They accepted, too, that the nature of these fields was indefinable, and only the laws of their behaviour could be sought. Similarly, most 'depth psychologists' – who believe that behaviour can be explained in terms of unconscious processes – have ignored questions regarding the whereabouts of the collective unconscious, seeking merely to discover and understand its laws by studying the effect that it has on human beings.

But just as theoretical physicists have gradually come to recognise various kinds of sub-atomic particles within the fields that they study and, with time, have deduced their laws of interaction, it may be expected that explorers of the psyche – that is, psychologists, psychoanalysts, and psychical researchers – will eventually discover more about the structure of the collective unconscious.

There are certainly many questions that remain. If, for example, the collective unconscious is indeed a psychic storehouse of all human experience, does it contain, like an electronic computer, the 'program' of everyone who has ever lived? And is it possible that sensitives who enter a psychic state gain the ability to activate and 'run' certain programs – the programs of those now dead?

Running such a program may not be in any way analogous to running a cassette on a tape recorder: the tape is passive, non-reactive and fixed in content. By contrast, there are pocket computers that are 'intelligent' enough to give one a very good game of chess; and it is possible to feed computers with medical programs that can 'converse' via a screen and a typewriter keyboard so fluently that the patient finds it difficult to believe that he is not dealing with a flesh-and-blood doctor.

Thus, when Rosemary Brown 'received' music from Liszt, Chopin and Beethoven, or Brazilian psychic artist Luiz Gasparetto's hands were apparently guided by Picasso or Toulouse-Lautrec, could it be that these two sensitives were interacting with programs stored in the collective unconscious – programs that contain information not only on the lives of these great men, but also their musical and artistic techniques, memories and personality traits?

It seems reasonable to suppose, if we accept the hypothesis of a collective unconscious stocked with such records, that such sensitives will also behave according to the beliefs and knowledge possessed by the originals. The deceased may, thereby, be invoking the aid of the living to solve the problems or unfulfilled artistic plans left behind at the end of their earthly lives. But the words, pictures and music passed on by the deceased could, of course, also be strongly influenced by the mind through which they are channelled – that is, the mind of the sensitive.

This concept of human minds influencing and being influenced by the collective unconscious raises the mind-brain problem with increased force. The mystery of how the will operates the brain, and hence the neurones (nerve cells) that control our muscles, has been tackled by – among others – the eminent physiologist Sir John Eccles. A highly simplified account of his theory runs as follows: the brain contains an enormous number of neurones, many of which are critically poised between firing and non-firing. Eccles suggests that tiny amounts of mental energy, well-directed by the mind, will operate such 'hair-trigger' neurones by psychokinesis (PK). Each neurone in its turn fires others, initiating in a fraction of a second a chain reaction involving hundreds of thousands of neurones.

In this mind-brain influence, which would also operate in the other direction, can be seen the possibility of a theory incorporating certain paranormal phenomena. If, for example, the minds of *A* and *B* connect at their deepest levels with the timeless collective unconscious, then sensory data entering *A*'s brain could – by means of psychokinetic influence – surface as imagery in *B*'s brain.

Various researchers have attempted to generalise quantum mechanics to include paranormal phenomena. The American physicist Martin Ruderfer, for instance, has suggested that *neutrinos* are responsible. Neutrinos are particles without electric charge and, to the best of our present knowledge, no mass. They react with matter extremely infrequently. In fact, they are ghost-like in behaviour: billions of neutrinos pass unimpeded through the Earth every second, and interstellar space is filled with them, created as they are in nuclear reactions within stars and travelling in all directions. It is this 'neutrino sea' that might be capable of initiating psychic phenomena.

Adrian Dobbs, a mathematical physicist, put forward a two-dimensional model of time and postulated the existence of 'psi-trons', particles that travel faster than light and can never be slowed below the speed of light. Within his closely argued theory (no more bizarre, in fact, than much of quantum mechanics), Dobbs tries to account for telepathy and precognition.

Also working on the nature of precognition, the physicist and parapsychologist Helmut Schmidt persuaded volunteers to try to predict single quantum processes – emissions of electrons from a radioactive strontium 90 source. The time of occurrence of such an event should be completely unpredictable, and yet Schmidt's volunteers obtained scores that would have been expected only once in every thousand million experiments. It is certainly difficult to explain Schmidt's experiments without invoking precognition or psychokinesis. If the former is involved, the mind is acquiring information about future events; if the latter, then the mind is causing events on a sub-atomic level, in a manner recalling Eddington's assertion that the world is made of 'mind stuff'.

We are still at the beginning of our understanding of such matters. Meanwhile, some new Newton or Einstein may already be waiting in the wings to show how a more generalised quantum-mechanical model will embrace paranormal phenomena.

TRAVERSING TIME

Psychics seem able to move back and forward in time, at will or spontaneously. How can this possibly fit in with the theory of a universe in which time is static?

Can certain people really see into the future and the past? And if so, do such abilities provide some sort of clue to the nature of time? Many philosophers and psychologists have taken seriously the evidence for precognitions and retrocognitions, accepting that our conventional ideas of time may actually be misleading, in the same way that theoretical physicists of the late 19th century came to realise that their ideas about space and time were wrong, especially in the subatomic and astronomical realms.

By 1908, German physicist Hermann Minkowski was suggesting that the Universe could be described in terms of four-dimensional space-time. In fact, he was introducing what has now come to be called the 'block Universe', a static universe with no past, present or future, except that introduced by the observer.

According to Minkowski, the observer's consciousness travels along his so-called 'world line' through the block Universe, like a spotlight moving over a dark landscape or field. Those bits of the field that the spotlight has already picked out, the observer terms the past; those that are yet to appear in the spotlight, he terms the future.

But what of the here and now? William James (1842-1910), the American psychologist, introduced the concept of the 'specious present'. This is seen as a small but finite chunk of space-time, containing everything that the observer is consciously perceiving at that moment.

The psychical researcher H. F. Saltmarsh (1881-1943) modified this theory somewhat, in an attempt to account for precognition and retrocognition. He supposed that the conscious mind's specious present was smaller than that of the subconscious. Thus, Saltmarsh argued, it is perfectly possible that an event that lies in the future of the conscious mind may lie in the specious present of the subconscious mind.

Importantly, if this event were unpleasant or likely to be dangerous to the person concerned, the subconscious might warn the conscious mind by presenting it with a premonition in the form of a dream. If the conditions were right, the premonition might even appear as a vision while the person was wide awake. Premonitory dreams are, however, more common. Indeed, many premonitions are received in a generally relaxed and receptive state of mind, while the subject is either emerging from or approaching sleep, or in a comfortable chair, while reading a book or watching television.

Saltmarsh did not, however, like the implications of his theory for the question of free will. If the future is simply a collection of events that make up the static block Universe, and if the events that make up a person's life are simply strung out in a line within the block Universe to be approached in a set order, then it seems there can be no free will. Saltmarsh therefore modified his theory in the light of this objection by assuming that the future is in some way plastic and modifiable, and that it is only when an event is experienced or becomes a past event that it becomes 'set', so that it cannot thereafter be modified.

It is possible, however, to construct a theory that goes some way towards accounting for the fact that, even if a premonition of a future event has taken place, this does not necessarily mean that the event itself is inevitable.

Let us suppose that the spotlight on the block Universe that contains everything consciously perceived by the person at that moment is surrounded by a hazy ring that represents the subconscious. Within this are all the events being perceived by the person's subconscious.

To take a concrete example, a girl is scheduled to sail on the *Titanic* in April 1912. She packs her bags, has them loaded into the hold, and is about to embark. But at that instant, the event of the liner's sinking is illuminated by the ring of her subconscious, although it still lies outside the spotlight of her conscious mind. The sinking is therefore still in her future, in common sense terms. But, somehow, a symbolic representation of the terrible scenes perceived by her subconscious manages to cross the threshold between subconscious and conscious, and she experiences a premonition of her own death. She therefore changes her mind about sailing, so that she avoids dying on the liner. She later reads about the liner sinking and no doubt congratulates herself on her premonition for saving her life.

The point to note is that the two events – the possible death of the girl in the *Titanic* disaster, and her change of mind and survival – are equally real in a potential sense, in that they are both events in the dark field of the Universe: the only difference between them is that the girl's conscious spotlight illuminated one, and not the other.

A further consequence of this theory is that, since the dark field of the Universe contains all possible events, many, many branches and junction points must exist, and the decision taken at any moment determines which branch of the tree of world lines the conscious and unconscious spotlight will travel along. This is reminiscent of the theoretical physicist Hugh Everett's concept of a multiple branching universe in which every probability is realised, but only one branch actually observed.

The experiences that make up a person's life, according to this theory, are rather like those of a man who enters an art gallery at night, his only illumination being a spotlight that he trains on the pictures of the corridor along which he is travelling. He sees scenes of his early childhood and boyhood, and then comes in the darkness to a T-junction. He can go either left or right, but chooses to go left and continues to shine his torch on the pictures on the wall of the left-hand corridor. He sees himself in these pictures as a youth carrying out various actions, going to various places, making various friends, until he becomes a man. He never sees the pictures of what his life would have been had he made a decision that took him right instead of left. He does not see, for example, that he would have died in a car accident at the age of 23. Instead, he sees himself completing his university studies, getting a good job, marrying and having children.

It may be that a psychic's subconscious field has the freedom to wander over the dark field of the Universe, probing until it intersects the world path of another person. There is also the possibility that if two subconscious fields – but not the corresponding conscious fields – intersect, then the right conditions for telepathic communication are created.

It has been suggested by a number of psychologists and psychical researchers that perhaps the ring of unconscious perception covers the whole lifespan of a human being. For example, the psychologist Aniela Jaffé has suggested that, at his deepest level, a human being has knowledge of his whole life. Dutch parapsychologist Professor Wilhelm Tenhaeff has taken this idea further and has remarked that the psychic may derive paranormal knowledge of his sitter through telepathy from the sitter's psyche.

The French philosopher Henri Bergson (1859-1941) speculated that one of the tasks of the brain may be to restrict this view of time to a particular moment – as in that theory of time in which the consciousness of the human being is confined to the present moment, but a higher self in sleep is allowed views of past and future events in his life. The American parapsychologist Lawrence LeShan, meanwhile, has pointed to the opinions of many mystics and psychics that, in their altered states of consciousness, time and space are irrelevant: there is no yesterday, today or tomorrow, and no passing of time. As the medium Eileen Garrett said: 'In the ultimate nature of the Universe, there are no divisions in time and space.' This is a view that is not fundamentally in disagreement with the teachings of modern quantum mechanics.

Masks such as the one above *are frequently worn by shamans during a trance state, as the soul supposedly leaves the body. On page 123, we take a journey to the spirit world.*

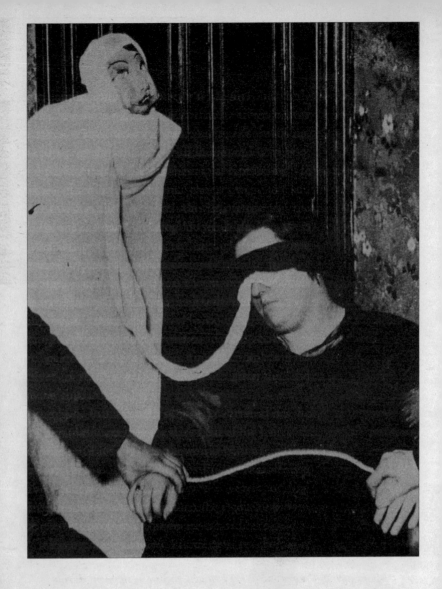

At a seance held at her home in 1933, the physical medium Helen Duncan produced the materialised form of her spirit guide, Peggy. Once researcher claimed it was made out of cheesecloth and a rubber doll. Other witnesses testified at Mrs Duncan's trial in 1944 to seeing many genuine spirit forms at her seances.

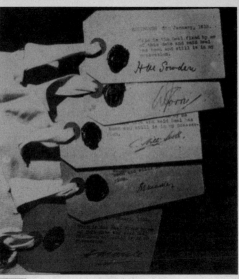

On page 113, we look at the controversial life of Helen Duncan. Could it be that her ectoplasmic materialisations were genuine or was she an accomplished fraud? In a court case in 1933, it was alleged that 'Peggy' was in fact a woman's undervest manipulated by Mrs Duncan; and a vest, left, was produced in evidence, together with the seals of witnesses who had attended the seance attached.

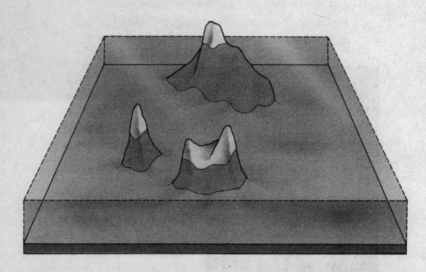

The drawing above illustrates the interconnection of human minds as conceived by psychologist Carl Jung. The conscious minds of individuals are separated, as i slands are separated by the ocean. But at the deepest level, each mind merges with the collective unconscious, a shared racial memory that unites individuals — just as the ocean floor links the world's islands. You can find out more about such views on page 95.

A SPIRITED DEFENCE

The conviction of a leading physical medium on a charge of conspiracy caused a storm of protest in Spiritualist circles. Was Helen Duncan guilty of deception or not?

The curtains of the cabinet in the darkened seance room parted and out stepped the figure of a woman. Vincent Woodcock recognised her immediately; it was his dead wife. In all, the young electrical draughtsman from Blackpool was to see the materialised spirit of his wife on 19 occasions during seances given by the medium Helen Duncan; but it was this particular occasion that changed his life.

Vincent Woodcock had brought his wife's sister with him to this seance; and when the spirit of his wife appeared from the curtained cabinet, she asked them both to stand. Then, with difficulty, the materialisation removed her husband's wedding ring and placed it on her sister's wedding finger.

'It is my wish that this takes place for the sake of my little girl,' the materialisation told the couple. A year later, they were married. At a subsequent seance, a further materialisation of the dead woman said how happy she was they had complied.

This touching story of true love was later recounted by Vincent Woodcock in court when he appeared as a witness for the defence in an astonishing trial that took place at London's Old Bailey. In the dock was the medium whose astonishing psychic powers had made possible his wife's return from the spirit world: Helen Duncan.

Back from the dead

Helen Duncan had been born in Scotland in 1898. She married at the age of 20, and her psychic talents were much in demand in the 1930s and 1940s, when she travelled around the country, holding seances in private homes and Spiritualist churches. She convinced thousands of people that the dead could return in physical form. But there were also sceptics who believed Helen Duncan's materialisations were in fact produced by trickery. She was said to have a spirit child, 'Peggy', who played an important role in her seances. But, in a court case in Edinburgh in May 1933, it was claimed that 'Peggy' was, in reality, nothing other than a woman's undervest that a policewoman succeeded in grabbing during a seance. The medium was found guilty of fraud and fined.

However, the verdict did not interfere with her career of mediumship. Indeed, during the Second World War, Helen Duncan's mediumistic powers were much in demand by the relatives of those who had died on active service, and she held many seances in Portsmouth, Hampshire, the home port of the Royal Navy. One of these seances, held on 19 January 1944, was raided by the police. A plain-clothes policeman who was present blew a whistle to give the signal, and his colleagues burst in. A grab was made at the ectoplasm issuing from the medium, and the seance ended abruptly in commotion. Although nothing incriminating was found, Helen Duncan, together with three others who were said actually to have arranged the seances, Ernest and Elizabeth Homer and Francis Brown, subsequently appeared at Portsmouth magistrates' court on a charge of conspiracy.

At the preliminary hearing, the Portsmouth court was told how Lieutenant R. H. Worth of the Royal Navy had attended Mrs Duncan's seances and suspected fraud. He bought two tickets for 25 shillings (£1.25) each for the night of 19 January and took a policeman with him – War Reserve Cross. Cross made a grab for the ectoplasm, which he believed to be a white sheet, but he was unable to retain it. No sheet was found by the other police officers when they entered the seance room. After the hearing, bail was refused, and as a result the medium was remanded in Holloway prison in London for four days before the case was resumed in Portsmouth.

The prosecution seemed to be uncertain on what charge the four accused should be indicted. On their first appearance at Portsmouth, they were charged under the Vagrancy Act of 1824; but the charge was then amended to one of conspiracy. When the case was eventually transferred to the central criminal court at the Old Bailey – where it was dubbed the 'trial of the century' by some newspapers – the Witchcraft Act of 1735 was cited.

Under this ancient act, the defendants were accused of pretending 'to exercise or use a kind of conjuration that through the agency of Helen Duncan spirits of deceased persons should appear to be present... ' Other charges were brought under the Larceny Act and they were accused of taking money 'by falsely pretending they were in a position to bring about the appearances of the spirits of deceased persons and that they then, *bona fide,* intended so to do without trickery'.

Spiritualists were dismayed by the use of the Witchcraft Act to bring a prosecution against such a famous medium. Under this Act, it appeared that Helen Duncan could be proved guilty whether or not her powers were genuine.

The prosecution clearly believed Helen Duncan was a fraud, and were not deterred by the absence of any props. During the trial, prosecuting Counsel John Maude produced a long piece of butter muslin and referred repeatedly to the theory put forward by a psychical researcher, Harry Price, that Helen Duncan achieved her results by swallowing muslin and then regurgitating it. Defence witnesses offered to produce a doctor's statement, as well as X-rays, to show that Mrs Duncan had a perfectly normal stomach, incapable of hiding any props that would produce the effect of materialisation. But these were not finally admitted in evidence.

A one-eyed spirit

The trial took place a few months before D-Day and lasted seven days. Numerous witnesses testified to events during Helen Duncan's seances that must have shaken many sceptics. Several people said, for example, they had seen the medium – who weighed all of 22 stone (140 kilograms) – and her tall, thin spirit guide, Albert Stewart, simultaneously.

Kathleen McNeill, wife of a Glasgow forgemaster, told how she had attended a seance at which her sister appeared. This sister had died just a few hours earlier, after an operation, and news of her death could not have been known to Helen Duncan at that time. Yet Mrs Duncan's guide, Albert, announced that the sister had just passed over. At another seance some years later, Mrs McNeill's deceased father strode out of the cabinet and came up to within 6 feet (1.8 metres) of her. She testified that he had only one eye, as indeed he had when alive.

Some of the most impressive evidence was given on the sixth day of the trial. Alfred Dodd, an academic who had written books on Shakespeare's sonnets, told the court that he had attended Helen

Duncan's seances on several occasions between 1932 and 1940. At one of these, his grandfather had appeared – a tall, corpulent man with a bronzed face, wearing a smoking cap just like the one he always used to wear. His hair, as always, was in a donkey-fringe style. After talking to his grandson, he turned to Dodd's friend, Tom, who had come with him to the seance. 'Look into my face, look into my eyes and you will know me again,' he said. 'Ask Alfred to show you my portrait. It's the same man.' The spirit then walked back to a curtained cabinet, clapped his hand on his leg three times and said: 'It's solid, Alfred, it's solid'.

Two journalists, H. Swaffer and J. W. Herries, were also called by the defence. The flamboyant Swaffer told the court that anyone who described ectoplasm as butter muslin 'would be a child': under a red light in a seance room, it would look yellow or pink, whereas the spirit forms had a living whiteness.

Herries, chief reporter of *The Scotsman* newspaper and a justice of the peace, affirmed that he had seen none other than Sir Arthur Conan Doyle materialise at one of Helen Duncan's seances. He had noted Doyle's rounded features and moustache, and had identified his voice. He further maintained that the idea that the spirit form of 'Peggy' could have been an undervest was ridiculous, and that the cheesecloth regurgitation theory was absurd.

Apart from the testimony of witnesses, the defence offered the jury an actual demonstration of Helen

Duncan's mediumship. At the start of the trial, the judge declined this offer and suggested instead that Mrs Duncan should be called as a witness. The defence replied, however, that Mrs Duncan could not testify, as she was in a trance during seances and unable to discuss what transpired. On the final day, the judge changed his mind about the demonstration, and asked the jury if they would like to have one. After some discussion, they turned down the offer.

Charge of guilty

The jury took 25 minutes to consider their verdict: they found the four defendants guilty of conspiracy to contravene the Witchcraft Act. They were discharged from giving verdicts on the other counts. The chief constable of Portsmouth then described Mrs Duncan's background. She was married to a cabinet-maker, had a family of six ranging in age from 18 to 26, and had been visiting Portsmouth for the past five years. In 1941, she had been reported for violating the security laws when she announced the loss of one of His Majesty's ships before the fact was made public. 'She is an unmitigated humbug and pest,' he said.

The judge deferred pronouncing sentence until after the weekend, and Mrs Duncan was led downstairs weeping. Between her tears, she declared in her broad Scots accent: 'I never heard so many lies in all my life'.

When he came to pass sentence, the judge said that the verdict had not been concerned with whether 'genuine manifestations of the kind are possible... this court has nothing whatever to do with such abstract questions'. The jury had found this to be a case of plain dishonesty, and he sentenced Mrs Duncan to nine months' imprisonment. The medium cried out, 'I didn't do anything,' and was led away moaning and crying. Of the other defendants, Mrs Brown was given four months (she had two previous convictions for larceny and shop-lifting) and the Homers were fined £5 and bound over to be of good behaviour for two years. An appeal for the case to go to the House of Lords was rejected.

Helen Duncan served her sentence in Holloway prison. The Spiritualist movement, shocked by the verdict, called for a change in the law to prevent such prosecutions. Many of Mrs Duncan's supporters believed she had been prosecuted to stop her leakage of classified war-time information.

When she was released from prison on 22 September 1944, Helen Duncan announced that she would not give any more seances; but it was not long before she changed her mind. In fact, she was soon giving so many that Spiritualists became concerned that she was over-sitting. The quality of the manifestations in her seances was said to have deteriorated, and the Spiritualists' National Union even withdrew her diploma.

But other reports suggested that her powers were in fact far from weakened. In the home of medium Susie Hughes, in Liverpool, for instance, Susie's spirit guide, 'Bluebell', was said to have appeared together with 'Peggy', Mrs Duncan's child guide. The two even sang and danced together in front of many witnesses. At another seance, Susie Hughes' father materialised. He greeted his wife and insisted that they walk into the brightest part of the room so that she could be sure that it was him. He then led her back to her chair and, with outstretched hands, took her in his arms and lifted her high above his head.

Emotional reunion

Alan Crossley, who wrote *The Story of Helen Duncan*, attended a seance with Mrs Duncan in 1954 at which he saw both the medium and Albert, her male spirit guide. He also saw the spirit of a man who had died just a few days earlier. The man's wife and son, present at the seance, were overcome with emotion when they recognised him.

In 1951, the Witchcraft Act of 1735 was repealed and replaced with the Fraudulent Mediums Act. Mrs Duncan's trial had certainly prompted this change in the law, but Spiritualist hopes that mediums would no longer be subjected to police harassment were short-lived. In November 1956, police raided a seance taking place in Nottingham. They grabbed the medium, searched her and took flashlight pictures.

121

They shouted that they were looking for beards, masks and a shroud. They found nothing. The medium conducting that seance was Helen Duncan.

The interruption of a physical seance is always regarded as extremely dangerous by Spiritualists, because the ectoplasm is said to return to the body too rapidly. In this case, it caused Mrs Duncan great discomfort. A doctor was called, she was treated for shock, and two burns were later discovered on her stomach. She was so ill that she returned to her family in Scotland and was admitted to hospital. Five weeks after the police raid, she left the hospital; and two days later she was dead.

The story of Helen Duncan is one of the most tragic and remarkable in the history of Spiritualism. She was either a brilliant fraud, able to make people see what they wanted to see by manipulating articles in the dark, or she was an exceptional medium.

Her story does not end with her death. Her daughter Gina revealed in *Psychic News* on 4 September 1982 that her mother had spoken to her for more than an hour through the direct-voice mediumship of Rita Goold of Leicester.

Most of the conversation was of a highly personal nature; and at the end of the seance, Gina declared: 'Yes, it is my mother. There is no doubt about it'. Some 26 years after her death, it seems that Helen Duncan was still working to prove that life does continue beyond the grave.

JOURNEYS TO THE SPIRIT WORLD

Some tribal shamans are able to enter a trance state and visit another realm in order to cure the sick. A number resort to psychedelic drugs to help them on such journeys.

The shaman, occupying an important position within many of the world's tribal societies, tends to see the physical world as inferior to, and conditioned by, the spirit world with which he communicates and to which he believes he travels when in trance.

Even the most ordinary physical events – a hunter's broken leg, or his failure to find game, for example – are seen as the results of supernatural happenings in which the hunter is perhaps the subject of an attack by malicious spirits, or has failed to show due respect to the gods and thus incurs their displeasure. Perhaps – and this is the worst possibility of all – a part of his spirit has wandered from his body without the hunter realising it, to become lost or imprisoned by evil demons.

In many shamanistic tribes, bodily sickness, particularly illnesses associated with high temperature and delirium, such as typhus and smallpox, are attributed to the latter cause. Thus, among the Altaic tribes of Siberia, the belief was – and still is for, in spite of many decades of communism, primitive communities still survive in this area – that really severe fevers were often caused by the imprisonment of the sick man's soul in the realms of Erlik Khan, one of the supreme rulers of the Underworld. It is clear that, in this context, the word translated into English as 'soul' means something more closely akin to 'vitality' or 'life force' than the 'soul' of Christian belief; for the Altaic tribesman believes it is perfectly possible to remain conscious, and even to conduct a rational conversation, when his 'soul' is absent from his body.

Just as it is believed that the shaman can travel upwards to the heavens while his body lies in trance, so it is thought possible for him to descend into the seven *pudaks* (literally, 'obstacles' – but the word 'hells' indicates the meaning of the word more precisely) of the infernal regions. This downwards journey is considered far more difficult and dangerous than the upwards transformation of consciousness into the nine heavens, so only the most powerful of shamans can undertake it. Even these supposedly risk death or madness when visiting the hells, and only the 'blue shamans' – men who are specialists in dealing with evil spirits – can make the journey in complete safety. And before a shaman will consider travel to Erlik Khan's black palace in search of the soul of a sick person, he will first set about searching more readily accessible locations.

The shaman therefore begins by entering a trance state, 'leaving his body', and looking for a strayed soul in the immediate vicinity of the sick person's yurt, or tent. If he finds the soul, he can usually coax it back into the body to which it properly belongs, so it is believed.

Hunting the lost soul

If, however, the soul is not nearby, the shaman searches further afield. He sends his spirit to examine the beds of lakes and rivers (both unlikely locations appear to be popular with truant Siberian souls), the depths of the forest, and the vast plains of the steppes. From all these places, the shaman's spirit can usually persuade the lost soul to return home, although the task is not quite as easy as when the soul has remained near its yurt. If the shaman's urgings are still in vain, and the soul will not return to its bodily home, the illness continues and the patient dies.

If the soul cannot be found, it is concluded that it is held hostage in the palace of Erlik Khan. The only way to get it back is to conduct a kind of infernal exchange of prisoners: Erlik will release a soul only if he is given another in exchange for it.

The shaman then negotiates a fee for the ransoming of the lost soul, either with the sick man's family or, if the patient is capable of conversation, the man himself. At the same time, it is decided whose soul shall be stolen and delivered to Erlik – most likely, some individual who has displeased both shaman and patient. While the chosen victim is asleep, the shaman enters a trance and leaves his body. He then transforms his spirit, usually into the form of an eagle or another bird of prey: shape-shifting is one of the arts in which shamans excel. The shaman-eagle now flies to the victim's yurt, dives upon his body, and seizes the struggling soul.

Then begins the journey downwards to Erlik Khan's palace. When this sinister dwelling, built of black boulders cemented together with black clay, is reached, the shaman politely asks the infernal ruler to make the exchange of souls, and the latter usually agrees. The shaman then returns the released soul to the body of the patient, who now begins an immediate recovery. But the man whose soul has been stolen and delivered to Erlik Khan falls ill, soon becomes sicker, and eventually dies.

Sometimes, a shamanistic procedure involving trance is undertaken, not so much for the sake of curing an illness but in order to determine its eventual outcome – to find out whether the gods have decreed life or death for the patient. A team led by R. Gordon Wasson has actually tape-recorded a Mexican ceremony of this type in its entirety.

This rite was performed on the night of 12 July 1958, in the Mazatic village of Huautla, by three shamans, two of them women, for the purpose of finding out whether a 17-year-old boy, Perfeto, would eventually recover from the chest illness – probably tuberculosis – with which he was afflicted. On the basis of divine messages they received at the height of the ritual, the shamans prophesied death, a gloomy prognosis that was to be fulfilled a few weeks later. These messages were directly heard by the shamans: any visions they saw were transitory and regarded by them as being comparatively unimportant.

Divine contact

The emphasis on what is heard, rather than what is seen, in Mexican shamanistic trance, is in marked contrast to its Siberian counterpart. Mexican shamans generally induce trance states by eating a particular type of semi-poisonous mushroom that is noted for its ability to produce auditory hallucinations. This 'divine mushroom' is unique only in that the hallucinations it produces are primarily aural rather than visual; for in every part of the world shamans use hallucinogenic plants as a way of 'loosening the girders of the soul', entering into trance and, so it is believed, coming into contact with gods, demons and lost souls. In Siberia, for example, shamans drink an infusion of the dried heads of *amanita muscaria,* the fly agaric mushroom or red, white-spotted 'toadstool' that often features in illustrated books of fairy tales as a quick method of achieving trance and vision.

The use of fly agaric has been, and remains, very widespread in Siberia. In the 18th century, Count von

Strahlenberg, a Swedish officer who had been a prisoner in Siberia for some years, described how the local population reached a state of 'drunkenness'. They did not, he reported, know the use of fermented liquors, but instead relied on an infusion of fly agaric, a sort of 'mushroom tea'. This drink, he added, was so highly valued by the tribesmen that the dried heads of the mushroom had become an article of commerce, a luxury that only the rich could afford. 'Those', added the observant Swede, 'who cannot afford to buy in a store of these mushrooms, post themselves... around the huts of the rich, and watch the opportunity of the guests coming out to make water; and they hold a wooden bowl to receive the urine, which they drink off greedily, as having still some virtue of the mushroom in it, and by this way they also get drunk.'

Bad trips

The 'drunkenness' observed by von Strahlenberg was very different from alcoholic intoxication, however. Steven Krassenikov, another 18th-century observer of Siberian tribal culture, remarked that those who underwent it were subject to various visions, terrifying or happy, depending upon differences in temperament. Some would jump, some dance, others cry and apparently suffer great terrors, while some might deem a small crack to be as wide as a door, and a tub of water as deep as the ocean. In other words, the drinking of fly agaric was often productive of something closely resembling both the 'bad trip' of the LSD-user.

Many anthropologists and students of ancient religion assert that the use of fungi and other plant substances to induce changes of consciousness is of great antiquity, probably almost as old as humanity itself. Thus, for example, in classical Greece, ergot – a fungus that grows on rye and other grasses – was administered to initiates of the mystery cult of Eleusis in order that they might be able to 'see the goddess'.

Similarly, in ancient India, a substance called *soma* was reputed to be both 'the food of the gods' and the chosen food of those wishing to come into contact with those gods. While the nature of soma has been the subject of much scholarly dispute – one eccentric academic of the last century believed it to have been rhubarb, a substance with laxative properties that seemed to him to be almost supernatural – it is now thought that it was some hallucinogenic substance taken by shamans in order to experience something supposed to resemble the life of the immortals.

But certain important questions remain. Do shamans have genuine supernormal powers? Can they transcend normal consciousness? Or are they simply inducing vivid hallucinations?

Roman Catholic priests, who accompanied Spanish soldiers and administrators to the Americas in the 16th and 17th centuries, had no doubt of the answer to these questions. Some shamans, they averred, were definitely able to obtain knowledge of the future and of things happening in distant places. But these supernormal abilities owed nothing, they said, to the personality of the individual shaman: rather, they were the gift of Satan, master of all shamans and wizards.

Ecstatic states

More than one Spanish chronicler asserted that the information given by shamans was 'perfectly exact'. Thus, Gonzalo d'Oviedo y Valdez stated that American-Indian shamans had some secret means of putting themselves into communication with spirits whenever they wish to predict the future. He had personally witnessed shamanistic rites and claimed to have observed the accuracy of the predictions made. The shaman, he wrote, 'appeared to be in ecstasy and to be suffering strange pains... while he lay senseless on the ground, the chief, or some other, asked what they desired to know, and the spirit replied through the mouth of the inspired man in a manner perfectly exact.'

Spanish-speaking theologians, particularly Jesuits, regarded shamanism as a dangerous and diabolical parody of the genuine physical and psychical phenomena associated with Roman Catholic mysticism. Indeed, priests were instructed to question Indian converts to Christianity closely as to whether they had drunk peyote – the favourite hallucinogen of Mexican shamans, made from cactus tops 'in order to find out secrets or discover the whereabouts of lost or stolen articles'.

The very nature of shamanistic activity dictates that there can be no hard scientific proof of the validity or otherwise of many of the claims made by its practitioners. On a purely anecdotal level, there is a good deal of evidence that some shamans do experience what seems to be genuine clairvoyance and clairaudience. And in the absence of hard scientific evidence, it has to be admitted that there is no proof that they do not leave their bodies to enter the spirit world.

AGAINST
ALL REASON

Statues that weep and bleed,
fish that fall from the sky and other
intriguing mysteries

Contents

Introduction

Since time immemorial, all sorts of strange happenings, contrary to the laws of nature as we understand them, have utterly perplexed the human race. Why, for instance, should portraits suddenly appear, as if from nowhere, on the floor of a Spanish house? What could cause holy statues or ikons to bleed or shed tears? Is it really possible to leave one's body on a spiritual voyage and experience what is known as astral travel?

Many of the bizarre events that you will read about in this book certainly seem against all reason. Orthodox scientists may even scoff at them; while by others they may be dismissed as fiction, figments of the imagination, or tricks that any competent magician could duplicate with the greatest of ease.

And yet, every now and then, researchers come up with new evidence that offers fairly conclusive proof for what previously we may have disbelieved. Professor Arthur Ellison, for example, carried out his own experiments in mind travel, with some amazing results. And, as we go to press, a new explanation has just been put forward for the Bermuda Triangle, within which so many ships have disappeared.

Some might at first be tempted to ridicule the tale of two strange, green-skinned children who appeared out of nowhere during the 12th century, according to monastic records. But, as recently as November 1995, in Denmark, an equally odd-looking green cat was found, for which there is current physical explanation.

Also late in 1995, the world's Hindu population reported what seemed to be a miracle. Certain statues in their temples – everywhere from New Delhi, India, to Neasden, England – were suddenly drinking offerings of milk. Thousands flocked to witness what was happening: the statues did indeed appear to be 'swallowing' the liquid. Scientists offered various possible theories but none was entirely acceptable. Eventually, the phenomenon stopped and the excitement died down.

Perhaps, then, our reactions to accounts of events that at first seem highly improbable should not always be coloured by complete and utter disbelief. The aim should be always to keep an open mind, which we trust you will indeed do as you turn the pages of this remarkable collection of tales of the unexplained.

WHEN FISH POUR DOWN LIKE RAIN

For centuries, there have been occasional incidents of fish falling from the sky. This strange, worldwide phenomenon is one of the least explicable quirks of nature.

On 28 May 1984, builder Edward Rodmell and his son were astonished to find that fish had rained on the house they were renovating in the London Borough of Newham. Dabs were lying in the yard; and there were also fish on the red-tiled roof and in the gutter. Then, on 7 June, a man living nearby found some 30 fish in his garden.

Extraordinary as such events may seem, they have occurred on many occasions On 16 February 1861, for instance, a violent earthquake shook the island of Singapore. For the following six days, rain fell in torrents. Then, later that year, after a last furious downpour, it stopped. François de Castelnau, a French naturalist staying on the island, reported what happened next to the Academy of Sciences in Paris. 'At 10 a.m the sun lifted, and from my window I saw a large number of Malays and Chinese filling baskets with fishes which they picked up in the pools of water which covered the ground. On being asked where the fishes came from, they answered that they had fallen from the sky. Three days afterwards, when the pools had dried up, we found many dead fishes.'

Although de Castelnau did not see the rain of fish himself, he was convinced that they had fallen from the sky. Dr A.D. Bajkov, an American marine scientist, was luckier. On 23 October 1947, he was having breakfast with his wife in a café in Marksville, Louisiana, USA, when shortly after a sudden shower of rain, he noticed fish lying in the streets: 'sunfish, goggle-eyed minnows and black bass up to 9 inches (23 centimetres) long'. More fish were found on rooftops, cold and dead, but nevertheless still fit to eat.

On their own, such accounts are not much to go on. Much of the evidence for fish falling from the sky is circumstantial – fish being found, usually after heavy rain, in places and on surfaces where no fish were before. But there are also eyewitness accounts. One of the best attested cases occurred at Mountain Ash, Glamorganshire, Wales, in 1859. In a paper published in the *Fortean Times* of autumn 1979, Robert Schadwald established, on the evidence of eyewitness accounts published at the time, that it had happened on 9 February 1859.

John Lewis, working in a timber yard at Mountain Ash, was startled at 11 a.m. when he was suddenly struck by small objects falling out of the sky. One of the objects fell down the back of his neck. 'On putting my hand down my neck, I was surprised to find they were small fish. By this time, I saw that the whole ground was covered with them. I took off my hat, the brim of which was full of them. They were jumping all about... The shed was covered with them... My mates and I might have gathered bucketsful of them, scraping with our hands. There were two showers... It was not blowing very hard, but uncommon wet... They came down in the rain... '

Wriggling myriads

A similar experience happened 86 years later to a certain Ron Spencer of Lancashire, while serving with the RAF at Kamilla, India, near the Burmese border. Speaking on BBC Radio 4 in April 1975, after another listener had described his experience of a fish fall, Spencer said that he had loved going out into the monsoon rains to wash himself. On one occasion, he was standing naked in the middle of this ritual when: 'Things started to hit me, and looking round, I could see myriads of small wriggling shapes on the ground and thousands being swept off the roofs, along channels and into the paddy fields. They were small sardine-sized fish. Needless to say, very shortly after the heavy storm, none were left. Scavengers had gobbled them up.'

Records are widely scattered and there is not a full study available that has collected all known cases. But it seems that only falls of frogs and toads are more abundant than fish. For example, Dr E.W. Grudger, of the US Museum of Natural History, collected accounts, and found only 78 reports. Seventeen of these had occurred in the USA; 13 in India; 11 in Germany, 9 in Scotland; 7 in Australia; and 5 in England and Canada. But Gilbert Whitley, working from the records in the Australian Museum, lists over 50 fish falls in Australasia alone that occurred between 1879 and 1971.

One of the earliest references to a fish fall is to be found in the ancient Greek text, the *Deipnosophistai*, compiled at the end of the second century AD by *Athenaeus*. These fragments, drawn from the records of nearly 800 writers, contain the report: 'I know also that it rained fishes. At all events Phoenias, in the second book of his *Eresian Magistrates*, says that in the Chersonesus it once rained fishes uninterruptedly for three days, and Phylarchus in his fourth book says that the people had often seen it raining fish.'

The earliest known case in England happened in Kent in 1666, and was reported in the *Philosophical Transactions* of 1698. But despite the wealth of authenticated and reliable reports that fish falls have occurred, no one has yet produced a convincing account of *why* they happen. One of the most plausible explanations is that they are caused by tornadoes, waterspouts or whirlwinds that lift water containing fish high up into a cloud mass and carry them inland. Other explanations include the

140

suggestion that the phenomenon is caused by fish 'migrating over land'; that fish-eating birds regurgitate or drop their food; that fish are left behind by ponds and streams overflowing; and that fish hibernating in mud are brought to life again by rain. But these do not account for the variety of eyewitness reports, the assortment of species found in the same place, the variety of terrain where fish have been found, and the sheer number of fish involved in some cases. And even though there are well-documented cases of whirlwinds and waterspouts transporting fish, this explanation is inadequate to cover all cases.

Orderly patterns

Whirlwinds, tornadoes and waterspouts are very messy, however, and tend to pick up anything in their way, scattering it in every direction. This conflicts dramatically with the great majority of cases of fish falls. In the Mountain Ash case, for example, the fall was restricted to an area 80 yards by 12 yards (73 metres by 11 metres); and in the Kent case of 1666, it was claimed that the fish were dumped in one particular field and not in any of the surrounding ones. Most falls, in fact, seem to follow this localised pattern. What is perhaps the most extreme example of this orderly fall of fish took place south of Calcutta on 20 September 1839. An eyewitness said: 'The most strange thing which ever struck me was that the fish did not fall helter skelter... but in a straight line

141

not more than one cubit [an ancient measurement deriving from the length of the forearm] in breadth'.

Whirlwinds, of course, move continuously; and there is considerable evidence that fish falls have lasted much longer than the time possible for them to have been caused in this way. The torrent of many hundreds of sand eels on Hendon, a suburb of Sunderland, north-east England, on 24 August 1918, for example, is a case in point. A. Meek, a marine biologist, reported seeing a fall that lasted a full 10 minutes and that was confined to one small area. But even if whirlwinds do retrace their path, some fish falls have occurred in such a rapid succession that they could not possibly have been caused by a single whirlwind. John Lewis of Mountain Ash, for example, witnessed 'two showers, with an interval of ten minutes [between them] and each shower lasted about two minutes or thereabouts'.

The length of time during which fish have been transported through the air seems, according to the evidence, to vary considerably. In many accounts, the fish are alive and thrashing when found on the ground: in other cases, they have been found dead, but fresh and edible. It is difficult to believe that fish could be hurled against the ground and not be killed, but evidence suggests that even those found dead were not killed by their fall. More puzzling still are the falls of dead fish. On two occasions in India, at Futtepoor in 1833 and at Allahabad in 1836, the fish that fell from the sky were not only dead, but dried. In the former case, the number of fish that fell was estimated to be between 3,000 and 4,000, all of one species. It is difficult to imagine how a whirlwind could keep so many fish in the air long enough for them to have dried out. But, despite widespread publicity in the Indian press at the time, no one came forward to report that a whirlwind had snatched up a valuable heap of dried fish!

Iced specimen

Perhaps even more extraordinary is the case from Essen, Germany. In 1896, a carp, encased in ice, fell out of the sky during a storm. Here, the fish must have been kept aloft by vertical currents, long enough to let it become the nucleus of an egg-sized hailstone. In falls of other animals and insects, there is a tendency for only one species to descend at any one time. But the evidence available concerning fish falls shows that they can be equally divided between falls of a single species and mixed falls. Up to six different species have even been identified in a single fall, for instance, lending support to the idea that the phenomenon is caused by a waterspout, scooping randomly from seas and lakes.

Falls of single species present many problems. The Mountain Ash fall in Glamorganshire, for example, was found to contain mostly sticklebacks, with just a few minnows. Sticklebacks live in freshwater streams and do not congregate in shoals. So how was it possible for a whirlwind to have scooped out such a vast quantity of sticklebacks from a single source and deposit them all in one place? Similar questions apply to other cases of fish falls involving just one species.

Another curious feature is the absence of any accompanying debris. Objects caught up in the currents of a whirlwind might be expected to be hurled out at different times and distances according to their mass, size or shape. Contrary to this expectation, however, fish falls often involve many different sizes of fish. At Feridpoor, India, for example, two species of fish fell in 1830, one larger and heavier than the other. Similarly, fish ranging in length from 6-12 inches (15-39 centimetres) fell in several gardens in Harlow, Essex, on 12 August 1968, according to the next day's newspapers.

Teleportation

Charles Fort, who spent a lifetime collecting accounts of strange phenomena, suggested that fish falls are the result of what he called 'teleportation', a force that can transport objects from place to place without traversing the intervening distance. Such a force, Fort claimed, was once more active than it is now, and survives today as an erratic and feeble semblance of its former self. Through this agency, fish are snatched away from a place of abundance to a point in the sky, from which they fall. Sometimes this point is not very high off the ground, which would account for the fact that the fish are often found alive. At other times, the point is very close to the ground, accounting for the many observations of fish that appear on the ground during a rainstorm. Fort further suggested that fish falls might be the result of a new pond 'vibrating with its need for fish'.

There is the case of Major Cox, for example, a well known writer in England after the First World War. In an article published in the *Daily Mail* on 6 October 1921, Cox reported that the pond at his Sussex home had been drained and scraped of mud. The pond was then left dry for five months before refilling with water in November 1920. The following May, Cox was astonished to find that it was absolutely teeming with tench.

Most fish falls occur during heavy rains, so the whirlwind theory seems to be partially acceptable. A look at the range of reported cases, however, shows that a number of falls have occurred in cloudless skies and quite independently of any accompanying strong wind. At present, the only rational explanation in terms of known causes seems to be the whirlwind theory. But this, as we have seen, cannot account for every single case. Some other unknown force must surely be at work.

SPANISH FLOOR SHOW

Portraits that appeared mysteriously on the floor of a Spanish kitchen are reported to have changed and decayed over a period of time, attracting thousands of sightseers and baffling psychical investigators.

On the morning of 23 August 1971, a housewife in the southern Spanish village of Belmez de la Moraleda went into her kitchen and was startled to find the likeness of a face, apparently painted overnight on the floor. It was not an apparition, nor was it an hallucination: the housewife – a simple peasant woman named Maria Gómez Pereira – could only assume that a paranormal phenomenon had taken place in her home.

The news spread quickly. Soon everyone in the village had heard about the strange happening and flocked to the house in Rodriguez Acosta Street in order to examine the face. It looked like a portrait in the Expressionist style, and the features seemed to emerge quite naturally from the blend of colours to be found in the floor cement.

In the end, the Pereira family tried to play down the extraordinary event that threatened to destroy their normally quiet everyday existence, and they decided to destroy the mysterious 'painting'. Six days after the appearance of the face, the Pereiras' son, Miguel, hacked up the kitchen floor and relaid it with fresh cement.

Nothing more happened for a week. Then, on 8 September, Maria Pereira again entered her kitchen, only to find a strange likeness of a human face in the process of manifesting itself in the concrete of the floor, in exactly the same place as the first one. This time, the delineation of a male face was even clearer than it had been before. It was impossible now to keep the crowds of curious spectators at bay. Every day, hordes of people queued outside the house in order to look at the 'face from another world'. It remained on the floor for several weeks: and although it did not disappear, the features started to change slowly, as if the face were ageing or undergoing some other degenerative process.

Recognising the importance of the faces, the mayor of Belmez decided that the second one, at least, should not be destroyed, but carefully preserved – rather like a valuable work of art. On 2 November 1971, a large crowd watched while the face was cut out of the ground, mounted behind glass and hung on the wall beside the fireplace.

By this time, the story of the second Belmez face had spread far beyond the village, and photographs of it had appeared in the local press.

The floor of the kitchen was then dug up in order to discover if there was anything buried there that might explain the mysterious appearance of the faces. At a depth of about 9 feet (2.7 metres), the diggers found a number of human bones. This discovery satisfied those Spiritists who were interested in the Belmez faces, since Spiritists believe that a restless spirit may haunt the place where its body is buried, or produce poltergeist phenomena there. Meanwhile, to the residents of Belmez, the discovery of the bones was not in the least surprising, since it was well-known that most of the houses in Rodriguez Acosta Street had been built on the site of a former graveyard.

Changing expression

The face that had been put behind glass was scrutinised by an art expert, Professor Camón Aznar, who expressed surprise at the subtlety of the 'painting's' execution. He described it as the portrait of a startled or astonished man with slightly open lips. But during ensuing weeks, the lines of the face started to decay, and the expression changed to one of irony.

Two weeks after the kitchen floor had been excavated, and then replaced, a third face appeared very near the spot where the first two were discovered; and two weeks after this, a fourth face appeared, the first to have obviously female features. After examining these two latest faces, Professor Aznar expressed the opinion that they were examples of paintings in true Expressionist style. Other observers, such as the painter Fernando Calderón and the parapsychologist Germán de Argumosa, considered them masterpieces of art, produced paranormally.

Stranger still, not long afterwards, around the fourth face, a quantity of smaller faces began to appear. Maria Pereira counted nine of them, while Professor Argumosa, who had taken up the case enthusiastically and who had become its principal investigator, was able to count eighteen.

At an international conference of parapsychology in Barcelona in 1977, Argumosa said that he inclined towards the view that the faces were the result of some form of poltergeist-like activity produced by disturbed spirits. Although his ideas were not very clearly formulated, he admitted to being 'most surprised when I was able to witness the formation of some of the faces from very crude lines to meticulously drawn portraits'.

On 9 April 1972, Argumosa had watched the formation of one face over a protracted period of time. Other witnesses present were the journalists Rafael Alcala from the newspaper *Jaén*, and Pedro Sagrario from *Patria*. It was incredible, Argumosa wrote afterwards, 'how the face slowly assumed contours before our astonished eyes ... I must admit my heart was beating faster than usual'. Pedro Sagrario also described what he had seen: the gradual appearance on the brick-built part of the floor of seemingly unconnected lines, which eventually composed themselves into an impressive and attractive 'painting' of a face. This face was photographed several times; but, oddly, it had virtually disappeared again by the end of the day.

Eventually, Argumosa invited his fellow parapsychologist Professor Hans Bender, of the Freiburg Institute in Germany, to help with the investigations. Professor Bender arrived in Belmez in May 1972, only to be met by a chaotic situation. Many people, including several priests, painters, parapsychologists and journalists, had witnessed the phenomena, and everyone had a different theory as to what might be the cause.

Different perceptions

After interviewing many of the local witnesses, Bender became convinced that the faces were genuinely paranormal in origin. However, Bender noted another dimension to the faces: they seemed to be perceived differently by different witnesses. The same face would appear to be that of a young man to one witness, and that of an old man to another.

Some of the faces also seemed to be constructed like a jigsaw puzzle, or to 'interlock' with other, larger faces. (This quality of one line being perceived in different ways is also often observed in the work of mediumistic artists.)

Attempts had been made to clean off the faces with detergents, and by scrubbing. But they persisted, evolving and decaying, seemingly in accordance with some strange law of their own.

Although Argumosa and Bender paid several visits to Belmez during the next few months, their investigations produced no conclusive results. But the 'haunted house' had become a place of pilgrimage for those interested in the occult, and people came from Spain, France, England and Germany to look at the faces, which they interpreted variously as demonic or sacred. They also brought tape recorders to record sessions with the 'spirits' that they expected to find lingering in the house. Quite a number of unusual recordings were obtained, including one made by Argumosa himself. On this can be heard loud cries, the noise of many voices talking all at once, and the sound of people crying. The tape was played in the Barcelona home of the psychical researcher Carole Ramis, and for her it certainly had an impressively eerie quality. Indeed, she was of the opinion that something very bad must have happened centuries ago at the house in Belmez – perhaps in some way connected with the graveyard beneath. But no entirely satisfactory explanation for the faces has yet been given: indeed, chemists who have examined the cement have been quite unable to account for the appearance of the mysterious Belmez faces.

SPIRITUAL JOURNEYS

Is it really possible to leave your body and travel spiritually? Professor Arthur Ellison carried out several personal experiments in astral travel, as described here.

It is often thought that if one has an out-of-the body experience – an OOBE – there remains no doubt about survival after death: that, in fact, an OOBE is a kind of mini-death, but with the option of returning to the body afterwards. Certain passages in religious literature certainly seem to confirm the similarity between death and OOBEs. Indeed, parts of The Bible can be interpreted to describe death as the breaking of a silver cord that joins the 'other' body to the physical body. 'Remember also your Creator in the days of your youth, before the evil days come... before the silver cord is snapped, or the golden bowl broken,' we find in *Ecclesiastes* 12, for instance.

The pioneering 'psychic' writers of the 19th and 20th centuries seized on such references, as well as similar passages in ancient Hindu scriptures, such as the *Upanishads*, to lend weight to descriptions of their own OOBEs. These frequently involved the soul's existence in another body made of some subtle material as yet unknown to western science, moving out of coincidence with the physical body and travelling away from it.

Until a few years ago, I myself thought that an OOBE would be an experience of great significance in which it would perhaps be possible to see dead relatives, converse with them, and bring back information that could be checked. All this would be of enormous help and significance in answering the ancient question of whether there is life after death. With this in mind, I tried hard, with various methods, to experience an OOBE.

A book by S. Muldoon and H Carrington, *The Projection of the Astral Body*, sets out a number of different methods of inducing an 'astral projection', as an OOBE was then called. All the procedures involved lying in bed on your back, and using the will and imagination in various ways. The principle was to loosen the grip of the physical body on the astral body by, for instance, imagining oneself in the astral body, consciously rotating about an axis from the head to feet, observing first the ceiling, then the wall, then the floor and the other wall. (Try it out, and you will find it is not at all easy.)

Other methods involved imagining yourself going up in a lift at the moment of sleep, and telling yourself that, at a particular point in the dream, you will wake up in a full astral projection. A third method involved going to bed very thirsty and imagining yourself going to the kitchen tap for a drink of water, pre-programming yourself to awaken, in an astral projection, on arrival at the tap.

Floating upwards

For one hour every night for a month, I tried these methods on retiring to bed. At last, I had success! The first sign was that, in accordance with the book, I found myself in a cataleptic state, unable to move a muscle. This was stated by Muldoon and Carrington to be the normal precursor to the experience. I used my will – or perhaps it was my imagination – to make myself float upwards, and the experience was quite fascinating. I felt as though I was embedded in the mud at the bottom of a river, and the water was slowly seeping into the mud and reducing its viscosity, so that eventually I was borne upwards by the water.

Slowly I floated upwards, still cataleptic, like an air ship released from its moorings. I reached the ceiling and floated through it into the darkness of the roof space. Then I passed through the roof tiles, and the sky, clouds and moon became visible. As I increased my 'willing' (or 'imagining'), my velocity of ascent up into the sky increased. To this day, I have the clear memory of the wind whistling through my hair.

From the moment of getting into bed to this point in the sky, I had no break of consciousness. Eventually, it all died down, and I was back in bed. I immediately wrote full and detailed notes on my experience, and recollected that I had read an account by a French writer, Yram, of similar experiences involving travelling up into the sky.

Thinking it over, it seemed a quite useless experience. Any sensible person would say that I had dreamed the whole episode. So I resolved that next time would be different – and it certainly was! The book stated that the catalepsy would disappear when the projection from the body exceeded 'cord activity range', and the projector would be free to walk about.

'Cord activity range' meant, according to Muldoon, that the distance from the body was great enough to reduce the 'silver cord' connecting the astral and physical bodies of the experimenter to a fine thread. The 'vital forces' (whatever they were) flowing through it would then be reduced to a low level and the catalepsy would disappear. If this occurred, it would be possible to walk into town, examine a shop window never seen before, memorise the contents, return to the body, write it all down, and carefully check the description the following day.

If this worked, surely no one would suggest that the whole experience had been a mere dream – especially if they were given the description before checking; and, even better, if they had themselves chosen the shop window to be 'astrally' visited! So I tried again. This time, it took only three or four nights to repeat the projection. However, on this occasion, I stopped the vertical movement at ceiling height and changed direction. Still cataleptic, I floated horizontally, feet first, towards the first-floor window of the room. Floating smoothly through the top of the window frame, I was aiming to describe a smooth parabola down on to the lawn. Here, I hoped, I should be outside 'cord activity range' and the real work of acquiring evidence could now begin.

Invisible hands

It did not happen like that. As I cleared the window and started the descent to the lawn, I had one of the most intriguing experiences to date. I felt two hands take my head, one hand over each ear, move me (still cataleptic) back into the bedroom and down into the body. I heard no sound, and saw nothing.

The experiences I have described took place in the 1950s. Since then, I have learned a great deal. First, I would say that lying on your back in bed and concentrating on a particular idea is a recipe for producing an auto-hypnotic trance. I have no doubt that I put myself into trance. Secondly, as I was expecting – and therefore suggesting to myself – that my experience would be what the book described, I entered a cataleptic state. Had I not anticipated that, I believe it probably would not have occurred. Thirdly, as I was expecting to float vertically upwards, that is the experience I had.

Other experimenters, with different ideas of what will happen to them, do not enter a cataleptic state,

156

and some times 'leave the body' horizontally, through the head, or sideways. A suggestion, to a good enough subject in a deep enough trance, that he or she will move around in a subtle body to other parts of the physical world, near or at a distance, will often be enough to produce that effect. Many people are even capable of having an OOBE as a result of suggestion under hypnosis. So, do they see the ordinary physical world? They do not have their physical eyes with them and clearly cannot. So what do they experience? It would seem what they go through is a dramatised reconstruction of a memory of the physical world: can it be anything else? But, sometimes the physical world seen in an OOBE does not quite match reality. There may be symbolic additions, like bars on the windows to prevent escape. Objects may also have a kind of luminosity. Muldoon even suggests that it is possible to awaken, projected, from an ordinary dream when observing an incongruity in the surroundings – for example, by noting that the paving stones do not have their long edges in the correct direction.

One of the best cases of a 'normal' projection into a 'duplicate physical world' involved Eileen Garrett, the famous psychic. She described in her autobiography how she projected her 'double' from a room in New York to a place in Newfoundland, the home of the doctor who had designed the experiment She could 'see', she wrote, the garden and the sea, the flowers and the house, smell the salt in the air and hear the birds. Entering the house, still quite conscious of her body lying in the room in New York, and able to speak to the experimenters there, she observed the doctor descending the stairs and entering his study.

Another person who experienced OOBEs regularly was Robert Monroe, an American businessman. One particularly important experience involved his projection to the location (unknown to him) of a woman friend, whom he found talking to two girls. He could attract her attention, he found, and she told him (mentally) that she knew of his presence but continued talking. He pinched her at about waist level, not expecting that she would feel anything. To his surprise, she cried out.

After the experiment, when she returned home, Monroe asked her (normally) what she was doing at the time of his projection. She described the scene, but remembered nothing of his 'visit'. Exasperated, he said: 'Did you not feel the pinch?' Very surprised indeed, she said that she had. Occasionally, Monroe felt that he was partly or wholly 'someone else'. Interestingly, this differs from the reports of many other experimenters, who talk of having consciousness both in the projected form and in the reclining physical body, and sometimes even of discussions between the two.

Disappearances in the Bermuda Triangle have been numerous, as you will discover in the chapter beginning on page 239. The reward poster, above, was circulated to draw the public's attention to just one such curious disappearance – the vanishing of the yacht Saba Bank, *while sailing from Nassau in the Bahamas to Miami, Florida.*

The phenomenon of fish falling from the sky has been the subject of eyewitness reports for centuries. The woodcut, above, shows an incident in 18th-century Transylvania, and the illustration, below, a similar event in Wales. You can read more about this extraordinary quirk of nature on page 137.

The world still wonders at the miracle involving Sadhu Sundar Singh, above, who managed to escape from a dry well, topped by a heavy iron lid and who has since become revered by many in the East as a saint. His story is told on page 172.

According to the traditions of Haiti, the dead can be restored to life, but only as mindless zombies. These figures, with their whitened faces and shroud-like wrappings, are seen here acting out the role of zombies at a street festival. But how genuine are the voodoo sorcerer's powers? Find out on page 218.

BLOOD AND TEARS

Can a plaster statue of Christ actually shed real blood, or a painting of the Virgin cry? These phenomena have been recorded many times, continuing to inspire – and also perplex – today.

One day in April 1975, just after Easter, Anne Poore of Boothwyn, Pennsylvania, USA, was praying for those who had turned away from the Church. She was kneeling in front of a 26-inch (66-centimetre) plaster statue of Jesus, given to her by a friend the year before. 'Suddenly I looked up at the statue,' she later told reporters, 'and my heart stopped beating. Two ruby-red drops of blood had appeared over the plaster wounds in its palms. I was terrified. I could see it was real blood. Since then, I've seen blood flow from the statue dozens of times.'

It is fashionable today to disbelieve in such things – or rather, to prefer to believe that such things do not happen. The closed or frightened mind often takes refuge behind an exaggerated rationalism. To such entrenched sceptics, accounts of objects of religious worship seen weeping tears or issuing blood are evidence of the deplorable survival of primitive and superstitious beliefs into this scientific age. But there is evidence that proves such things do happen at times, as the following stories show.

In the 1950s, an Italian physician, Dr Piero Casoli, made a prolonged study of weeping Madonnas. There was no shortage of them, for he concluded that they occurred on average about twice a year in Italy alone. And the records of the British *Fortean Times* show that such occurrences have been recorded throughout modern history, reports being received from all over the world. In 1527, for instance, a statue of Christ in Rome wept copiously and was taken as an omen of the fall of that city. In July 1966, a crucifix owned by Alfred Bolton of Walthamstow, London, shed tears on at least 30 occasions. In December 1960, a statue in a Greek Orthodox church at Tarpon Springs, Florida, streamed 'little teardrops'. And in January 1981, a statue of the Virgin Mary at Caltanisetta, Sicily – said first to have wept in 1974 – began to bleed again from the right cheek.

Faced with such seemingly 'impossible' occurrences, we are prompted to ask the rational question: can these stories be dismissed as 'mass hallucinations'? There are certainly records of people gathered around a religious image that is said to bleed or weep, their anticipation fired by rumour, who have 'seen' the miracle, possibly when the most suggestible person present cried out: 'Look, the Madonna is weeping!'

The American psychical researcher Raymond Bayless himself discovered just such a case. It began on the evening of 16 March 1960, when a tinted portrait of the Blessed Virgin Mary began to weep tears inside its glass frame. It was owned by Pagora Catsounis of New York, who immediately called in her priest, Father George Papadeas, of St Paul's Greek Orthodox Church, Hempstead. He said: 'When I arrived, a tear was drying beneath the left eye. Then, just before our devotions ended, I saw another tear well in her left eye. It started as a small, round globule of moisture in the corner of the eye and slowly trickled down her face'. At the bottom of the frame, the slow but steady trickle did not collect, as expected, but appeared to vanish before it had a chance to form a puddle.

Weeping Madonnas

In the first week, 4,000 people filed through Mrs Catsounis' apartment to stare and to pray, while tears flowed intermittently. The painting was subsequently transferred to St Paul's. Then, almost beyond belief, another weeping Madonna turned up in the family. It was owned by an aunt of Mrs Catsounis, Antonia Koulis. The circumstances seemed suspicious, but the phenomenon was vouched for by the Archbishop himself. The portrait was said to weep copiously; and when Father Papadeas let reporters handle it, the picture was still damp. Samples of the fluid were taken for analysis and found not to be human tears. This painting was also enshrined in St Paul's. Mrs

Koulis was given a replacement, and this too began to weep. It was at this point that Raymond Bayless began his investigations, as reported in the magazine *Fate* in March 1966.

Close examination of the surface of the painting revealed stains below the eyes that consisted of crystallised particles, something like those of a serum. The accumulations, being dried, had not moved downwards. When Bayless examined the image a second time, these raised 'tears' were still in the same place. He found no pinholes or other openings through which liquid could have been introduced into the central area of the painting, and stated: 'During our first visit... one woman, who was acting as interpreter, suddenly cried out that a new tear was descending from an eye. I looked immediately but in my opinion such was absolutely not the case. Some viewers and worshippers were convinced they saw tears appear and move on the surface of the icon while my friend and I were both present. On the other hand, we both were convinced, because of our careful examination, that... the tear was not liquid and did not flow or even descend a fraction of an inch'.

The case of Anne Poore's bleeding statue is quite different. When she recovered from her shock at its sudden bleeding, she made the statue the centrepiece of a shrine on her front porch where a great many people saw it. On Fridays and holy days, the flow of blood was particularly strong, streaming downwards, in a cyclical recurrence that parallels the regular bleedings of some stigmatics. Eventually, the statue was moved to St Luke's Episcopalian Church at Eddystone, Pennsylvania, and installed on a platform 10 feet (3 metres) above the altar. Father Chester Olszewski, pastor of the church, said: 'It has bled as long as four hours. I know there can be no trickery. I have seen the palms dry, then, minutes later, have observed droplets of blood welling out of the wounds... Incredibly the blood seldom runs off the statue. Its robes are now encrusted with dried blood'. Another priest, Father Henry Lovett, said he came to see it as a sceptic and went away convinced it was a miracle. 'I've personally taken the hands off the statue – they are held in place by wooden dowels – and examined them. They're solid chalk. And the statue has bled profusely even as I watched.'

The Blood of Christ?

In this case, there is no doubt that a blood-like liquid flowed mysteriously from the sites of Christ's wounds on the statue. But was it actually blood? Dr Joseph Rovito, a respected Philadelphia physician, conducted his own investigation. X-rays revealed no trace of a reservoir or other trick mechanism concealed in the statue, but the result of the blood tests was not so straightforward. Although identified as human blood, the low red cell count was curious, and indicated great age. The fact that the blood flowed quite a distance before coagulating indicated that it was fairly fresh, but fresh blood contains millions of red cells. Father Lovett, and other Catholics, therefore jumped to the conclusion that this was actually the blood of Christ.

Such images are almost always objects of worship, and so the mysterious appearance of liquids on or near these images is bound to be interpreted in a religious context. But outside this context, there are almost identical accounts of a variety of related phenomena: bleeding-tombstones, for instance; persistently wet or recurring bloodstains in a few haunted houses (evidence of a legendary murder, perhaps); or the constant distillation of substances such as clear oils or blood-like fluids that appear to come from the relics of some saints.

Once trickery and natural explanations, such as condensation, have been discounted, and the flow of blood has been established as not coming from inside the statue, then we have to accept that the liquid is appearing on the surface of the object, materialised there from an unknown source by the mysterious phenomenon of teleportation. The same probably applies to the appearance of tears on statues or icons. Yet appearances of these liquids are not random; in fact, they are remarkably consistent, for they restrict themselves to sites where either faith or legend leads us to expect miraculous happenings. Further consistency is observed in the association between bleeding and images of Christ, and weeping and images of the Virgin Mary. This regular association suggests either that the teleportative force is created by an unknown intelligence or that it acts automatically in response to especially powerful images in the human mind, on an instinctive or unconscious level.

Tears of joy

American parapsychologist, D. Scott Rogo, told the story of the Reverend Robert Lewis who, on the day of his ordination, recalled how his grandmother – his first spiritual mentor – had wept with joy the day he said he wanted to join the ministry. However, she died before his ordination and he deeply regretted not being able to share the happiness of his success with her. He glanced at her photograph on his dresser, and suddenly accused his companion of playing a joke.

The friend, the Reverend William Raucher, later wrote: 'I went over to see what was troubling him. I was astounded. The photo of Bob's grandmother was soaking wet, dripping with a small pool of water spreading on the dresser under it. Examining the picture, we found that it was wet inside the glass... The back of the picture, made of dyed imitation velvet, was so wet the velvet had streaked and faded. Removed from its frame, the photo didn't dry quickly. When it did dry, the area about the face remained puffed, as though the water had originated there and run downwards from the eyes.'

Rogo suggested that Lewis had unconsciously used a telekinetic ability to project a strong emotion into his immediate environment. 'Lewis underwent a mini-trauma when he passed his ordination exams,' wrote Rogo. 'His grandmother often wept with joy... He wanted to share his joy with her; he wanted to see her cry with happiness, so he used his psychic ability to stage the event.'

Rogo made the further suggestion that this was not a freakish power of one individual, but that we all may possess this ability to cause dogmatic changes in our environment by projecting outside ourselves powerfully felt or suppressed emotions. This type of paranormal projection, in which events are related to the spiritual or psychological tensions of those involved, takes two classic forms: overtly religious phenomena, and the disturbances known as poltergeist activity. In both cases, contemporary theorists relate the outburst of activity, or sudden manifestation of phenomena, to some inner crisis. Such a crisis may take many forms, such as the onset of puberty and its attendant physical and emotional complications, or the mounting pressures of illness, frustrations and inadequacies.

To the faithful, the sudden appearance of blood or tears constitutes a miracle: to others, though, it indicates a form of hysteria – that is, the unconscious mind stages such apparently mystical events in order to break a vicious circle of depression and self-pity.

Many of those unfortunate enough to be the focus of poltergeist phenomena certainly do seem to have been suffering from traumas, crises or major changes. When Mary Jobson, a 13-year-old poltergeist victim, developed patches of anaesthesia on her skin, as well as swellings, and convulsions, her bedroom furniture moved, music and voices came from mid-air, and raps emanated from the walls. At times, quantities of water were also seen to fall, apparently from nowhere, on to the floor.

Such phenomena undoubtedly occur – but we can only guess at how or why. The facts are suggestive of a teleportation of liquids, but from where remains a mystery at present. Intriguing, too, is the difference between certain types of paranormal projection and the way in which they affect those who are troubled by them. As researcher Dr Nandor Fodor observed: 'Religious ecstasy of the weeping Madonna type restores, whereas the poltergeist senselessly frightens and destroys'.

A MIRACLE IN TIBET

It seemed as if Sadhu Sundar Singh's fate was sealed when he was sentenced to die in a deep, dry well – but, miraculously, he survived.

All faiths have their saints, mystics and visionaries who have experiences expressed to them in the vocabulary of their own culture. A Roman Catholic may see a vision of the Virgin Mary; a Quaker may receive a revelation from the 'inner light'; a Muslim may experience a communication from Mohammed; a secular poet may find himself for an instant at one with the Universe and spend the rest of his life trying to express the glory of that moment's insight.

Such experiences can be used as propaganda for this or that form of belief. But the fact that they are shared by individuals of so many faiths and non-faiths surely means that they cannot be accepted as evidence for one particular form of truth.

The story of Peter's miraculous escape from prison, when chained between two guards (*Acts* 12), is one that even many Christians find difficult to accept. Yet a 20th-century Christian, Sadhu Sundar Singh, not only claimed to have had a similar experience but also spoke of witnessing an extraordinary vision, one that was to change his life. Sundar Singh's story begins in India, in the early 1890s, when he was still a young boy growing up in a wealthy Sikh family. His mother, a deeply religious woman, had taker Sundar to visit a *sadhu*, a holy man who had chosen the life of a homeless wanderer in search of truth. The meeting between the young boy and the old mystic had a profound effect on Sundar, and he at once made it his resolve to search for God.

Christian vision

When he was 14, his quest was intensified by the deaths of his mother and elder brother. A year later, possibly as a result of the missionary influences that were prevalent in India at the time, he struck out against western religion. Christianity was anathema to him; and to show his hatred, he stoned local Christian preachers and publicly burned The Bible in his village. Three days after this denouncement, Sundar is said to have received the sign he had been so fervently looking for. After praying all night, he had a vision. In the vision, Jesus Christ appeared to him and said in Hindustani: 'How long will you persecute me? I have come to save you. You pray to know the right way. Take it.'

Sundar's search had ended; and no one was more surprised than he that it should end with a revelation from a Christian God. But this was only the beginning of Sundar's story: with his personal quest now over, a new journey of evangelism had begun. He was baptised into the Christian Church in 1905; but, after taking an Anglican ordination course, he decided that the conventional priesthood was not for him. His new found faith was not a fragile thing, but then neither was his sense of Indian culture and tradition. Sundar believed he could spread his own vision of Christ only if he remained unfettered by denominational bonds: not for him the dog-collars and suits that he had seen other converted Indian priests wearing. Nor was he willing to block out his awareness of the ever-present spirit world, a world also close to the hearts of some of the villagers among whom he lived and later preached.

To resolve his dilemma, he took the unique step of becoming a Christian *sadhu*, preaching the Gospel without material resources and relying on charity. As such, he was allowed access to areas that would have otherwise been closed to him; and as an Indian holy man, albeit a Christian one, he was less likely to alienate the very people he was trying to convert.

Sadhu Sundar Singh made it his special business to evangelise in Tibet. And it was in that mysterious country that the miracle is said to have taken place. He crossed the Himalayas several times on foot and, though it was not easy to make converts in a Buddhist country, his zeal remained undiminished. It was during one of these trips that he was arrested and condemned to death for preaching Christianity.

Buddhist law forbids a true disciple to kill, so criminals are executed in ways that, by means of legal fictions, exonerate Buddhists from direct responsibility. Sundar's death sentence could have taken a variety of forms. One method was to sew the victim into a water-saturated bullock's skin: the skin would then be put out to dry, and as it slowly contracted, so the person within would gradually be smothered to death. Sundar's fate was to be just as unpleasant. He was beaten, stripped of his clothes and then violently thrown down a dry well, topped by a heavy iron lid. By his own account, the floor of the well was carpeted with the human bones and putrid flesh of previous victims.

It was only a question of time before either Sundar Singh would be suffocated by the terrible stench of death or he would die from starvation. One thing, however, sustained him. When he had first seen his vision of Christ, he reported experiencing a strong sense of peace and joy. This feeling, he claimed, remained with him always, even at times of distress and persecution. The effect of the vision – which, he maintained, was objective and entirely different from many other mystical experiences he was to have later on – was permanent; and that feeling of peace and joy stayed with him throughout the duration of his incarceration in the well.

Sundar passed the time in prayer until, on the third night, he heard a key grating in the lock above and the rattle of the withdrawn cover. He claimed that a voice now called to him to seize the rope that was lowered. His arm had been injured during the beating he had received, but fortunately there was a loop in the rope into which he placed his foot. He was then hauled up the well and was free. He claimed he now heard the lid being replaced and relocked. Once he was out in the fresh air, the pain in his injured arm simply disappeared and he is said to have rested until morning, then returning to the local caravanserai, an inn where groups of travellers would seek refreshment. He remained there for a short while before resuming preaching.

Divine intervention?

The reappearance of a man thought to be dead and safely entombed caused a furore. Sundar was arrested, brought before the head Lama and ordered to describe how his escape had taken place. His explanation of what had happened only enraged the Lama, however, who declared that someone must have stolen the key. But when he found it was still on his girdle, which never left him, he was said to have been terrified. The Lama, apparently cowed by the possibility that the escape was indeed a product of some kind of divine intervention, ordered Sundar to leave immediately and to go as far from the city as possible.

This, then, was the miracle in Tibet, when Sundar Singh was supposedly plucked from certain slow death. But was the hand that saved him divine or human? Certainly, Sundar's account has its weaknesses. How was it that, after his release, he was able to make it all the way back to the caravanserai without anyone commenting on his nakedness? In fact, such a sight was not as unusual in Tibet as it would have been in Britain, say. There is, however, no getting away from the fact that someone could have stolen the key in order to secure Sundar's release, subsequently replacing it in the Lama's girdle, or there may have been a duplicate.

A sceptic would have strong grounds for pointing out that the tale rests on the unsupported witness of a single man. That man, besides being subject to a constant stream of mystical visions, had experienced many other wonders. He claimed to have made contact with a secret Indian Christian brotherhood whom he urged to declare themselves publicly; and to have met a *rishi* (hermit) of great age, the Maharishi of Kailash, in the Himalayas, who dwelt in a cave 13,000 feet (4,000 metres) above sea-level and imparted to him a series of apocalyptic visions. These, however, were never recorded; and the secret Christian brotherhood never declared themselves.

But miracle or no miracle, the event cannot overshadow the fact that Sundar was a genuinely good man who, in his own lifetime, was revered by many as a saint. In fact, Sundar himself always tried to play down his psychic and mystical experiences, as well as his possession of a gift of healing. He found that a reputation for miracle-mongering pandered to the public's taste for the bizarre and that he thereby risked diverting attention to himself and away from Christ. His own view of the affair in Tibet was that it had been heavenly forces at work. However, he would probably have been the last person to have wanted to make a production out of the so-called miracle. Glorification of himself, or even the name of the God he served, was entirely foreign to him.

By the 1920s, Sadhu Sundar Singh had become something of a household name. He made many trips, financed by friends, to Ceylon, Burma, Malaysia, China, Japan, America, Australia and Europe. Through these, he made a deep impression on thousands of ordinary people of many races. But there were just a few who regarded him with suspicion and branded him a confidence trickster. He continued to visit Tibet, and the country that had been the source of his deepest revelation also turned out to be the place where he finally disappeared, without trace, somewhere in the Himalayas, in 1929.

SURPRISES FROM THE PAST

Modern research suggests that our ancient ancestors may have had technologies that were far more advanced than our own.

In a museum in Cairo, Egypt, a small wooden model was on display. No one could mistake what it was: one glance showed the wings, fin, tailplane and deep, bulky body of some kind of aircraft. The model was just under 6 inches (15 centimetres) long, and its wingspan extended to just over 7 inches (18 centimetres). Made of light sycamore wood, it would glide a short distance when thrown from the hand. It would not have been a great surprise to see a model like this in a science museum. But this model had pride of place as an exhibit in Cairo's Museum of Antiquities, and it probably dated from around 200 BC.

This ancient model is a glaring challenge to our ideas about the development of technology. And it is only one of innumerable oddities and enigmas that fuel speculation about the scientific knowledge and engineering skill of our ancestors. No one had connected the wooden model with the idea of artificial flight when it was first found in 1898 – five years before the Wright brothers had even made their first successful powered flight – in a tomb in the ancient Egyptian city of Saqqara. It had been stored there in a box together with figurines of birds. Dr Kahlil Messiha, who rediscovered it in 1969, was astounded by its evident resemblance to a modern aircraft.

A committee of archaeological and aeronautical experts studied the model, and they pointed out the cambering of its wings – that is, the curve of the upper surface, which generates lift – and the 'anhedral' or downward droop of its wingtips, which provides stability. They conjectured that the craft was a model of a full-sized aircraft. It would have been a 'powered glider', designed to carry heavy loads at very low speeds – probably less than 60 miles per hour (95 km/h). It could even have been propelled by an engine mounted at the rear, at a point where the model's tail is now broken.

The committee was sufficiently convinced of the importance of their find to devote a special display to it in Cairo, and the discovery prompted a fresh look at 'bird models' in other collections. Over a dozen similar 'gliders' were found in other tombs. Could they really be models of ancient aircraft? The idea of ancient aeronauts is possibly almost as surprising as that of ancient astronauts; but it seems aeromodellers may also have been at work in South America as early as the first millennium after Christ.

The supposed aircraft models that have come to light are a number of small gold ornaments that have been found in Colombia, Costa Rica, Venezuela and Peru. Aeronautical experts and biologists have compared these ancient objects with the forms of bats, sting rays and birds.

Ancient jet fighter?

One example was spotted in a collection of ancient art objects from Colombia by Ivan T. Sanderson, head of the *Society for the Investigation of the Unexplained* in the United States. It was a pendant, 2 inches (5 centimetres) long, intended to be worn on a necklace or bracelet.

The Colombian archaeologists had classified it as 'zoomorphic', or animal-shaped; but in fact it looks much more like a delta-winged jet fighter than any animal or bird. It has triangular appendages that resemble the wings of several types of modern supersonic aeroplane, a small straight tailplane, a tail fin and what appear to be insignia on one side of the fin. Yet the ornament is attributed to the early Chimu (who are also called Mochica), a pre-Incan society that flourished in South America from about 200 BC to 800 AD. Being so small, and made of solid gold, the model does not, of course, fly, but the resemblance to certain advanced aircraft built since World War II is so remarkable that one is inevitably left wondering whether it was indeed produced as a replica.

However, although these objects look like jets, how safe a guide is that? Curiously, the symbol on the

Colombian ornament's 'tail fin' clearly resembles the Semitic 'beth', or letter B. Some researchers have therefore jumped to the conclusion that the aircraft perhaps originally came from the Middle East. Over-enthusiastic interpretation may lead some people to regard all extravagant claims for ancient objects with suspicion, but it becomes necessary to pay serious attention when a functioning device from an 'impossible' date is discovered. The Saqqara glider is one example; and an equally impressive one is the 'Baghdad battery'. Externally, the battery is a clay pot under 6 inches (15 centimetres) tall. It is stoppered with bitumen, in which is mounted a copper cylinder that runs down about 4 inches (10 centimetres) inside the pot. The cylinder is made from strips of copper soldered together, and is closed with a copper cap. Inside the cylinder is an iron rod that been heavily corroded, probably by acid. The pot was found in Baghdad, and dates from some time during the Parthian domination of this part of Iraq, which lasted from 140 BC to AD 224.

When the archaeologist Wilhelm Konig came across the 'Baghdad battery' in a museum in Iraq in 1937, he immediately saw how it could have been used to generate an electric voltage. Experiments made with modern replicas some years later confirmed Konig's belief that it could indeed have served this purpose. To generate a voltage, it would be necessary to pour a suitable liquid into the cylinder. A large variety of fluids could have been used, including acetic acid or citric acid (these are the main constituents of vinegar and lemon juice respectively), or copper sulphate solution. This arrangement will generate between 1.5 and 2 volts between the copper cylinder and the iron rod. If a series of such cells were to be linked (forming a 'battery' in the proper sense of the word), the available voltage could be increased substantially.

Ancient electricity

The most likely use for electricity among the Parthians would have been the electroplating of figurines, an advance on the art of gilding which dated back centuries before them. The battery could have been used to apply a voltage between a metal statuette and an ingot of gold while both were immersed in an electrolyte. Gold would have been transferred through the liquid to be deposited as a thin film on the figure's surface.

Similar clay pots have been found at other sites near Baghdad. They are a salutary reminder that our conceptions of mankind's historical development are often based as much on ignorance as on knowledge of skills of a particular period.

Static electricity was known to the ancients: they knew, for instance, that when amber (in Greek, *elektron*) was rubbed, it would attract light objects such as dust and hairs. So the technique of generating electrical current – which is electric charge in motion – could have been an equally haphazard, isolated discovery centuries before its generally recognised initial use. Neither finding seemed to lead to further technological development or insight into the causes of the phenomenon, however, although some enthusiasts have claimed that the Parthians – and, before them, the ancient Egyptians – used electric light.

There are, indeed, enough soberly accredited anomalies of technology from the past to keep us well aware that some of our ancestors did develop their technology – and to astonishingly high levels.

Treasure ship

In 1900, sponge divers found the wreck of a treasure ship, almost 2,000 years old, off the Greek island of Antikythera, between the Peloponnesian peninsula and Crete. It was laden with bronze and marble statues, and may have been sailing to Rome when it went down in about 65 BC. In its cargo was found a mass of wood and bronze, the metal so badly corroded that it could just be made out as the remains of gearwheels and engraved scales.

Only in 1954 did Derek J. de Solla Price of Cambridge University finally deduce that the mechanism was a kind of astronomical clock, far ahead of anything that was to be seen in Europe again for hundreds of years. In fact, the mechanism, when new, must have borne a remarkable resemblance to a good modern mechanical clock. The device consisted of at least 20 gearwheels, supported on a number of bronze plates, the whole mounted in a wooden box. When a shaft that passed through the side of the box was turned, the pointers moved at different speeds over dials, which were protected by doors. Inscriptions in Greek explained how to operate the machine and how to read the dials.

The device was a working model of the celestial bodies – the Sun, the Moon, and the planets then known to the Greeks. Their relative positions in the sky were shown with great accuracy. The time of day was also indicated by the pointers. In Price's words: 'Nothing like this instrument is preserved elsewhere. Nothing comparable to it is known from any scientific text or literary allusion'. He goes on to say that: 'It seems likely that the Antikythera tradition was part of a large corpus of knowledge that has since been lost to us, but was known to the Arabs'. Mechanical calendar devices were indeed made by them centuries later, and they are said to have inspired the clock-makers of medieval Europe.

But what other remarkable inventions might such a body of knowledge have contained? What forces, benevolent or malevolent, might the ancients have commanded that did not stay alive in the memory of their descendants? That, of course, remains a mystery.

TANTRIC SEXUAL RITES

Some believe that certain secret cults have found the key to eternal youth. What truth is there behind this amazing claim that life can be prolonged through sexual indulgence?

Although most western writings on the subject of Tantra are somewhat vague about its inner mysteries, certain works by Kenneth Grant – known as *The Typhonian Trilogy* – go some way towards revealing and analysing this ancient eastern system. In these books, Grant unfolds some of the arcana underlying the symbolism of so-called Left-Handed Tantrism, as practised in the West.

According to Grant, the lotus – sacred flower of the Orient – is a symbol of the female genitalia and of psychic energy, and is composed of all the mystical essences. Its secretions are therefore said to be collected for use in various magical rites and for the consecration of talismans. As Grant explains, quoting from an initiate:

'What is not (generally) known is that these secretions are not mere excretions but are valuable fluids which contain in themselves the secretions of the endocrine glands in a much purer form, and more fit for human use than the gland extracts and desiccated gland products of the present-day organotherapy... The secretions of women are made in the laboratory of the Deity, the Temple of the Mother, and they supply just what is needed by the human.

'Of the three kinds of fluids, the urine is the least and the weakest; *rajas,* or menstrual secretion, is next; and *bindhu,* the last, is a secretion not at present known to the West, and obtainable only by means of the Shakta-Tantra and their analogies in Mongolia, Tibet, China, Peru, Mexico and elsewhere; a fluid that bisexualises... and rejuvenates to an extraordinary extent.'

The commentator goes on to say that at least 16 different types of bodily fluid from women are used in the eastern Tantric system – the sixteenth, *sadhakya kala* (also known as the ray of the Moon) being the most secret. To lend some support to these assertions, Grant cites Havelock Ellis, the pioneer sexologist. In his book *Studies in the Psychology of Sex,* Ellis says that only 14 of the bodily secretions known in Tantrism are recognised by western science.

Exactly how the various essences are obtained and applied, however, is not revealed. Nor are the precise results of their supposed effects. But there are indications that, in some way, they are able to retard or even halt the ageing process – a most remarkable effect, certainly, if true.

One highly secret group that would appear to have been successful in this technique is known as the Cult of Priapus and Ayana, thought still to function in Britain, Europe and the United States. The cult was named after two ancient gods. Priapus was the fertility god, venerated by the ancient Romans, Etruscans, Greeks and Pompeians and symbolised by his large phallus. His consort Ayana had three breasts, and she was regarded as submissive to him.

Eternal youth

According to the Roman author, merchant and traveller Lucius Marcellus, the Cult's followers would present their daughters to the Temple of Ayana, and here they would be trained as priestesses. In return, they were admitted to the inner sanctum where they were taught extraordinary magical powers, including the secret of eternal youth.

The onset of Christianity and its persecution of pagan religions caused the Cult to go into hiding, however, and it has remained underground ever since. Like the Tantrics, the Ayana cultists practised indiscriminate sex, incest and other forms of sexual rites considered to be morally degenerate. But despite the persecution of its adherents, the Cult apparently survived and later spread.

One of the ways in which the Cult stays secret is by dispensing with regular mass gatherings. Its aspirant priestesses are usually trained individually, or in small groups of two or three, by a priestess with whom they reside. The inner sanctum of the Cult's various branches meets only twice a year, and always at different venues.

The survival of the cult into contemporary times was discovered in the late 1950s by an American occultist, James McNally. But McNally's discovery was quite by chance and, being a devout Christian, he was horrified at what he found. Consequently, he uncovered little more about the cult and its activities. Another investigator, Justin C. Tanner, gleaned additional information. He found that there were three temples of the Cult in the United States, one in Denmark, one in Britain, and possibly others.

Another researcher, meanwhile, Arnold Weech, gained the confidence of the inner circle of the British temple and, in 1978, published a pamphlet about his assessment of the Cult of Ayana. But he reported that he did not think the Cult had any powers greater than those claimed by other occult groups he had encountered.

Weech did confirm, however, that the group appeared to have the power to arrest the ageing process. In his opinion, a further 20-40 years could be added to normal life expectancy, together with the retention of a youthful appearance. When he first encountered what he accepted ultimately as evidence of age-retarding, Weech found it difficult to believe. He met a young girl who looked about 18 years of age and reported: 'Only after I had met her daughter and granddaughter (who did not possess this power) did I even begin to believe that such a power existed.'

Later, however, Weech met another member of the Cult, a man who appeared to be in his mid-thirties. 'And by sheer chance I was able to check and completely confirm his claim that he was born before the turn of the century.' The man mentioned that he had served on *HMS Iron Duke* during World War I. Weech happened to know a man in his home village who had been an officer on the same ship at the same time and arranged a meeting between the two.

Photographic proof

The meeting duly took place, according to Weech, and within the first few minutes it became obvious that there could no longer be any doubt. They spent nearly five hours discussing old times and past events; but the clincher came when our host produced a collection of photographs. One was of a gun crew standing in front of a gun turret; and there, smiling at the camera, with the same tell-tale scar on the point of the chin, and looking only a little younger, was the Cult member.

As a result of his investigations, Weech came to the conclusion that initiates of the Cult did have the power to arrest the ageing process, along with 'the ability to alter or change certain physical characteristics and develop mental powers to a very high degree, and one other power, which I have promised not to disclose.'

This secret power appears to comprise some manner of ensuring that each member will remain absolutely submissive to the Cult and will not disclose its existence nor its secrets to anyone. According to Weech, the Cult of Ayana does not charge at all for membership, nor does it even accept voluntary donations. Moreover, it does not actively seek new members for its ranks and certainly does not pander to the curious.

Would-be members have their life thoroughly checked before being admitted to the Cult and, if any of the details they have given turn out to be false or misleading, they are immediately rejected. Those who are admitted are then put in touch with a mentor, who remains their only contact with the Cult until the preparatory period is over. At this point, the candidate is then given the choice of joining – for life – or of withdrawing.

The Elders have complete control, and any member who offends an Elder is subjected to severe penalties, including corporal punishment. Weech states in his monograph that none of the members with whom he came in contact had any regrets. A young married man told him: 'We have literally to grovel sometimes. Our particular Elder has total power over us and can use us as he wishes, we can only obey. If he desires my wife, then he takes her and

I have no say in the matter. Some of the ceremonies strip away all human dignity and yet we have no regrets. The diminishing of one's ego is a small price to pay for the priceless powers we now command.'

Illegal acts

In an attempt to investigate the cult further, Magdalene Graham, editor of the quarterly *Occult World,* which originally published Weech's pamphlet, was contacted. She gave her opinion as follows: 'Unfortunately, the Cult of Priapus and Ayana has now gone deep underground and severed all links with other organisations.' Asked if she believed the Cult used Tantric methods to attain their age-retarding process, she replied: 'I should think it extremely unlikely that the Cult used Eastern methods as they . . . were extremely scathing of Eastern mysticism. They did state that they used sexual magic but, from the deliberately vague hints, it is obvious that this took somewhat unusual forms and probably consisted of acts which even in these enlightened times remain illegal.'

It is clear that there are indeed cults in Britain, Europe and the USA today that practise sex magic. Even if they deny the Tantric source, it is almost certain that the ancient cult of Tantra, based upon the symbolic union of the god Shiva and his consort Shakti, provided the initial impulse for such practices and beliefs.

Certain places are often associated with strange phenomena –
Stonehenge, for instance, and the Devil's Garden in Cheshire, where
in 1978 two silver-suited figures were seen emerging from a shiny
round object, as above. On page 197, we investigate whether such
spots are in fact gateways to another dimension.

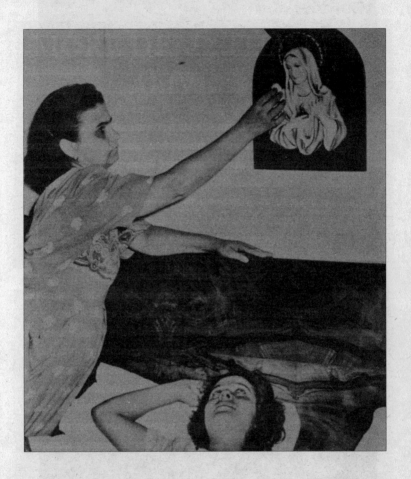

Witnesses were astoundeed when a portrait of Christ, far left, *in a French church, began to ooze blood over a period of months. Likewise, the mother of Antonietta Janusso, of Sicily, marvelled at the shedding of tears from a plaster Madonna over her daughter's sick-bed, shown in the photograph,* above. *Researchers put forward their theories about such holy blood and tears on page 163.*

The artist's impression, above, shows the two terrified children, found at the entrance to a cave in Banjos, a tiny village in the Spanish province of Catalonia. What was most peculiar was the odd green tone to their skin. Find out more about such bizarre 'evergreen' mysteries in the chapter starting on page 206.

WINDOWS ON ANOTHER WORLD

Why is it that certain areas of the world seem to be focal points for mysterious happenings such as the sightings of UFOs or hauntings? Could it be that such 'window areas' are gateways to the unknown?

It has been observed, on more than one occasion, that there exist peculiar haunted regions upon the face of this planet. These enigmatic 'window areas', which serve as focal points for UFOs, mystery animals, and all manner of unusual phenomena, are often as puzzling as the 'things' they host. This was the opinion offered by American phenomenologist David Fideler as he opened a major survey of one such 'window area', in Michigan, USA, for the magazine *Fortean Times*.

The possibility of windows, doorways, gateways or portals into the unknown has long been discussed; and, for sure, local legend often associates paranormal happenings with certain spots. Knowes, or Neolithic burial mounds, for example, are often regarded as such magical places. One story tells of two Orkney fiddlers who were walking past a knowe when, suddenly, in the middle of a sentence, one disappeared. Years later, the remaining fiddler was passing the mound when suddenly his companion was back, his eyes still as bright and his beard still as black as before, and on his lips the end of the very sentence he had been uttering at the point when he disappeared.

Space warps

Such mysterious disappearances and reappearances are also favourite science-fiction themes. The famous movie *2001 – A Space Odyssey*, for example, shows star travellers reaching their destination via a time and space warp. Even modern music ensures that this concept remains in our consciousness. The rock group *The Moody Blues*, for instance, had a hit with a song called *Slide Zone*, describing the effects of falling through a window in the framework of space. So clearly this is a familiar idea. But just what evidence is there for the existence of such windows?

David Fideler, a member of the Michigan Anomaly Research Group, which was set up to investigate the window concept scientifically, cited the following as examples of the kind of case that his team put on record, and which they believed show that Lake Michigan may well constitute just such a window area.

On 31 March 1897, a brilliant white light appeared in the sky over Galesburg, Michigan, accompanied by a strange crackling sound. Ten days later, fishermen at Pine Lake observed an 'alien' animal, something like a panther – but, of course, panthers are not indigenous to Michigan. It made a 'terrible noise' and was blamed for the slaughter of local livestock.

Other strange events occurred in the Lake Michigan area, too. On 6 February 1901, a mysterious fall of dust-like material descended on the town of Paw Paw on a perfectly calm day. In May 1954, a motorist at La Porte (a pleasingly suitable French name that means 'the door') observed three oval UFOs that gave out beams of light. His car engine and radio failed while the UFOs were flying by overhead.

Five years later, a young mother was the first to experience what became a wave of sightings of gorilla-like 'furry' humanoids, similar to the bigfoot or sasquatch, again in the Lake Michigan area.

Then, on 1 January 1970, a gigantic explosion rocked Pullman, a lakeside suburb of Chicago, just after midnight. Windows were broken, things fell from shelves, and a mysterious large hole appeared in the frozen surface of the lake, 200 yards (180 metres) from the shore, throwing great chunks of ice high into the air. The unexplained blast was felt 4 miles (7 kilometres) away.

In August 1976, several witnesses at New Buffalo saw a misty white object floating over a field. It was interpreted by one witness as a ghost, and by another as an angel. All these, and many other weird experiences in the vicinity of Lake Michigan, certainly indicate that there is something strange about the place.

Sceptics may claim that any populated area would reveal a similar catalogue if researched thoroughly enough, but there is sufficient evidence to prove that certain areas definitely record far more than their fair share of mysterious phenomena.

Interestingly, language sometimes provides a clue to the discovery of window areas. For if an area has always experienced a large number of strange events, this may be reflected in its name. Loren Coleman, an American writer on the paranormal, once conducted a study of locations with names that refer to the Devil, or the equivalent in the local language. He theorised that these places often received their names because of their reputation, since rumours of terrifying encounters would, in ancient times, have been directly linked with the Devil.

Coleman analysed many such places throughout the USA, and found that they were frequently rich in a variety of peculiar events. He concluded: 'Geographical "Devil names", worldwide, may indicate locales high in Fortean energy and strangeness. These places deserve some extra attention... '

Likewise, David Fideler pointed to an area around Draguignan in France (the name is possibly derived from 'dragon') and a nearby hill, known as Le

Malmont, which translates into English as 'the evil mountain'. Several strange incidents are reported to have taken place there – including the appearance of mysterious floating balls of light, and the mountain-top confrontation between a car and humanoid figures that emerged from a 'glow'.

Floating object

One of Britain's most frightening close encounter events took place at the Devil Garden, a secluded spot beside the River Weaver, near Frodsham in Cheshire. The date was 27 January 1978. At 5.45 p.m., four men in their late teens were wandering through some meadows close to a weir. They had to admit that they were poaching which meant that they were rather unwilling to discuss their story. But on this night, they were to bag rather more than they had bargained for, when they saw a strange object floating along the surface of the river from the direction of Weaverham. It was about 20 feet (7 metres) above the ground, and at first they took it to be a satellite that was out of control. (A Soviet satellite had crashed in Canada a few weeks earlier, so this was a natural assumption.)

The 'satellite', a round silvery object with a small skirt underneath, floated down into the nearby undergrowth, emitting flames as it did so. It then sat there, immobile and eerie, making a sound like rushing wind. The men were very scared, of course, but well hidden in the bushes, so they felt reasonably secure. They gazed in amazement as a peculiar bluish glow, which may have been ultra-violet light, emanated from the object. It hurt their eyes to stare at it; but just as they were about to run, with thoughts of radioactivity now uppermost in their minds, a 'man' appeared around the side of the object. He surveyed some cows in a nearby field, which were standing unnaturally still, perhaps through fright. A moment later, he went back round the craft and returned with a colleague. Between them, they were carrying a frame-like structure, not unlike a cage. The humanoids wore silver suits and helmets that bore lamps. They placed the large frame-like structure, which appeared to be very light, around one of the cows, and then proceeded to take measurements by moving some struts up and down.

The four men had by now had enough and fled the scene, no doubt thinking that they might be next on the list for inspection, and not relishing the thought. Off they ran, but one of them felt a strong sensation tugging him backwards by his genitals. These were sore for some days afterwards, and red as if sunburnt – out of the question in an English winter!

'Light ball' phenomena are in fact the commonest occurrence in such 'window areas'. The similarity to ball lightning is obvious. Ball lightning, however, seems to occur in well-defined meteorological conditions, whereas there appears to be no restriction as to when and where window area light balls can arise. It seems likely that the light balls, just like ball lightning, are electrical effects; but whereas ball lightning is thought to be caused by a static electrical charge in the atmosphere, light balls may be caused by a charge in the ground itself, produced by some kind of magnetic anomaly.

The catalogue of events that have occurred in Aveyron region of France is typical of experiences at a window area. Francois Lagarde was the author of an excellent study of the affair, as covered in *Flying Saucer Review* and the French UFO journal *Lumières dans la Nuit*. Clearly, the balls of light that seem so often to invade 'window areas' are very odd things indeed, and are capable of inducing quite disturbing effects.

Floating balls

The story concerns a farming family who had lived in the depths of the countryside for many years. On 15 June 1966, they saw a series of light balls, which were about 4 feet (1.2 metres) in diameter, floating about their large farmyard, climbing over hedges and seemingly inspecting things. They disappeared by 'blending into' a large opaque vertical cylinder of light in a nearby field. Over the next few years, these light balls were seen frequently, the cylinder always appearing with them.

It was on the night of 11 January 1967, however, that the family experienced what appears to have been the most bizarre phenomenon of all. The farmer's son decided to take his car and pursue one of the light balls. He saw some of them blend into the cylinder, only one of them remaining outside it. But, as he approached the object, which was hovering above the road, his car lights and engine cut out. Desperately, he tried to restart the car and turn on the internal light – but nothing happened. He had no power at all, and felt unable to move. Suddenly, a small saucer-shaped object flew towards him, straight across the fields. It had two small domes on top, and inside, surrounded by a greenish haze, were two humanoid figures wearing green overalls. The UFO came closer, and then departed with a blast of heat. The metallic road sign close to him then began to vibrate visibly as the UFO flew away. Eventually, the witness recovered and was able to return home, but he suffered strange reactions for some time afterwards. At first, he could not sleep; then he slept for 20 hours or more. At times, he found himself floating as if out of his body; he also experienced temporary limb paralysis on several occasions.

The major proponent of the 'window area' theory has been American journalist and collector of oddities, John Keel. His restless pursuit of the myths and monsters, falling frogs and flying saucers that haunt his native land has been pervaded by the wry humour that also characterised the writing of Charles Fort. Keel also undoubtedly means us to take very seriously indeed what he has to say.

One 'window' Keel claims to have found is in West Virginia. For months during 1967, local citizens were plagued by an horrific apparition, a winged humanoid dubbed 'Mothman'. There were also cold spots, space messages and meandering light balls. Warnings were received telepathically from mysterious aliens, stating that the current Middle East situation might escalate into a third world war, and that a nationwide power failure was imminent. Few people took any notice of these reports, but Keel knew better. On 15 December 1967, he sat watching the television news, sure that something was about to happen.

Over in West Virginia, it was the busy evening rush hour. At Point Pleasant, an old steel bridge carried the road across the Ohio River. Under the abnormal load of a traffic snarl-up, it creaked and groaned, tottered and swayed. Then, suddenly, it snapped. Cars and screaming people were plunged to their doom. Thirty-eight people were dead. Meanwhile, local residents, who had been spared the disaster, looked into the sky and saw, bobbing up and down above the river, meandering balls of light. Point Pleasant, it has now been generally recognised, is right in the middle of John Keel's West Virginia 'window area'.

RIDDLE OF THE GREEN CHILDREN

Thirteenth-century monastic records tell of the mysterious appearance, in the small Suffolk village of Woolpit, of two strange, green-skinned children. Their origin, and that of other oddly-coloured humanoids, has caused considerable speculation over the years.

The reign of Stephen, last of the Norman kings, was a dark period in the history of England. Stephen, who seized power in 1154, was a weak and foolish ruler who diminished the monarchy's immediate power by a policy of giving away titles, lands and royal rights to anyone prepared to support him, who fought a costly civil war, and who allowed the governmental machine to run down and his subjects to lose touch with the Crown. For the vast majority of ordinary people, it was a time of anxiety and strife.

Life went on, of course, in the towns, manors, villages and fields; the land was tilled and the harvests gathered, but it was hard to make a living and constant fear of war or invasion unsettled economic life to a marked degree. And, as often happens in times of great hardship, the suffering, uncomplaining thousands clung with increasing desperation to the emotional shelter offered by the Church. As Dorothy Stenton remarks in her *English Society in the Early Middle Ages*: 'Their lives... were hard and brief and they accepted unquestioningly a religion that offered to the poor and hungry an eternity of satisfaction'.

If anything, this understates the case. Religion was the very crux of medieval life, and with religion went a belief that the unworldly, or noncorporeal, existed as fact. What the eye could not see was every bit as real as the visible world; that spirits were invisible to human eyes was only an indication of Man's distance – through sin – from God. To some people was given the gift of seeing spirits; and at certain times, these incorporeal beings were apt to appear, either spontaneously or through invocation. For Saint Isidore of Seville (AD 560-636), demons, for instance, were quite real. In his *Etymologia*, he describes them as creatures that: 'Unsettle the senses, stir low passions, disorder life, cause alarms in sleep bring diseases... control the way lots are cast, make a pretence at oracles by their tricks, arouse the passion of love... when evoked, they appear; they take on different forms, and sometimes appear in the likeness of angels.'

A paranormal event would have been greeted quite differently in medieval times from the way in which we would regard it today: then, it would have excited fear, awe, interest – but not, on the whole, surprise. And with this attitude went, unavoidably, what we would now regard as credulousness. Clearly, the veracity of any inexplicable occurrence of the medieval period must be considered in the light of such an outlook – and with extreme caution.

A marvel witnessed

Monastic chroniclers of the time understood this. Among them was William of Newburgh – a monastery in Yorkshire – who, looking back to Stephen's reign in 1200, began his account of the strange green children who materialised at Woolpit, near Bury St Edmunds in Suffolk, with the following words: 'I must not there omit a marvel, a prodigy unheard of since the beginning of all time, which is known to have come to pass under King Stephen. I myself long hesitated to credit it, although it was noised abroad by many folk, and I thought it ridiculous to accept a thing which had no reason to commend it, or at most some reason of great obscurity, until I was so overwhelmed with the weight of so many and such credible witnesses that I was compelled to believe and admire that which my wit striveth vainly to reach or follow.'

After this diffident preamble, the chronicler continues more confidently: 'There is a village in England some four or five miles 17 or 8 kilometres from the noble monastery of the Blessed King and Martyr Edmund, near which may be seen certain trenches of immemorial antiquity which are named in the English tongue, Wolfpittes, and which give their name to the adjacent village. One harvest-tide, when the harvesters were gathering in the corn, there crept out from these two pits a boy and a girl, green at every point of their body, and clad in garments of strange hue and unknown texture. These wandered distraught about the field, until the harvesters took them and brought them to the village, where many flocked together to see this marvel.'

Abbot Ralph of Coggeshall, a monastic scribe working in Essex, some 30 miles (50 kilometres) south of Woolpit, was less sceptical about the green children, but also less definite about the colour of their skin, claiming only that they were 'tinged of a green colour'. He continued: 'No-one could understand their speech. When they were brought as curiosities to the house of a certain knight, Sir Richard de Calne, at Wikes, they wept bitterly. Bread and other victuals were set before them, but they would touch none of them, though they were tormented by great hunger, as the girl afterwards acknowledged. At length, when some beans just cut, with their stalks, were brought into the house, they made signs, with great avidity, that they should be given to them. When they were brought, they opened the stalks instead of the pods, thinking the beans were in the hollow of them; but not finding them there, they began to weep anew. When those who were present saw this, they opened the pods, and showed them the naked beans. They fed on these with great delight, and for a long time tasted no other food. The boy, however, was always languid and depressed, and he died within a short time. The girl enjoyed continual good health; and becoming accustomed to various kinds of food, lost completely that green colour, and gradually recovered the sanguine habit of her entire body. She was afterwards regenerated by the laver of holy baptism, and lived for many years in the service of that knight... and was rather loose and wanton in her conduct.'

Sunless origins

The girl apparently married and settled down in Kings Lynn. Here, she was often asked how she and her companion had arrived at Woolpit. The two monastic accounts differ at this point, though not substantially. Abbot Ralph records that they came from a country that was entirely green, inhabited by green people. It was also said to be sunless but twilit. They had been tending their flocks one day when they came to a cave: 'On entering which they heard a delightful sound of bells; ravished by whose sweetness, they went for a long time wandering on through the cavern, until they came to its mouth. When they came out of it, they were struck senseless by the excessive light of the sun, and the unusual temperature of the air; and they thus lay for a long time. Being terrified by the noise of those who came on them, they wished to fly, but they could not find the entrance of the cavern before they were caught.'

In William of Newburgh's account, on the other hand, the children are found in a cornfield, not a cave. The girl says: 'We are folk of St Martin's land; for that is the chief saint among us... One day we were feeding our father's flock in the field, when we heard a great noise, such as we hear now when all the bells of St Edmund's peal together. When, therefore, we were listening with all our ears to this marvellous sound, suddenly we were rapt in the spirit and found ourselves in your harvest field.' She adds that theirs was a Christian land with churches of its own, a land separated from a land of light by what she called a wide stream – presumably a sea.

That two alien, mysterious children turned up somewhere near Woolpit and were discovered there by the local villagers seems fairly credible. Times were hard, and it is not difficult to imagine that a family, too large and unable to provide for all, might choose to offload two of its younger members. In those impoverished times, it happened frequently. It even happens today. But it is the children's greenness and the other 'facts' of the case that make this such an extraordinary incident – and at the same time call upon a number of medieval superstitions and beliefs that cast considerable doubt upon the entire story.

The reports claim that the children were green, or green-tinged. No other colour has such supernatural

211

significance. In folklore, it has a curious dual significance: it is the colour of life and fecundity, but also a magical and slightly sinister colour, often associated with fairies. The most famous example of the association that the colour green had in medieval times is the 14th-century anonymous poem *Sir Gawaine and the Green Knight*. The weird hue of the Green Knight who turns out, as his colour suggests, to be an ambivalent character, neither good nor evil, immediately identifies him with the world of faerie.

Phantom from fairyland

In Brian Stone's translation from the Middle English, the description of the Green Knight runs as follows: 'The assembled folk stared, long scanning the fellow. For all men marvelled what it might mean, that a horseman and his horse should have such a colour as to grow green as grass and greener yet, it seemed, more gaudily glowing than green enamel on gold. Those standing studied him and sidled towards him with all the world's wonder as to what he would do. For astonishing sights they had seen, but such a one never; therefore a phantom from Fairyland the folk there deemed him.'

If Woolpit's two foundlings were green, it is likely that they would have been regarded as in some way supernatural by the villagers. But what if someone who was present at their sudden appearance decided that they were, in any case, supernatural: how long would it be before their colour became part of the legend, the 'fact' evolving from the rumour? This is a contrived theory, but not a difficult one to swallow. Further evidence to support this argument is provided by the Woolpit children's predilection for green beans. Traditionally, beans are the food of the dead and of ghosts, and the souls of the dead are said to dwell in bean fields. But beans have good properties, too – scattered round the house, they are said to ward off evil spirits; and in witch country, a bean was to be kept in the mouth to be spat at the first witch one encountered. The detail of the two children eating nothing but beans merely compounds their other-worldly image. There is therefore more than a hint here that someone has included this detail for emphasis, and that it is not intended to be taken literally.

What is most likely is that two foreign children had been abandoned by their nomadic parents, and were later found in a state of near exhaustion and starvation. Their greenness could have been some form of jaundice or even secondary anaemia. Perhaps, on the other hand, they were just green with queasiness – the simple effect, maybe, of eating far too many green beans.

An interesting postscript to the Woolpit tale is the story of the green children of Banjos, a tiny village in the Spanish province of Catalonia. The story goes that in August 1887, some peasants found two strange children crying at the mouth of a cave. The young

boy and girl spoke in a tongue incomprehensible to
the villagers; and, it was claimed, specialists called in
from Barcelona failed to recognise it. They were clad
in clothes that were made from an unknown material:
but, strangest of all, their skins appeared bright green.
What is more, their odd colouring appeared to be due
to natural pigmentation.

Diet of green beans

The children seemed terrified at first. The mayor of
the village offered them food, but they refused, and
for five whole days they starved, drinking only spring
water. Then they spotted a basket of raw green beans
and ended their fast. Thereafter, they lived solely on
green beans and water; but the boy had been gravely
weakened, and died within a month. His sister, on the
other hand, thrived and soon began to learn Spanish.
Eventually, she could speak well enough to be able to
describe the place that she and the boy had come
from. The sun never shone there; but its natural
boundary was a large river across which could be seen
another land bathed in sunshine.

Life had been peaceful, until one day a great noise
deafened the children, and they suddenly found
themselves transported to sundrenched Banjos. On
hearing this, the intrigued villagers searched for an
entrance to this hidden world, but without success.
The girl, meanwhile, reconciled herself to her new
life. Her skin gradually lost its green hue, and she

214

died peacefully five years later, taking with her the mystery of her origin.

The story sounds strangely familiar. In fact, its similarity to the story of the green children of Woolpit at first seems uncannily close: the only differences lie in that the Banjos children are described as having 'almond-shaped, Asiatic eyes', and that the girl dies after five years. But when we learn that the name of the mayor who looked after the children is Ricardo de Calno, credulousness is stretched beyond its limits. A certain Sir Richard de Calne had met with the Woolpit green children, remember. So unless there is some extraordinary Fortean coincidence at work, it can probably safely be assumed that the green children of Banjos are a complete fabrication.

But how did the Banjos story ever come to be accepted as true? Until the 1950s, the Woolpit tale was little known, but in 1959 Harold T. Wilkins included the story in his popular book *Mysteries Solved and Unsolved*. It was Wilkins who first suggested that these children might have come from a 'fourth dimensional world [that] existed side-by side with ours'. He also felt that the story could 'imply that they had been teleported from some world in space . . . where men live underground'.

Wilkins's extravagant views encouraged an unscrupulous author – as yet unidentified – to update and relocate the story. An imaginary village in a remote part of Catalonia was invented – there is no such place as Banjos – making checks difficult for anyone who knew nothing of the tale's ancestry. And so the story came to be accepted as fact, even though no one has ever produced testimony of any kind for the account – despite a claim that 'documents concerning the case exist, together with all the evidence given under oath by witnesses who saw, touched and questioned the children'.

The blue humanoid

Science fiction stories frequently feature accounts of aliens in the form of little green men. An actual sighting some 25 years ago, however, seems to indicate a somewhat different shade of humanoid colouring. In January 1967, on a rather bleak day, several young schoolboys were walking home together over Studham Common in Britain's Chiltern Hills when one of them thought he had spotted a strange figure, subsequently described as a small, blue man with a tall hat and a beard, lurking behind a bush in the distance. The lad immediately pointed him out to a friend and, curious, they both determined to approach him. Gingerly venturing towards the man, they got to within about 60 feet (18 metres) of him, but he promptly vanished into thin air, in a puff of smoke, as if anxious not to be seen. Utterly intrigued by now, because of what they had witnessed, the two boys got their pals to join in a hunt for the little blue man; and, sure enough, before too long he reappeared not far away, only to vanish again and then return – a trick he kept repeating.

The boys also reported hearing odd, foreign-sounding voices at the time, and soon began to feel distinctly nervous about the whole episode. They mentioned the occurrence to their teacher; and, questioned later by investigators who had been looking into reports of recent UFO sightings by local people, the boys wrote independent accounts of their adventure. The blue man, they all agreed, had been about three feet in height and had sported a tall hat. Mysteriously, too, he had worn a wide, dark belt with a six-inch (15-centimetre) square box at the front where a buckle might have been. The purpose of this was not, however, obvious.

To this day, the boys' experience remains unexplained, as do the humanoid's peculiar blue colouring and his persistent vanishings and reappearances. But it is not only people who occasionally take on strange hues, so it seems. In November 1995, animal-lover Pia Bischoff of Denmark found a stray cat with green fur near a hay loft. It was quite healthy and normal – apart, that is, from its copper patina which would not wash out. Scientists remain utterly mystified by its odd appearance

MORE DEAD THAN ALIVE

*The dead can be restored to a semblance of life –
as zombies, the mindless slaves of evil magicians
– so those steeped in voodoo tradition believe.*

'Near her, the black fingers of one silent guest were
clutched rigidly around the fragile stem of a wine glass,
tilted, spilling. Terror pent up in her overflowed. She
seized a candle, thrust it close to the slumped, bowed
face, and saw the man was dead. She was sitting at a
banquet table with four propped-up corpses...'

This is the vivid account of a voodoo wedding
breakfast held in the 1920s, as recounted to the
American journalist, William Seabrook, by friends
who had been present. The propped-up corpses were
intended to be turned by sorcery into zombies – half-
animate bodies living a twilight existence as the slaves
of the magician who was the banquet's host. (In fact,
according to Seabrook, the magician's intention was
thwarted, he fled and the corpses promptly
disappeared.)

There is only one country in the West where such
a ghastly celebration might have taken place: Haiti,
birthplace of voodoo. But do voodoo sorcerers really
have the power to reanimate newly-dead corpses? Or

is the notion of the zombie pure self-deception on the part of voodoo practitioners? The word 'zombie' appears in many African languages. In the Congo, it means a fetish; in Benin, it refers specifically to the python god. In modern voodoo, it seems that a snake deity is called upon to animate the zombie at the whim of the sorcerer who has become the corpse's master. The rites involved combine aspects of African magic and religion, with elements derived from both western occultism and popular Catholicism.

Voodoo actually played a part in the revolution in which Haitians threw off French rule. In August 1791, France was in the throes of the turmoil that had begun some two years previously. The King and Queen were prisoners, the nobility and clergy had seen their power torn from them, and Liberty, Equality and Fraternity had been adopted as the watchwords of the new order.

Little seemed at first to have changed in St Domingue, the western third of the Caribbean island of Hispaniola, the brightest jewel in the French colonial crown. There, 40,000 Frenchmen controlled half-a-million black slaves and 30,000 mulattos, growing crops of cotton, sugar, coffee and indigo. The first effect of the disturbances in France had been to improve the lot of the mulattos. Then the darker-skinned Haitians grew restless, helped by the agitation of a mysterious priest-sorcerer, named Boukman, who had found his way to St Domingue from Jamaica.

On 14 August 1791, Boukman summoned those who wished to follow him to a rendezvous deep in the forests. According to contemporary accounts, thousands of slaves slipped away along secret forest trails to the meeting, during a colossal tropical storm that must have lent extra terror and awe to the proceedings that followed.

Blood ritual

Boukman then conducted a blood ritual, sacrificing a pig and asking all who wished to be free to drink of the still-warm blood. The ceremony ended with a wild dance of 'divine inebriation', after which the participants melted away again, into the forests. The whole ritual closely resembled the activities of the Mau Mau during the Kenyan war of independence of the 1950s – and it had a similar result.

During the next few days, most of the great plantations were overrun and their owners killed. Although the stronger French colonists clung on for a further 12 years, the final result of the nocturnal gathering was the complete defeat of the French and the establishment, under the leadership of President Toussaint l'Ouverture, of the independent black republic of Haiti – home of voodoo.

According to the beliefs of the Haitian peasantry and, often enough, of the educated elite, it was also the home of the zombie, that sinister, animated, but reputedly soulless corpse. The zombie is the slave of an evil sorcerer, known as a *bokor*, who has removed a newly dead body from its grave and, by means of spells, endowed it with the shadow of life. It is an incomplete existence. Although the zombie eats, breathes, excretes, hears and even speaks, it has no memory of its previous life and no understanding of its own true condition. In other words, a zombie is a fleshy robot, a biological machine.

The Haitian peasant, ever alert for evil or dangerous aspects of voodoo, has several signs by which he can spot a zombie. It tends to lurch from side to side as it walks, to carry out other physical actions in a mechanical way, to have glazed eyes, and to have a nasal quality in its voice. This characteristic is particularly associated with death in Haitian folklore, probably because it is the local custom to plump out the nostrils of a corpse with cotton wool. The *guede* – sinister, lecherous gods of death in the voodoo pantheon – are notable for speaking in this way. When a voodoo devotee is possessed by one of the *guede*, he or she always speaks with a strongly nasal intonation. A further link between zombies and the death gods is suggested by the fact that one of the most prominent of the latter, Captain Guede, is often given the title 'Captain Zombie'.

Almost all Haitians fear the possibility of deceased relatives being transformed into walking cadavers, and the various preventive measures taken to avoid this possibility are readily noticeable, even in present-

221

day Haiti. Even the poorest peasants will borrow money to build heavy stone coverings over the graves of their immediate relatives. In rural areas, graves are dug as near as possible to a public road or footpath, so that sorcerers will be unable to go about their nefarious work, for fear of prying eyes. Sometimes, a bereaved family will watch over a new grave for night after night until they are certain that the body is sufficiently decomposed to be useless for the purposes of a *bokor*. On occasions, the dead are buried in the safety of a peasant farmer's compound. Some carry out even more extraordinary precautions to prevent their dead entering the misty half-world of the zombie. They have been known to inject poison, for instance, into the body, mutilate it with a knife, or even to fire a bullet into it, thus 'killing' it twice over.

Impossible tasks

A less drastic measure includes placing eyeless needles and balls of yarn in the grave, along with thousands of tiny sesame seeds. It is thought that the spirit of the deceased will be so busy with the impossible tasks of threading the needle and counting the seeds that it will be unable to hear the voice of a *bokor* calling it from the tomb. Alternatively, a knife, with which it can defend itself, may be placed in the corpse's hand. Sorcerers sometimes control whole troops of zombies and on occasion have gone so far as to hire them out as labourers. One such alleged case was recorded by

William Seabrook. During a bumper sugar crop in 1918, the Haitian American Sugar Corporation offered a bonus for new workers on its extensive plantations. Soon, little groups of villagers, including whole families, made their way to the company's labour office. It was customary for such village groups to work collectively, and the pay for the entire work force would be given to a foreman who would share it out when the party returned home.

One morning, an old village headman, Ti Joseph, and his wife Croyance, led a band of nine ragged and shuffling men into the Hasco office. They were, explained Joseph, backward and ignorant hill farmers who spoke only an obscure rural dialect and could understand neither Creole nor French. In spite of this disadvantage, he continued, they were excellent workmen, strong and healthy, who would labour happily at whatever tasks they were given.

Hasco's labour manager took on the gang, agreeing with Joseph's suggestion that they should work far from other groups: the head man explained that they were so primitive that they would become shy and confused near others. But his real reason for insisting on his workers' isolation was his fear that one or other of them would be recognised by a relative or former friend. For every one of Ti Joseph's work gang was a zombie.

Ti Joseph's labourers worked steadfastly through the hours of daylight, stopping only at dusk for their

223

meal of unsalted millet porridge. (Voodoo tradition holds that if a zombie tastes meat or salt, it becomes conscious of its true condition and, weeping bitter tears, makes its way back to its grave.)

The taste of salt

One Sunday morning, Ti Joseph left his wife Croyance to look after the zombies while he took the day off. Croyance led them into the nearby town: there was to be a church festival and she apparently thought that the zombies would be pleased to witness a religious procession. But the zombies were as unmoved by the spectacle as by anything else that happened around them. Dumbly and vacantly, they continued to stare into space. Croyance, pitying them, decided that sweetmeats might please them.

She bought some tablettes, which are made of brown sugar, coriander and peanuts, and put a piece into each zombie's mouth. But the peanuts had been salted before the tablettes had been made. As they chewed the delicacy, the zombies realised that they were dead, and that they did not belong to Haiti's bright sunlit world, but to the darkness of the tomb. With an appalling cry, they rose and shuffled out of the town into the forests, towards their home village in the mountains. When at last they arrived there, they were recognised by the relatives and friends who had buried them months before. As they reached the graveyard, each approached its own grave, scrabbled away the stones and earth that covered it, and then fell to the ground, a mass of decomposition.

Ti Joseph's power, which had preserved their bodies from decay, had vanished. The villagers inflicted their revenge on Ti Joseph and paid a local sorcerer to cast a spell on him. But before it could take its effect, some of the men had ambushed him and cut off his head.

Seabrook was told this tale by Constant Polynice, a Haitian farmer. Shortly after telling this story, he showed Seabrook a group of three supposed zombies. They were digging with machetes, under the supervision of a young woman. Seabrook looked into the face of one of the men and said: 'And what I saw then, coupled with what I had heard previously, or despite it, came as a rather sickening shock. The eyes were the worst... They were in truth like the eyes of a dead man, not blind, but staring, unfocused, unseeing. The whole face... seemed not only expressionless, but incapable of expression.'

Seabrook reassured himself that these men were 'nothing but poor ordinary demented human beings, idiots, forced to toil in the fields'. But his Haitian friend was not convinced. Writing in the 1950s, the French anthropologist Alfred Metraux heard a good deal of evidence both for and against the existence of zombies. But when he was shown one in the flesh, he concluded that she was 'a wretched lunatic'. Indeed, the following day, the person he had seen was identified as a mentally deficient girl who had escaped from the locked room in which she was usually kept.

Another American writer, Zora Hurston, met and photographed a girl who was alleged to have been a zombie for no less than 29 years. In 1907, Felicia Felix-Mentor had died of a sudden illness, and was buried by her husband and brother. In 1936, a girl dressed only in a thin, torn cotton smock was found wandering in a road near the brother's farm. She appeared to have lost the power of speech completely. Felicia's relatives identified her as the long-dead girl. Taken to a hospital, she cringed fearfully when anyone approached, as if expecting ill-treatment.

It was there that Zora Hurston took her picture and tried to speak to her. Afterwards she wrote: 'The sight was dreadful. That blank face with the dead eyes. The eyelids were white all around the eyes as if they had been burned with acid. There was nothing you could say to her or get from her except by looking at her, and the sight of this wreckage was too much to endure for long.'

Was the girl who had been found merely a wandering lunatic? The firmly entrenched belief of the Haitians that relatives and loved ones have been seen after their burial, living the half-life of the zombie, throws doubt on this theory. There must surely be something deeper to the legend of the zombie.

HOWLS OF
HORROR

*The image of someone turning into a wolf is one
that has haunted human imagination for
centuries. It finds its chief expression in the
terrifying legend of the werewolf. But could there
be more to such tales than mere superstition?*

Towards the middle of the 19th century, on a
picturesque hill near the Vistula, a river in Poland that
flows past Cracow and Warsaw, a large gathering of
young people were celebrating, with music, singing
and dancing, the completion of the harvest. There
was food and drink in abundance, and everyone
indulged freely.

Suddenly, while the merry-making was in full
swing, a terrible, blood-curdling cry echoed across the
valley. Abandoning their dancing, the young men and
women ran in the direction from which the cry had
come and discovered, to their horror, that an
enormous wolf had seized one of the village's prettiest
girls, who had recently become engaged to be
married, and was dragging her away. Her fiancé was
nowhere to be seen.

The most courageous of the men went in pursuit
of the wolf and eventually confronted it. But the

furious monster, its mouth foaming with a fiendish rage, dropped its human prey on the ground and stood over it, ready to fight. Some of the villagers ran home to fetch guns and axes; but the wolf, seeing the fear of those who remained, again seized the girl and vanished into the nearby forest.

Many years elapsed; and then, at another harvest feast, on the same hill, an old man approached the revellers. They invited him to join in the celebrations, but the old man, gloomy and reserved, chose to sit down to drink in silence. A countryman of roughly the same age then joined him and, after looking at him closely for a moment or two, asked with some emotion: 'Is it you, John?'

The old man nodded, and instantly the countryman recognised the stranger as his older brother, who had disappeared many years before. The merry-makers quickly gathered round the old visitor and listened to his strange tale. He told them how, having been changed into a wolf by a sorcerer, he had carried his fiancée away from that same hill during a harvest festival and had lived with her in the nearby forest for a year, after which she died.

'From that moment on', he continued, 'savage and furious, I attacked every man, woman and child, and destroyed every animal I came across. My trail of bloodshed I cannot even now completely wipe away.' At this point he showed them his hands, which were covered with bloodstains.

'It is some four years since, having once again changed back to human shape, I have wandered from place to place. I wanted to see you all once more – to see the cottage and village where I was born and grew up to be a man. After that... well, I shall become a wolf again.'

No sooner had he uttered these words than he changed into a wolf. He rushed past the astonished onlookers and disappeared into the forest, never to be seen again.

The fairy-tale aspects of this story do, of course, make it very difficult to take seriously. Could too much drink have enhanced the already colourful imagination of the peasant folk? Could detail have been built upon detail with each new telling until the story reached its present apparently fanciful form? It is a strong possibility... and yet, like so many werewolf horror stories of its type, it is reported by many mythologists and historians, folklorists and psychologists as pure fact.

Horrific evidence

In one period of little over 100 years – between 1520 and 1630 – France could record a staggering 30,000 cases of werewolfism – a fact documented in the proceedings of werewolf trials that are still preserved in the public records.

In 1573 at Dôle, near Dijon in central France, a werewolf named Gilles Garnier was accused of devastating the countryside and devouring little children and, after confessing to the crimes, was burnt at the stake. Years later, in 1598, in a wild and desolate area near Caude, a group of French countrymen stumbled across the horribly mutilated, blood-spattered body of a 15-year-old boy. A pair of wolves, which had been devouring the corpse, ran off into a nearby thicket as the men approached. They gave chase – and almost immediately they found a half-naked man crouching in the bushes, sporting long hair, an unkempt beard and long, dirty claw-like nails, which were clotted with fresh blood and the shreds of human flesh.

The man, Jacques Rollet, was a pathetic, half-witted specimen under the curse of a cannibal appetite. He had been in the process of tearing to pieces the corpse of the boy when disturbed by the countrymen. Whether or not there were any real wolves in the case, except those that excited imaginations may have conjured up, it is impossible to determine. But it is certain that Rollet supposed himself to be a wolf, and killed and ate several people under the influence of this delusion, a psychiatric condition known as *lycanthropy*. He was sentenced to death, but the law courts of Paris reversed the sentence and charitably shut him up in a madhouse – an institution where most suspected werewolves should probably have lived out their days, rather than being executed.

Another significant werewolf case occurred in the early 17th century. Jean Grenier was a boy of 13, partially idiotic and of strongly marked canine physiognomy – his jaws jutted forward, and his canine teeth showed under his upper lip. He believed himself to be a werewolf. One evening, meeting some young girls, he terrified them by saying that, as soon as the sun had set, he would turn into a wolf and eat them for supper.

A few days later, one little girl, having gone out at nightfall to tend to the sheep, was attacked by some creature that, in her terror, she mistook for a wolf, but that afterwards proved to be none other than Jean Grenier. She beat him off with her sheep-staff, and fled home.

Pact with the Devil

When brought before the law courts of Bordeaux, Grenier confessed that, two years previously, he had met the Devil one night in the woods, had signed a pact with him and received from him a wolfskin. Since then, he had roamed about as a wolf after dark, resuming his human shape by daylight. He had killed and eaten several children whom he had found alone in the fields, and once he had entered a house while the family were out and taken a baby from its cradle.

A careful investigation by the court proved that these statements were true, certainly as far as the cannibalism was concerned. There is little doubt that the missing children were eaten by Jean Grenier, and there is no doubt that the half-witted boy was firmly convinced that he was a wolf.

In more recent times, the werewolf phenomenon has retreated somewhat into the realms of fantasy, but has done so without losing any of its grim horror. Nevertheless, tales of real werewolves have cropped up from time to time this century. Three werewolves were said to haunt the forested Ardennes area of Belgium just before the First World War, for instance; while, in Scotland at about the same time, a hermit shepherd in the area of Inverness was rumoured to be a werewolf. In 1925, a whole village near Strasbourg testified that a local boy was a werewolf; and, five years later, a French werewolf scare terrorised Bourg-la-Reine, just south of Paris.

Werewolf scares have indeed occurred the world over. In 1946, for instance, a Navajo Indian reservation was frequently plagued by a murderous beast that was widely reported as a werewolf. (Navajo traditions are rich in werewolf tales). Three years later, in Rome, a police patrol was sent to investigate the strange behaviour of a man suffering from werewolf delusions: he regularly lost control at the time of a full moon and let out loud and terrifying howls.

In Singapore, in 1957, police were again called to look into a long series of werewolf attacks a nurses' hostel. One nurse awoke to find a horrible face, with hair reaching to the bridge of the nose, and long protruding fangs, glaring down at her. The mystery was never solved.

In 1975, Britain's newspapers were full of the most extraordinary reports about a 17-year-old youth from the village of Eccleshall, Staffordshire. In the awful belief that he was slowly turning into a werewolf, he terminated his mental agonies by plunging a flick-knife into his heart. One of his workmates told the inquest jury that the youth had made a frantic telephone call to him just before his death. 'He told me,' said the witness, 'that his face and hand were changing colour and that he was changing into a werewolf. He would go quiet and then start growling.'

Born to be wild

Some 'wild men' take other forms. The French anthropologist, Jean-Claude Armen, for instance, reported that, on several occasions during the 1970s, he saw a 'human gazelle' in the Syrian desert.

The creature, was a 10-year-old boy who galloped 'in gigantic bounds amongst a long cavalcade of white gazelles'. According to Armen, this 'gazelle boy' seemed to have adapted himself to the life of the herd, licking and sniffing at the animals in the friendliest of ways.

This seemingly well-authenticated account is just one example of many reports dating back to the Middle Ages of encounters with human children who have supposedly been reared by wild animals.

But the most frequently-featured foster-parents in such accounts are undoubtedly wolves – animals that haunted the ancient forests of Europe and beyond, and that became a staple element of folk tales.

One of the earliest of wolf stories is that of Romulus and Remus, the legendary founders of Rome, who as babies were suckled by a she-wolf. In modern times, however, one of the most intriguing cases of children supposedly reared by wolves occurred in India in 1920. Two girls, aged two and eight, were allegedly found in a wolf-lair at Midnapore in West Bengal by an Anglican clergyman, the Reverend J.A.L. Singh.

Singh kept a diary of his efforts to humanise the two, whom he named Amala and Kamala. Civilising them proved a difficult task, for they ran on all fours, howled like wolves, and ate only raw meat. The younger child, Amala, died within a year of being found, but Kamala lived for a further nine years, learning to walk upright and to speak over 30 words.

It remains a mystery as to whether these children and their like were truly reared by wolves or whether, as it was asserted by the child psychologist Bruno Bettelheim, they were abandoned autistic children who had simply crawled into an animal's den.

The werewolf tradition, meanwhile, may be built on ignorance and delusion, but its influence on the mind of the weak and sick has always been powerful and most probably will remain so.

The face, above, *appeared overnight on the floor of a home in the Spanish village of Belmez de la Moraleda. Over the next few months, however, it began to degenerate. Scientists and parapsychologists were utterly baffled by the occurrence, as described in detail on page 146.*

This painting by Austin O. Spare shows the ancient god of fertility, Priapus. The modern secret cult of Priapus and Ayana emphasises sexual rites and claims to be able to halt the ageing process by certain magical practices, as outlined on page 186.

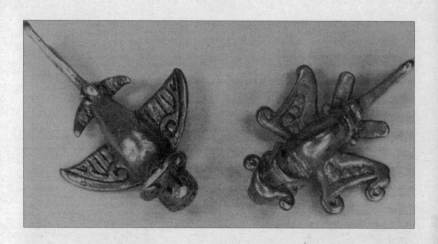

One of the ancient gold ornaments, top, *resembles a modern delta-wing jet; and those,* below, *seem to be arithmetical models of the solar system. On page 179, we ask how Man could possibly have been so technologically advanced at such early dates.*

The 19th-century Indian miniature, above, *depicts the story of Usha, who experienced astral travel. During these journeys, she would leave her body for voyages of the mind. Such out-of-the-body experiences, as recounted on page 152, have occurred frequently in the West, too.*

SUNK WITHOUT TRACE

What is the secret of the Bermuda Triangle,
where over the years numerous craft seem to have
vanished in strange circumstances?
Is there some mysterious power lurking there, or
could disappearances be due to far more
mundane factors?

The Bermuda Triangle, an area in the western Atlantic where scores of ships and aircraft have disappeared without trace, has been described as one of the greatest true-life mysteries of all time. This is not simply because ships and aircraft have vanished there, but because – according to numerous writers and researchers – the disappearances are without explanation and therefore seem to be caused by some force or phenomenon as yet unknown to science.

It is a very disturbing, if not highly alarming claim – for precautions can be taken against the known dangers of the highway but not against the unknown forces of the Bermuda Triangle. Every crossing of the region is said to be potentially fatal, in much the same way as every pull of the trigger in Russian roulette is hazardous. For as well as being subject to all the natural dangers of the sea – such as storms, hurricanes and waterspouts – the Triangle is also home to the Gulf Stream, a fast-moving body of water that can carry an unwary or inexperienced sailor miles off course just in a matter of hours and quickly disperse wreckage, too.

Few writers seem to agree about the Triangle's precise size and shape. The American Vincent Gaddis, originator of the phrase 'Bermuda Triangle', placed it within a triangle linking Florida, Bermuda and Puerto Rico. Richard Winer thinks it is a trapezium, however, while John Wallace Spencer sees it as a scalene triangle. Ivan T. Sanderson refers to it as 'a sort of funny blob'.

Strangely, in spite of the Triangle's notoriety, the number of disappearances within it is far from high. About 150,000 boats cross the Bermuda Triangle every year. On average, about 10,000 send a distress call, but only about 100 losses are recorded annually. And while 100 losses are 100 too many, of course, it is not a significant proportion of 150,000 – 0.07 per cent, in fact.

Charles Berlitz, perhaps the best-known of those who have written about this area, stated that: 'All ship losses are mysterious, inasmuch as relatively few captains set out to lose their ships. When the fate of a ship is established, or even assumed, the mystery ceases. This has not been the case with the many ships which have disappeared in the Sargasso Sea.'

It is there, or near there, that the majority of

Bermuda Triangle losses have taken place, Berlitz says. The British ship *Bella,* for example, is said to have vanished in 1854 on a voyage from Rio de Janeiro to Jamaica. She is known to have been overloaded and is presumed to have capsized. But author Alan Landsberg has wondered why the vessel should have had a perfectly safe voyage until she entered the deadly Triangle.

A search in the records at Lloyds reveals a ship of that name built in Liverpool in 1852, but there is no suggestion that it suffered any misfortune. The only ship corresponding with the Triangle's *Bella* is a vessel of that very name, sometimes associated with the famous 19th-century case of the 'Tichborne inheritance'. This concerned the attempt of butcher Arthur Orton to impersonate the heir to the Tichborne estate, Sir Roger Tichborne, who had been lost at sea after leaving Rio de Janeiro aboard the *Bella* of Liverpool. Unlike Tichborne's ship, of which no trace was found, the *Bella* heading for Jamaica did, apparently, leave wreckage, which was found six days after having left Rio. So assuming perfect sailing conditions and maximum speed, the nearest that this vessel could possibly have been to the Bermuda Triangle when disaster struck was some 2,000 miles (3,200 kilometres) away.

A similar case is that of the German ship *Freya.* She is said to have sailed from Manzanillo, Cuba, in 1902, and to have been found in the Triangle, abandoned by her crew and giving every appearance of having been caught in a particularly violent storm. Weather records reveal that only light airs prevailed in the region at the time, however. The *Freya* was, though, in an area where submarine volcanic activity had been reported at about the same time as the ship was abandoned, and it is believed that this probably prompted the crew to abandon ship. Whether or not this explanation is correct does not really matter because records show that the *Freya* did not sail from Manzanillo, Cuba, but from Manzanillo, Mexico, and that she was not found abandoned in the Bermuda Triangle, nor in the Atlantic Ocean, but in the Pacific.

In fact, no hint of mystery was ever attached to either the *Bella* or the *Freya* until writers began searching for Triangle fatalities. And it is questionable whether other ships – such as the *Lotta, Viego,* and *Miramon* or *Miramonde* – also supposedly lost, ever even existed.

During the 19th and early 20th centuries, ships did not carry radio equipment, so we cannot be certain of where they were when disaster struck or what form any disaster took. The *Atalanta* (not *Atlanta* as many authors call her), for example, disappeared on an intended voyage of 3,000 miles (4,800 kilometres), only 500 miles (800 kilometres) of which were reportedly through the dreaded Bermuda Triangle. We do not know where she was when she was overwhelmed, but we do know that she had a crew of very inexperienced cadets, and that severe storms swept her route.

Cyclops capsizes

The first radio-carrying vessel claimed by the Bermuda Triangle was the 19,000-tonne American collier *Cyclops* in March 1918. As with the *Atalanta,* her route was in the path of a severe storm, winds reaching speeds of 84 miles per hour (135 km/h). So it is quite likely that she capsized. Her top-heavy superstructure and the nature of her cargo – which may not have been properly secured – would naturally have ensured that the *Cyclops* sank very quickly.

The Japanese freighter *Raifuku Maru* is also said to have vanished, in 1925, after sending a strange radio message: 'Danger like dagger now. Come quick!' The message, picked up by the White Star liner *Homeric,* but distorted by electrical interference, was in fact 'Now very danger. Come quick!' The *Homeric* sped to the freighter's assistance but encountered mountainous seas, and only arrived in time to see the *Raifuku Maru* sink with all hands.

Some writers about the Bermuda Triangle state that the 395-foot (106-metre) freighter *Sandra* and her crew of 28 sailed into oblivion in calm seas and under blue skies in June 1950. But the only correct details are the freighter's name and nationality. The *Sandra* was 185 feet (55 metres) long, carried a crew of 11, and vanished in hurricane force winds in April 1950.

Hurricanes and storms also prevailed when the freighter *Anglo-Australian* vanished in 1938, when the yacht *Connemara IV* was abandoned in 1958, and when the *Revonoc* and its owner Harvey Conover disappeared in 1958. Similar explanations are, in fact, available for the bulk of Triangle disappearances.

The cornerstone of the Triangle myth, however, is the disappearance of five US Navy bombers – Flight 19 – and a sea plane, all on 5 December 1945.

The enigma of flight 19

On 5 December 1945, fourteen US Navy crewmen in five, single-engined Avenger torpedo-bombers, left Fort Lauderdale, Florida, on a training exercise. They were to fly east, make a practice bombing run on a target shipwreck north of the Bahamian island of Bimini, fly north and then head back to base. All went to plan until their return flight. An hour after they set out, the squadron leader, Lieutenant Charles Taylor, radioed in to say he and his planes were off-course, and lost. Their compasses, he said, were 'going crazy'.

Two hours later, the Fort Lauderdale control tower could still hear the crewmen trying to work out where they were. Contact with the squadron eventually grew fainter and the last words the tower heard were: 'Entering white water... we are completely lost.' That was not all. A flying boat, sent up to find them, also failed to return.

For 45 years, the riddle of Flight 19 endured. Then, in May 1991, deep-sea divers searching for Spanish treasure claimed to have found the five bombers some 12 miles (120 kilometres) off the Florida coast in 750 feet (230 metres) of water. One of the planes' tail serial numbers, 28, seemed to match that of the lost squadron's lead aircraft. In June, however, salvage experts announced the bombers were not the lost squadron, but older planes, lost in separate accidents. Robots, sent down to the sea-bed, found that the plane serial numbers did not match those of the lost Avengers either. As to the number 28, a researcher discovered that the US Navy re-uses serial numbers after a plane is destroyed. Thus, the Bermuda Triangle still keeps the Flight 19 mystery intact.

Among other aircraft to have vanished in the Bermuda Triangle were the British airliner *Star Tiger* and a Douglas DC-3, both in 1948. The *Star Tiger*, a Tudor IV aircraft, mysteriously vanished towards the end of a flight from the Azores to Bermuda on 30 January of that year. Contrary to legend, the last message from it was an acknowledgement of a radio bearing requested several minutes earlier, and not 'Weather and performance excellent. Expect to arrive on schedule.' The weather was, in fact, anything but excellent. Cloud cover throughout the flight had prevented accurate navigation; and the aircraft had battled against severe headwinds, forcing the pilot to revise his estimated time of arrival, thereby reducing the safety margin of extra fuel. The airliner disappeared at the most critical stage of her flight. She had insufficient fuel to reach any airport other than Bermuda, and was forced to fly at 2,000 feet (600 metres) because of the headwinds. Had anything gone wrong – fuel exhaustion, complete electrical failure or engine breakdown – the *Star Tiger* would have plummeted into the sea within seconds.

Distorted evidence

The case of the Douglas DC-3, lost on 28 December 1948, is an example of how facts have sometimes been omitted and distorted to imply a greater mystery than probably exists. The aircraft, carrying 27 passengers, had left San Juan, Puerto Rico, bound for Miami, Florida. The pilot, Captain Robert Linquist, is said to have radioed that he was 50 miles (80 kilometres) from Miami, could see the city lights, and was standing by for landing instructions. Miami replied within minutes, but the aircraft had vanished. The water over which the aircraft was flying was only 20 feet (6 metres) deep, yet search-craft failed to locate any wreckage.

The DC-3 is actually known to have had a defective radio, so sudden silence does not mean that the aircraft was overcome immediately after sending the message to Miami. It also removes any mystery attached to the lack of a distress call. Furthermore, the pilot did not say he could see the lights of Miami. It seems that some writers have quite literally put these words in the pilot's mouth because he said that he was only 50 miles (80 kilometres) from Miami (from which distance the lights of the city would be visible).

Linquist is known to have been compensating for a north-west wind, but wind direction had changed during the flight and it is not known whether the pilot ever received radio notification of the fact. If not, he might well have missed the Florida peninsula and flown into the Gulf of Mexico. Although the depth of the sea over which the DC-3 was flying at the time of the last message is in places only 20 feet (6 metres) deep, in other areas it suddenly plunges to depths of up to 5,000 feet (1,520 metres). Nobody is actually certain where the aircraft went down.

As a rule, every air disaster is the subject of an exhaustive enquiry to establish the cause, and such investigations rely largely on minute examination of wreckage. If there is no wreckage, however, it is virtually impossible to hazard a guess at what happened. So, since none of the accepted causes of an air crash can positively be eliminated, how can we be absolutely sure that some unknown phenomenon was alone responsible?

A few years ago, it was claimed that the strange forces of the Bermuda Triangle also reached into space when it was learned that a weather satellite malfunctioned over the Bermuda Triangle, and *only* over the Triangle. But the satellite was not, in fact, malfunctioning. Its job had been to collect visual and infra-red data on cloud cover and to transmit the information to Earth. For convenience, the infra-red signal was transmitted direct, while visual signals were stored on a loop of tape for later transmission. At certain times, the tape became full and therefore had to be rewound, so no visual signal was transmitted. By pure coincidence, the tape was rewinding when the satellite's orbit brought it into position over the Bermuda Triangle.

A final unexplained case – as reported in *The Evidence for The Bermuda Triangle* by David Group – is said to have occurred in 1970, in Florida. A National Airlines' Boeing 727 was about to land at Miami Airport when it apparently disappeared from the control radar for 10 minutes. It then reappeared and landed. A subsequent investigation discovered that every clock and watch aboard was 10 minutes slow, suggesting that, for a while, the craft had ceased to exist in some way.

Human fallibility and mechanical failure may account for most of the disappearances. But, in December 1995, it was suggested that a natural phenomenon may be to blame and that the disappearances could perhaps be due to a massive build-up of methane gas under the Atlantic. Be that as it may, many still think it more likely that some mysterious force is at work in the Bermuda region.

SOUNDS
MYSTERIOUS

Why do sands around the world produce weird booms, roars, squeaks and whistles, while coastal waters sometimes echo to mysterious explosions? Some of the intriguing sound effects created by nature are analysed here.

The British physicist, R. A. Bagnold was travelling on a field-trip in the desert area of south-west Egypt when he and a companion had a strange and unnerving experience.

'It happened on a still night – suddenly a vibrant booming so loud that I had to shout to be heard by my companion. Soon other sources, set going by the disturbance, joined their music to the first with so close a note that a slow beat was clearly recognized. This weird chorus went on continuously for more than five minutes before silence returned and the ground ceased to tremble.'

The phenomenon of booming sands is only one of the weird sound effects nature can produce. Sands that sing, bark, roar, squeak and whistle have cropped up in travellers' tales for over 1,500 years. Earliest references are in chronicles from the Middle and Far East. Marco Polo, for instance, described an example of the phenomenon that occurred in the Gobi Desert in medieval times, and Charles Darwin remarked upon a case in Chile in the 19th century.

A seventh-century account taken from the *Tun-Huang-Lu* manuscript, preserved in the British Museum, gives a description of a rumbling dune that appears to have been used as a kind of fairground side-show at festivals in the oasis town of Ho-t'ien (Khotan) in north-west China. In Khotan is a sand hill that at certain times gives out strange noises. The account reads as follows: 'The hill of sounding sand stretches 80 *li* [25 miles or 40 kilometres] east and west and 40 *li* [13 miles or 20 kilometres] north and south, and it reaches a height of 500 feet [150 metres]. The whole mass is entirely constituted of pure sand. In the height of summer, the sand gives out sounds of itself, and if trodden by men or horses, the noise is heard 10 *li* [3 miles or 5 kilometres] away. At festivals, people clamber up and rush down again in a body, which causes the sand to give a loud rumbling sound like thunder.'

Booming sands

A similar example was reported by an early investigator, A D. Lewis. He described a rumbling dune in the Kalahari Desert of South Africa in 1935 in this way: 'By sliding down the slope in slow jerks on one's "sit-upon" ... a very loud roar is produced. In the still of the evening and early morning, natives were kept sliding down the slope in this way, and the noise was easily heard at a distance of 600 yards [550 metres], like the rumbling of distant thunder.'

But what causes sands to boom? It is known that the continuous internal movement of sand within the dune, whether it occurs naturally or as a result of intervention, can – under certain conditions – produce a low-frequency vibration. This is audible as a hum which can sound like the pure note of an organ or a double bass. The presence of overtones, meanwhile, can produce a sound more reminiscent of the rumble of thunder, the drone of bumble-bees or low-flying aircraft. Seismic waves accompanying the sound have also been recorded; and these ground vibrations may even manifest themselves as mild electric shocks.

The actual mechanism that produces such vibrations is, however, far from completely understood. It has been conjectured that the hum may originate as an oscillation of individual grains caught between sliding masses of sand. But the key to the phenomenon is sometimes said to lie in the way in which the grains are packed together. Windy conditions and dryness are essential for producing booming sand, a fact giving rise to the suggestion that booming sand may also be common on the windy and waterless deserts of Mars.

Sand dunes are generally found in remote regions, far from what might be called the 'noise pollution' of the 20th century. Acoustic phenomena that occur in more densely populated areas, meanwhile, are often more difficult to isolate, and run the risk of being misidentified. So it is with certain seemingly distant explosions, heard all around the European coast and as far into the Atlantic Ocean as Iceland. These so-called 'mist pouffers' are also heard on the North American and Asian coasts. The most famous example, found in Barisal, now in Bangladesh, is known as the Barisal guns because of the nature of its sound. G.B. Scott gave this report in *Nature* magazine in 1896:

'I first heard the Barisal guns in December 1891, on my way to Assam from Calcutta through the Sunderbans [tidal forests]. The weather was clear and calm, no sign of any storms. All day the noises on board the steamer prevented other sounds from being heard; but when all was silent at night . . . the only sounds the lap of the water or the splash of earth, falling into the water along the banks, then at intervals, irregularly, would be heard the muffled boom as of distant cannon. Sometimes the reports would resemble cannon from two rather widely separated opposing forces, at others from different directions but apparently always from the southward, that is seaward.'

Suggested explanations for the Barisal guns have been many and varied. They could result, perhaps, from explosions of vast methane bubbles rising from the ocean floor. They could be caused by seismic activity on the ocean bed – although, curiously, there is no correlation between the mysterious detonations and seismic records. They may be caused by the sonic boom of meteorites falling through the atmosphere faster than the speed of sound. The explanation remains elusive: and the question, for some reason, has become one of those curiosities of the natural world that are generally overlooked.

Anger of the gods?

The inhabitants of the small town of East Haddarn, Connecticut, USA, are used to hearing mysterious noises. The rumblings – known to the local American Indians long before the Europeans came – have shaken buildings, rattled crockery and even, on one occasion, allegedly thrown someone out of bed. Variously likened to cannon fire, a heavy log falling, thunder, or the passing of a lorry, the sound was believed by the original inhabitants to be the ragings of the god Hobbamock. This god supposedly lived inside Mount Tom, which is situated to the north-west of the town; and in the 17th century, the Indians would inform newly-arrived European colonists that the god was expressing his anger at them as unwelcome settlers. The area in which the noises are most often heard is the hilly part called Moodus, which takes its name from the Indian *Matchitmoodus* ('place of bad noises').

Intriguing though these noises are, they rarely appear to harm people or property. 'There's nothing to be afraid about; we're so used to it', Frances Kuzaro, the town librarian once said. 'Usually, your dishes will rattle and you might think it's the furnace in the cellar ready to blow up.' Other locals are equally dismissive. James Meyer, a high school biology teacher who devoted his thesis to the noises, commented: 'A lot of people don't bother listening to them any more. You hear a noise and assume it's something else – sonic boom, traffic'.

The noises do, however, definitely exist; and their origin has been studied by a group of seismic experts headed by Dr John E. Ebel. He placed a network of five seismometers within a 10-mile (16-kilometre) radius of Moodus. This 'net', which was extremely sensitive, showed tiny earthquakes that matched reports of noises recorded by listeners whom Ebel employed in Moodus. 'Every one I've heard has been verified' said Cathy Wilson, one of Ebel's volunteer listeners, 'except one, which turned out to be a gunshot.'

Ebel concluded that the noises are the result of shallow, low-magnitude so-called 'micro-earthquakes'. 'The surprising and unexpected result of my study', Ebel commented, 'is the fact that the micro-earthquakes are so very, very shallow that they shake the surface in a way that makes it act like a loudspeaker, sending off the boom.'

This explanation seems more likely than previous ideas, which ranged from gaseous and chemical reactions far below the surface of the Earth to exploding gemstones. But how exactly does it happen? And why only at Moodus? Scientists are puzzled; and the precise way in which the geology of the area allows the Earth's crust to act as a sounding board remains unknown.

Curious blasts

A quick explanation was sought with urgency, however, when a series of mysterious explosions hit the east coast of North America in December 1977. Residents of New Jersey and South Carolina in the United States and Nova Scotia in Canada reported mysterious booms accompanied by explosions. Mrs Hattie Perry, of Barrington, Nova Scotia, who monitored the reports of the phenomenon, described the occurrence as follows:

'Some say it sounds as though a car has hit the side of a house. Others think that some missile has landed on the roof. One woman, lying in bed, was terrified to see the tiles on her ceiling pull apart, then close together again.'

The booms were registered on sensitive seismic equipment at Columbia University's geological observatory, just outside New York City, and the explosions were estimated as equivalent to the detonation of between 50 and 100 tonnes of TNT.

So what caused the blasts? One explanation was that deposits of methane gas hidden under the continental shelf or along the shore, suddenly ignited. Another was that they could have been due to the sonic boom created by Concorde as it flew close to the North American seaboard. True, the blasts were not heard at the time that Concorde flew over; but, it was argued, in the extremely cold weather conditions that prevailed at the time, it would have been possible for the sonic boom wave, travelling upwards, to be reflected from a boundary between layers of cold and warm air. The reflected sound wave could then have reached ground level some considerable time after Concorde had flown over the spot. A third suggestion was that the sonic wave came from unscheduled military test flights in the area.

Few scientists were prepared to lend support to the methane theory, and the Pentagon quickly denied any supersonic activity by military aircraft at the time. That left the possibility that the culprit was indeed Concorde.

The Canadian government, however, took this idea seriously enough to request the British and French air authorities to change Concorde's route: there had been reports of Concorde flying as close as 20 miles (32 kilometres) to the Canadian coast. As a result, from 17 February 1978, Concorde pilots were instructed to maintain a minimum distance from the Canadian coast of 50 miles (80 kilometres). But reports of booms heard in the region of Nova Scotia still persisted.

What, then, are we to make of such evidence? It is, of course, perfectly possible that the booms were caused by military aircraft engaged in supersonic manoeuvres; and, interestingly, the Naval Research Laboratory, which was commissioned by the United States government to investigate the phenomenon, remains evasive on this particular point. All one can do for the moment is to agree with the comment of Ernest Jahn, a scientific investigator for the National Investigations Committee on Aerial Phenomena (NICAP), who said: 'It is some kind of physical phenomenon which we simply don't understand'.

MINDPOWER

Feats of the human brain that are almost
beyond belief

Contents

Introduction

Dr J. B. Rhine, researcher into psychic abilities at Duke University, North Carolina, USA, never ceased to be amazed by the potential of the human mind. As he put it: 'It staggers my imagination to conceive all the implications that follow now that it has been shown that the mind, by some means as unknown and the mind itself, has the ability directly to affect material operations in the world around it.'

The powers of the ordinary brain are wonderful enough. But some people, it seems, can use the mind in almost unbelievable fashion. They can hypnotise, inflict curses, move objects, wage war, exercise mass mind control or even wipe out whole military installations through psychic means alone. Some even claim to be able to travel in mind only, visit a particular location, and then report back to describe it – all without leaving the comfort of an armchair. Others, meanwhile, have such vivid imaginations that life is led as a succession of fantasies. But such extraordinary feats not only occur while an individual is awake; for even during dreams, the mind is also remarkably active and hard at work.

Remarkable, too, are the powers of those gifted individuals who seem to be able to make miracles happen, by curing the infirm without the apparent need for drugs or operations.

Interestingly, scientists have discovered that it is the right hand side of the brain that may be responsible for such talents as insight, imagination and creativity.

What else, then, do we know about the workings of the human brain? This fascinating book looks deep into its many facets, and marvels at its powers. What is more, you are invited to tune in to telepathy and take part in some entertaining experiments, specifically designed for you to try with friends and family. Read on, and get wise to some mind-blowing possibilities.

THE SPLIT BRAIN

Science has revealed that the human brain is split into two – that, quite literally, we all have two independent brains. What are the implications of this most extraordinary of discoveries?

One of the greatest achievements of the famous French mathematician Henri Poincaré (1854-1912) was the resolution of a difficult mathematical problem concerning what he called 'Fuchsian functions'. He says in his memoirs that he studied the problem diligently and logically for some time but failed to get a suitable answer.

In the midst of intensive mathematical work on the problem, he took a short break to go on a geological excursion, where the excitement of the travel made him forget all about mathematics. So, with his mind full of geology rather than Fuchsian functions, he waited for the bus that was to take him on a field visit. The bus arrived – and as he got on, the solution to his problem came to him in a kind of intuitive, unthinking flash. He was so confident that he had the right answer that he did not bother to verify his intuitive insight until he had returned from the excursion. The insight turned out to be correct and succeeded where logic previously had failed.

There are lots of instances in history of such 'flashes of insight' – many of them occurring in dreams – that suddenly provide a person who is worrying over some problem or other with the correct solution. What is especially interesting is that these insights often occur when the person concerned is not consciously thinking about the problem. It is as if, by 'letting go' and allowing itself to wander away from strictly logical thinking, the brain can somehow provide the answers.

So does Poincaré's experience, and others like it, mean that the brain can work in two distinct ways – either in a systematic, step-by-step way, or intuitively, without conscious control?

According to a growing number of physiologists and psychologists, the brain does seem to operate both logically and intuitively, and will oscillate between these two distinct forms of behaviour according to circumstances.

Work carried out by anatomists and neurophysiologists, who study the brain, supports this claim. Anatomically, we know that the human body is roughly bilaterally symmetrical. It is possible to draw an imaginary line through the middle of a person, bisecting the nose and ending between the feet and, with a few rather important exceptions – such as the heart – the right side of the body is a mirror image of the left. On a general anatomical level, this also holds true for the brain.

Looked at from above, the brain is made up of two cerebral hemispheres. Joining these two hemispheres is a bridge that comprises about 200 million nerve fibres called the *corpus callosum*. This structure is one of several bundles of nerve fibres, linking equivalent centres on the two sides of the brain. Now, although each hemisphere of the brain appears to be the approximate mirror image of the other, this is not actually the case: when the hemispheres are examined more closely, profound differences emerge between the functions of the left and right sides.

Roots of dexterity

There are, of course, other instances of seemingly symmetrical parts of the body that, although mirroring each other anatomically, are actually rather different functionally. The most obvious example is our hands: 90 per cent of people write using their right hand and are termed 'right-hand dominant'. In these people, the left hand is termed the 'minor' hand. The 10 per cent of people who write with their left hand are 'left-hand dominant'.

The two hemispheres of the brain also show this 'dominant-minor' distinction, but in this case, the left side of the brain is usually the dominant side (for 96 – 98 per cent of the population), the right hemisphere taking the 'minor' role.

It may seem curious at first that, although the left hemisphere of the brain is dominant, it is the right hand, in most people, that is dominant. But there is a straightforward anatomical explanation: in the hindbrain (the rearmost part of the brain, continuous with the upper end of the spinal cord), many bundles of nerve fibres 'decussate' (cross over) from right to left, and vice versa. This decussation of fibres is responsible for the fact that the left side of the brain generally controls the right side of the body, and vice versa. So it is that the dominant left hemisphere of the brain controls the dominant right hand.

But what exactly does it mean to say that the left hemisphere of the brain is dominant? Dominance in a hand is quite clear. It is stronger and more dextrous. The brain, however, encased in its hard skull, is much more of an enigma. Perhaps not surprisingly, it was not until 1844 that it was proposed – by A. L. Wigan, in his book *The Duality of Mind* – that the fact that the brain has two hemispheres might mean that people have two separate minds. This extremely controversial idea was suggested to Wigan by a post-mortem examination he carried out on a man with no history of mental illness, whose brain turned out to have only one hemisphere. The fact that half his brain was missing had apparently produced no noticeable effect during his life.

This was the first recorded instance of extreme one-hemisphere dominance. Although more recent anatomical evidence has been less dramatic, neurophysiologists probing the brain have found many examples in which one hemisphere dominates the other in specific ranges of functions.

Split-brain research

One important method of examining the functions of the two sides of the brain is 'split-brain' research. Splitting the brain means carrying out a commissurotomy – that is, cutting the *corpus callosum* which, as we have seen, is a thick bundle of nerve fibres connecting the two halves of the brain. Originally, this rather drastic-sounding treatment was carried out, in the early 1960s, by Joseph Bogen of California to ease the pain of sufferers of extreme fits of epilepsy. By cutting the *corpus callosum* and the anterior commissure, another bunch of nerve fibres joining the two hemispheres of the brain, epileptic seizures were kept from spreading from one side to the other. The patients who underwent this surgery stopped having fits and in every respect appeared quite normal.

This fact was a source of puzzlement to neurophysiologists, because they found it impossible to understand why such major surgery apparently had no negative effects on the patients. Perhaps A. L. Wigan was right: perhaps, after all, humans did have two separate minds, and cutting the connecting links simply enhanced their independence.

However, it was not until R. W. Sperry and his colleagues at the California Institute of Technology started studying 'split-brain' effects in cats and monkeys and then extended their research to 'split-brain' humans that some curious anomalies in behaviour emerged. Sperry and his fellow researchers had reasoned that cutting the human *corpus callosum* meant that the speech and writing areas located in the dominant left hemisphere were no longer in contact with the right hemisphere that controlled the left side of the body. Therefore, they argued, if an object were presented in the left-hand side of the field of vision (which was perceived by the right hemisphere of the subject's brain), the 'split-brain' patients would be able to see the object, but could not explain what it was, nor write about it, since these functions were a left-brain activity.

Sperry and his team set up a series of simple experiments to explore these ideas. In one such experiment, a 'split-brain' patient sat on one side of a screen. Behind the screen, out of his view, was a collection of small, simple objects such as a hammer, a knife, a nut, a bolt, and so on. The name of one object was flashed for one-tenth of a second on to the screen in such a way that it was recognised only by the right hemisphere. When the patient was asked to name the object, he failed; but if he felt behind the screen with his left hand, he was able to select the correct object.

Many other controlled scientific experiments on this theme have been carried out, together with investigations of brain activity using electro-encephalographs to compare neural activity in the two hemispheres when the subject is carrying out a number of varied tasks.

Taking sides

In essence, the left brain controls speech, writing and numerical abilities; its mode of thought is analytical, logical, and rational; and it proceeds by rigorous step-by-step analysis of the problems it is set. The right hemisphere, meanwhile, controls the ability to visualise in three dimensions, a 'sense of direction' and musical ability; it is perceptual, intuitive, imaginative, and discerns things as wholes or in terms of patterns rather than by analysing them logically in the manner of the left hemisphere.

Such findings lead us to interesting conclusions. The reason why, for most people, the left hemisphere of the brain appears to be dominant, for instance, is that its abilities in the verbal, analytical and logical areas are those that are the most highly regarded – in western culture, at least. The mathematician is trained so that his left-brain functions are developed to a high degree, whereas the value of his right brain can go unnoticed until the left brain relaxes its hold over thought processes. Poincaré's insights, remember, came to him in a flash, demonstrating that the processes of his right brain were largely unconscious, coming to the fore when not actively called upon.

There are of course, the artists, sculptors, mystics and people who 'drop out' of the system and counter this left-brain domination by trying to assert the value of right-brain activity but they still remain, in general, a barely tolerated minority on the fringes of our society. Nonetheless, their presence may indicate that they are the vanguard of a new form of consciousness – a consciousness that embraces both right-brain and left-brain thought and behaviour. But this new form of consciousness will have a difficult struggle if it is to counter the powerful forces that favour left-brain dominance. Since the left brain controls the right side of the body, we would expect that, under the regime of the old consciousness, right-sidedness would be favoured, while in certain cultures the left side would have a flavour of disrepute about it.

Evidence confirms this: *The Bible,* for instance, indicates that God 'shall set the sheep on his right hand, but the goats on his left' (*Matthew* 25:33). The goats are not only placed on the left: they are ultimately destined to be thrown to the Devil.

In the Greek tradition of Pythagoras – a patriarchal tradition – the right side was associated with the light and the Sun, the straight, the good and the male, whereas the left corresponded to the dark and the Moon, the crooked, the evil and the female. In ancient Egypt, however – a matriarchal society – the Isis cult honoured the female, Isis, rather than the male, Osiris. Night was revered rather than day, and the Isis processions were led by priests holding an image of the left hand.

Western society, with its patriarchal, male-dominated view of the world, inherited from the Greeks, has suppressed the matriarchal view of the Egyptians – and there seems little alternative but to conclude that this is because a rival order constitutes a threat to the dominance of the right side.

Sinister activities

It is perhaps significant that western society sees as *sinister* (from the Latin for 'left-sided') such activities as magic and mysticism, because there appears to be no rational logic behind them. But activities such as meditation, yoga, faith healing, parapsychology, divining and achieving altered states of consciousness through the use of drugs all defy left-brain logic, and are practised by increasing numbers of people.

The growth in the pursuit of these 'sinister' activities has arisen, it seems, because more and more people are rebelling and reacting against the alienation, depersonalisation and rationalisation imposed by western technological existence, and are seeking to let their right brains come alive, thereby restoring the balance between left and right brains. The right brain can be seen to be reasserting itself in all aspects of life, ranging from an increasing willingness to take paranormal occurrences seriously to an interest in mystical systems.

Mysterious powers that lie hidden in our right brain may even prove to be the origin of a whole range of experiences that defy rational explanation. Among them are a number of psychic abilities.

Water diviners, for instance, often dowse in a relaxed, almost trance-like state in which the left brain does not assert its dominance and the right brain can act freely. It is possible that the right brain even recognises the presence of water and causes the arm muscles to contract involuntarily, making the dowsing rod move. The involvement of the right brain in psychic abilities may explain, too, why phenomena like metal bending, telepathy and clairvoyance are so notoriously difficult to reproduce in the laboratory: the scientific environment of the laboratory may repress psychic abilities by actively accentuating the dominance of the left brain.

There is another startling possibility. Perhaps telepathy – apparently an elusive ability that surfaces only fitfully – is actually simply the way our right brains speak to each other. To restore the balance between left and right brains might therefore be to restore latent telepathic abilities.

If this rebellion by the right brain is to generate a new consciousness of life, it is important to keep a sense of perspective. What is necessary is not left- or right-brain dominance, but harmony between the two hemispheres of the brain. This harmony can arise only through an open dialogue between the halves of the brain, each contributing its own strengths and abilities. To this end, we may be able to train ourselves to use our right brains more consciously through, for example, biofeedback, giving time – from school age onwards – to 'right-brain' activities, and training ourselves to realise when to 'let go' or forget a problem so that the right brain can help to resolve it.

The renowned physicist Albert Einstein, it seems, was well practised in this. During his most enlightened moments, he seemed to relax and then allow his mind to wander, thinking in symbols rather than in words and sentences. Indeed, it is believed by some that the very use of language somehow imposes logic and thereby restricts potential creativity.

We may also be able to learn from the Chinese, who have long held the view that all existence is represented by the integration of opposites known as *yin,* the female principle, and *yang,* the male principle – opposites that also, broadly, delineate the contrast between the right and left brains. The philosophers of ancient China, it seems, were wiser than we are: they knew – centuries before western neurophysiologists began to discover the same truth – that without this active union of opposites we are, to put it simply, but half-brained.

THE MARVEL OF MEMORY

What are memories? And where are they stored?
A startling new theory presents us with much
food for thought.

We are all brought up to believe that recollections are stored inside the brain. It is an old and respectable idea, and many of us may not even think of questioning it. Nevertheless, it now seems that some theories of memory may be open to doubt.

One early theory was put forward by the 4th-century Greek philosopher, Aristotle. He went so far as to compare memory with impressions that have been left on soft wax by experience – the sealing wax, the impressions left upon it, and the persistence of these impressions in the wax all providing an analogy with the process of memory.

Since Aristotle, this same trace theory has been repeatedly modified in accordance with latest advances in technology to provide more and more up-to-date analogies. Currently most popular is the theory that memory is stored in the brain in the same way that information is contained in a hologram. This is a sophisticated version of the trace theory of Aristotle, but it is still essentially the same.

Aristotle's trace theory applies to long-term memory specifically. But there is also another kind of memory that is short-term. This is the kind of memory you have when you look up a number in the telephone directory. You remember the number for as long as it takes you to dial it, and then immediately forget it. It is possible that short-term memory is explicable in terms of a kind of reverberation in the brain's neural circuits. It is long-term memory, however, that presents us with problems.

The hypothesis of formative causation suggests one possible answer. According to this theory, the development of form in living creatures is governed by a so-called 'morphogenetic' field – a kind of biological field that can, by a process that is known as morphic resonance, be 'tuned in to' by other members of the same species and so influence their development. This hypothesis can also explain memory to some degree.

If organisms enter into morphic resonance with previous organisms of the same species on the basis of similarity, then there could be a very interesting consequence, for the thing that an organism resembles most closely in the past is itself. Although it is obvious that the development of individual living things is not governed simply by their own forms in the past, we nevertheless have the fascinating possibility that organisms may be subject to morphic resonance from their own past states.

Memory may thus consist of a kind of tuning in to the past states of our own organism through the process of morphic resonance so that the past is, as it were, continuously present to us. According to this theory, it is not necessary to suppose that all memory traces are actually stored inside the brain.

Conclusive evidence?

So why do we take the trace theory of memory for granted? There are two pieces of evidence that, for many people, seem to provide conclusive and overwhelming evidence for the existence of memory traces, and that lead to the unquestioning acceptance of the idea that memories are stored inside the brain.

The more important of these is evidence from brain damage – that various types of brain damage can lead to loss of memory. A standard interpretation of this is that damage could remove those parts of the brain tissue that contain memory traces. But this is not the only possible interpretation. To see the fallacy in the argument, take the analogy of a television set. If you were to damage a television set by cutting out part of the wiring or removing a few transistors and condensers, and completely lost reception of one channel as a result, you would not automatically assume that this proved that all the people – actors, musicians and announcers – you saw on the programmes of that channel were contained within the condensers and transistors that you had removed.

And yet, if you were embedded in that way of thinking, you might easily think so. And you might think you had proved you were right when you saw that, when you replaced the parts you had removed, the channel reappeared.

Loss of memory through brain damage does not prove in any way that memory is stored inside the brain. It merely proves that a normal brain is essential for the effective recall of these memories. It is in fact possible that the effects of brain damage on memory can be explained in terms of the loss of the ability to recall or tune in to past states of the brain.

A second piece of evidence often cited in favour of the trace theory of memory is related to the work of Wilder Penfield on electrical stimulation of the brain tissue of epileptics. He found that this enabled some patients to recall particular scenes from their past with great vividness: indeed, the electrical stimulation seemed to reawaken memories. The most obvious interpretation of this result is that memories must be embedded in or near to the stimulated tissue, and that the electric current somehow reawakens them. But again, such supposed evidence is quite inconclusive. Think of the television analogy. If you were to apply electric currents to the tuning circuits inside a television set, you would find some very strange things happening – jumps from channel to channel, possibly, and distortions of the picture. But, again, this does not prove that the figures you see on the screen are actually located inside the television, any more than in the previous analogy.

Further objections spring from the nature of the trace theory itself. Although the traces are taken for granted, their nature is still very much a matter of dispute in the scientific community. One popular and well-established theory suggests that memories may depend on reverberating circuits of electrical activity in the brain – loops of electrical current within the actual tissue.

Conflicting theories

Another theory, which was much in vogue during the early 1970s, is the idea that memory is stored in the complex molecules of ribonucleic acid (RNA), a substance that is similar to DNA. The memory traces are, according to this theory, in some unspecified way laid down inside these molecules. However, this theory has rather gone out of fashion because there is very little evidence to support it, and it is not yet clear how a chemical or set of chemicals inside the brain can fulfil as complex a function as the encoding of memory.

But the third and most popular of theories is that of synaptic modification. The synapses are connections between the nerve cells, and the idea is that they somehow become modified as electric pulses – nerve signals – pass through them, making it more likely that the same signals will pass through them again. This is similar to the hydraulic theory of memory, as proposed by the philosopher and scientist René Descartes (1596-1650). Descartes suggested that memory depends on the flow of fluids through pores. The more often the fluid flows, the more it will enlarge the pores, making it easy for the fluid to flow in that direction again.

The main evidence for the theory of synaptic modification comes from a series of experiments carried out on a species of snail, *Aplysia*. This snail has exceptionally large nerves, which are therefore easy to study, and it reacts in simple ways to simple stimuli: if you go on prodding it with a needle, for example, it gets used to this after a while and, instead of withdrawing into its shell, it simply ignores the prodding – if, that is, it has established that the stimulus is harmless. This is a well-known kind of learning, termed *habituation*, whereby animals simply ignore stimuli that do not threaten them.

Detailed and very elegant experimental work has shown that changes occur in the synapses of *Aplysia* during the process of habituation, but the reason for these changes is still unclear. There is evidence to show there certainly are, in some cases, changes in the brain during learning in the higher organisms – but can these changes entirely explain the phenomenon of memory?

The most damning piece of evidence against the trace theory of memory comes from a series of experiments carried out by K. S. Lashley. He set out with the hypothesis that, if memory traces do indeed exist in the brain, it should be possible to locate them. The idea was to cut out portions of the brain and identify the bits of memory that disappeared. He spent a great deal of time doing this and, after many years, ended up completely frustrated with this line of research.

Experimental extraction

Lashley's experiments were on rats, and he found that loss of memory occurred only when large portions of the brain were removed. Importantly, loss of memory was proportional to the amount of nervous tissue removed, rather than its location. Lashley called this the law of mass action: the idea was that it was the mass of tissue removed that was important, not the specific bits. The experiment was repeated with octopuses, and the same results were obtained: again, loss of memory was proportional to the mass removed, rather than the particular portion of the brain that was extracted.

Clearly, all attempts to find localised traces within the brain have failed. This, of course, has posed great difficulties for the trace theory of memory, which had earlier seemed straightforward. It is, in fact, the main reason why the holographic theory of memory was developed – a modification that suggested that there are, indeed, memory traces, but spread all over the brain – so that if you cut out parts of it, you will not make much difference, since all memories are localised everywhere. But this theory also has its problems. A hologram works on the principle of light waves and interference patterns stored on photographic film. There is nothing of the sort to be found in the brain.

This is the present state of research into memory. The idea that memory traces are stored inside the brain is really an aspect of the mechanistic theory of life, stemming from the theory that everything to do with the mind is explicable in terms of matter, and is reducible to things inside the brain. If you share this conviction, then you have to believe that memories are stored inside the brain.

However, when you consider the possibility that the brain may not be a memory storage device but, rather, a tuning system that enables memories to be picked up, this failure to find localised memory traces in the brain certainly makes sense. Several hitherto unexplained phenomena also begin to seem less surprising from a scientific point of view.

The collective unconscious

According to the new theory, we normally tune in to our own memories – but it is conceivable that the process of morphic resonance may allow us to tune in to other people's memories, too. Telepathy can thus be explained as the almost instantaneous transfer of very recent memories; and clairvoyance could be the result of tuning in to the memories of distant people. There is also, of course, the possibility of tuning in to memories from the distant past. This could be one way of explaining how some people can have access to memories of past lives, often through hypnotic regression. It could even explain why many of the memories produced under hypnotic regression are patchy, or seem to be the result of the overlapping of memories of entirely distinct lives. It could perhaps be the result of tuning in to more than one morphogenetic field at the same time, and jumbling the information received in this way.

This new concept of memory as an aspect of morphic resonance also lends theoretical support to the well-known notion of the collective unconscious, put forward by psychologist C.G. Jung. We may be influenced, perhaps, not only by memories of particular people in the past, but also by a sort of pooled or collective memory from countless previous human beings – in other words, there may exist a sort of species memory. Indeed, rather than existing separately, our minds may be influenced directly by others, including countless people in the past, through the interconnectedness of memory, whether we realise it or not. In turn, our own ideas and memories may be adding to the collective memory of mankind, and may persist to influence future members of the human race, too.

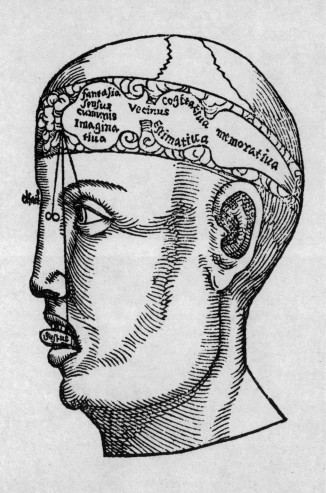

On page 274, we address the question of how memory works and where it is sited. The illustration above, *from* Margarita Philosophica *by Gregor Reisch, shows the seat of memory as situated just above the ear.*

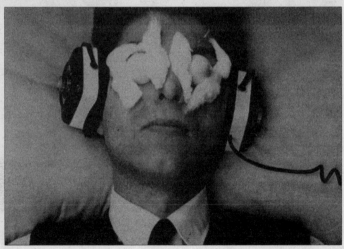

Tests such as these have shown the mind to be active even during sleep, and psychic abilities to be located in the right part of the brain.

Are the creatures in Goya's The Sleep of Reason Brings Forth
Monsters, above, *the product of our own unconscious minds, or
could they sometimes be intruders from outside? Evidence that our
minds may not in fact enjoy undisputed possession of our bodies is
presented on page 325.*

Some unfortunate individuals suffer terrible mental torment as their minds play hosts to a number of different personalities, some inhibited, some outrageous – just as actress Joanne Woodward, above, did in the film The Three Faces of Eve.

MAKING MIRACLES HAPPEN

*Can praying to the Virgin Mary or a saint
actually effect a 'miraculous' cure? Or are there
more down-to-earth explanations for such
sudden releases from serious illness?*

When faced with an illness over which we have no
immediate control, we tend to worry, perhaps even
panic. This is a perfectly natural reaction; and the
more critical the pain or the malady we know we
have, or believe we have, the more fervently we wish
it would pass. For many of us, that wishing is but a
small step from praying – in the belief that, if we do
so, some external agency (God, our guardian angel or
one of the saints) will put an end to our suffering.

One of the possible outcomes of being ill is that
we recover; another is that we die; a third, covering
the majority of cases, is that we come to terms with
the illness, mentally and physically, with the help of
medical treatment and natural resistance, inherent in
the human body. In the case of serious – even
apparently terminal – illness, few doctors will deny
that a small number of their patients experience
temporary periods of remission. In some rare
instances, they acknowledge, too, that the remission

can be sudden, and lasting. Sometimes the body seems to mend in just a few days or perhaps hours, even where it has been broken down by some form of cancer, for example. Remission is not a fantasy, or a rumour, or even a matter of misinterpretation of the facts: it happens.

Bearing in mind our natural tendency to wish away our illnesses or to pray for release from them, it is hardly surprising that sometimes remission coincides with our most fervent prayers, or a more sophisticated form of attempting to secure divine intervention – the petitioning of a religious figure such as the Virgin Mary, or visiting a place of pilgrimage, such as Lourdes, for instance. But had the prayers remained unsaid, the Saint not called upon, and the pilgrimage not been undertaken, might the remission – be it temporary or permanent – have happened anyway?

The tradition of healing persists, and in the West it persists particularly as a belief in divine intervention, whether or not a human agent, such as a priest or a healer, is involved. In cases where healing is apparently brought about by contact with religious objects, such as relics, or by visits to shrines or recognised places of pilgrimage, the 'divine' influence is said to be 'direct'.

The Roman Catholic tradition of healing is undoubtedly the greatest repository of varied and vociferous claims for divine healing in the modern world, and healings that have apparently taken place within that tradition are frequently termed 'miracles'.

The *Shorter Oxford English Dictionary* defines a miracle as: 'A marvellous event exceeding the known powers of nature and therefore supposed to be due to the special intervention of the Deity or some supernatural agency; chiefly an act (e.g. of healing) exhibiting control over the laws of nature, and serving as evidence that the agent is either divine or is especially favoured by God.' George Bernard Shaw, on the other hand, in his play *St Joan*, chose to describe a miracle as 'an event which creates faith'.

Back to life

Both of these definitions apply to the healings of Sathya Sai Baba, the Indian mystic who is widely respected in both the West and the East. Many of his followers regard him as being a manifestation of God in this age. But even if we ignore such extreme claims, Sai Baba has certainly impressed those who have witnessed his 'miracles'.

His most spectacular healings have been two cases where he is said to have brought the dead back to life. Of the two, the most widely reported was his raising of V. Radhakrishna, aged 60, at an ashram (a religious community) at Puttaparti. There was no question in this case that the man was dead, for he had already begun to decompose when Sai Baba raised him to life, three days after pronounced dead by doctors.

This is as direct an example of a miracle cure as one can expect to find; and it is either true or not. If it is false, then many people have been duped. But Sai Baba's record of producing other miraculous phenomena – such as 'apporting' hot food or 'sacred ash', apparently from nowhere – makes this raising from the dead more credible. Yet, as with many of Christ's miracles, there seems to be an obvious question left unanswered: if Sai Baba was able to revive the man from death, why did he permit him to die in the first place? What possible benefit could three days of widowhood have had for the man's wife? Does it become more of a self-promoting trick than a miracle in this context? The glib theological answers – that God's purpose is subtle but sure, and that miracles make us 'glorify the Lord' – do not seem to help that much.

Certainly much simpler and more straightforward in their motivation were the miraculous cures associated with Linda Martel, a hydrocephalic child who spent her short life in Guernsey, dying aged five in 1961. At the time of her death, the media were full of stories about her supposed cures, but gradually her name has faded into comparative obscurity, remembered only by her family and, presumably, by those whom she cured.

During her few years, Linda – who also suffered from spina bifida and whose legs were paralysed – showed herself to be very advanced intellectually, and often her most perceptive remarks were deeply religious. She would, for example, speak of 'my Jesus Christ' with a conviction that seemed to smack of experience; yet her family was not particularly religious, and are unlikely to have inculcated such an attitude in her. Like other leading healers, she seemed to have some power of diagnosis, as well as that of healing; but, again, such a small child is highly unlikely to have learned the 'skills' in the conventional way, as an adult might have done.

Healing clothes

Her healing was occasionally direct, and she cured by touch in the presence of the sick; but most frequently it was brought about by the sufferer touching an item of clothing that Linda had worn. Such healings are reported to have occurred both before and after her death, and the illnesses and problems cured are said to have included a spinal injury, haemorrhoids, eczema, warts, cartilage trouble, and cancer of the throat. A multitude of such cures were claimed in the years following her death.

In the case of Linda Martel, one must conclude either that those who claimed to have been cured with her direct or indirect help were deceived or deceiving – or that the cures were genuine. Healing by the power of the mind – by faith – no doubt accounted for a great many of the claims: cures were even attributed to her grave. But if the claims regarding the curing of spinal injuries or cancer are to be accepted as genuine, then we must start considering what the concept of 'miracle' means in this context. Could such a small and helpless child have the power to heal, and to impart that power in some way to the clothes she wore? Or was some external power working through her, so that those who associated themselves with her simple and naïve faith in Christ could benefit from his legendary healing powers? It is not an easy case to assess, but at least we do not have here any suggestion of self-promotion.

There is something compelling about some of the claims made for Linda Martell, despite the lack of a great deal of conclusive and verifiable evidence. Yet there is an American case, of some fame, in which there is both photographic evidence and abundant personal testimony that, though it fits the definition 'miracle', and undoubtedly concerns cures of a kind, many still find absurd and unacceptable. It concerns the healing ministry of Willard Fuller, a former Baptist minister with a marked evangelistic style.

Initially, he healed all kinds of ailments; but one day a man, whose ulcer he had cured, came to him and said: 'Preacher, I have one cavity in a tooth back here. I believe that if God can heal an ulcer, He can fix this cavity for me. Will you lay hands on me and pray for me for the meeting of my dental needs?' Fuller duly did so, and the tooth was found to be 'miraculously' filled.

Bryce Bond, writing in *Alpha* magazine about Fuller's dental ministry, stated: 'Those who have seen a filling gradually form describe it as a small bright spot which becomes larger until it fills the whole cavity, like the speeded-up picture of a rose blooming. Porcelain fillings are common occurrences and are of particular interest because they form fast enough for witnesses to watch the growth, but slowly enough to give many people a chance to witness at first-hand what is happening... '

Divine fillings

The minister of a church where Willard Fuller appeared and demonstrated his skills in 'miracle dentistry' in 1967 reported to an astounded congregation: 'Right before our eyes, teeth have been filled with gold, silver and porcelain – not just one night but every night. Over 200 people have experienced this miracle in two weeks. Last night, one man received seven silver and two gold fillings. This is done in such a way that there can be no doubt.'

Many apparent healings have a natural cause, and demonstrate no more than the exceptional potential of the body to heal itself in the right circumstances. But there can be no argument about teeth that suddenly fill with gold, or silver, or even porcelain – it is a remarkable event that defies explanation. Yet its very banality – after all, there are plenty of dentists in the USA, and presumably they all know how to fill

293

cavities with a variety of materials – seems to argue against any sort of direct divine intervention in Willard Fuller's 'miracles'. Many people wonder why the Almighty should fill the teeth of fortunate Americans, while leprosy – and worse – rage unabated in the Third World. If Fuller had this power, then it could be argued that it must be his, not God's. Or, if it is divine in origin, it seems to point to a somewhat whimsical deity.

Shock healing

But there are many examples to show that healers do not always concentrate their powers on the poorest or the most sick; and in this light, it is worth mentioning Dzhuna Davitashvili, the Soviet healer, who is said to have done much to sustain the late President Brezhnev during his prolonged last illness. The *Sunday Times* of 29 August 1982 reported that: 'The healer's credentials include testimonials from high Soviet officials, stage and literary celebrities and numerous distinguished foreigners who have written thanking her for curing stomach ulcers, hernias, double pneumonia, kidney ailments and malignancies.'

She is said to have healed by the laying on of hands, which apparently gave patients a sensation rather like a mild electric shock; and, although a Christian, she did not claim to work miracles on those she treated. But then, of course, in the Soviet

Union at that time, discretion may have been the better part of valour.

With so much research yet to be done on the nature and process of healing, it is surprising that those established churches that claim to demonstrate the power of God through healing by ordained priests have no clear idea of the nature of the gift, nor how it operates. In the early 1980s, there was a debate about faith healing in the *Church Times* – the Anglican newspaper – that one week gave an excited account of the spectacular healings said to have taken place in a Bristol church. Yet, only a short time later, it printed the warnings of another writer who said: 'Beware! For Satan himself masquerades as an angel of light. Not all healing is good and in Jesus' name; but happily there is the gift to distinguish between Spirits. Satan can "heal", and he does.'

TUNING IN TO
TELEPATHY

It is said we all once had telepathic abilities which have been largely lost. The experiments described here have been designed to test for this hidden talent.

Imagine sitting in a comfortable chair in a darkened room, wearing headphones through which you can hear the roar of a waterfall cascading down a Welsh mountain. Your eyes are covered with halved ping-pong balls on which a red light shines, and all you can see, as you relax, is a diffuse red glow.

This extraordinary situation is part of an experiment designed to test for telepathy. As someone who has agreed to take part in the test, you are first welcomed by the experimenter, and then asked to fill in a 'mood report' describing your attitude to the experiment and your general emotional state. The experimenter then seats you in a comfortable chair, puts headphones over your ears, and adjusts the level of waterfall noise until it is comfortable. He or she next plays another sound at such a level that you can just hear it through the waterfall noise, and then drops the noise level by five decibels so that you cannot hear it at all.

The experimenter now places palmar electrodes on your left hand so that any physiological response you may experience can be monitored. Then, halved ping-pong balls are placed over your eyes, and a red light is adjusted so that it is 18 inches (45 centimetres) from your face.

The gentle waterfall sound and ping-pong eye covers should block out all external conditions and visual distractions, relaxing you into what is known as the *Ganzfeld* state. (*Ganzfeld* – from the German for 'uniform field' – refers to the unchanging or uniform level of stimulation caused by blocking external sensation.)

Finally, the waterfall sound is switched off and you are next played a tape containing the suggestion that you will now become aware of subconscious information. The waterfall sound is then switched on once again.

Deprived of outside sensory stimulation, you turn mentally inwards, becoming aware of thoughts, images and memories that are the expression of your subconscious mind. At the same time, another person – the sender – begins to pass information to you by playing a tape through your headphones, so quietly that it is impossible for you to hear it against the waterfall noise. This is known as subliminal stimulation: the stimulus is physically real, but is too quiet to be perceived consciously. Instead, it is picked up at the subconscious level. The target tape, in this experiment, carries five thematically related words, and is chosen at random from four such tapes by the sender after the beginning of the experiment. Thus no one knows, for the duration of the experiment, what the tape contains.

While in this state, you are asked to voice whatever comes into your mind. What you say is recorded and, after the experiment is over, you are asked to order the sets of target words according to which of them you feel corresponds most accurately with the impressions gained while in the *Ganzfeld* state.

Word association

You now complete another mood assessment form and undergo a word association test for each of the four target tapes, in which you are presented with the four sets of five words, including the set heard subliminally, and asked to think of the individual target words, saying whatever first comes into your head. The tape of your impressions is then submitted to three independent judges, who analyse it and estimate its correspondence with the four target tapes.

In the *Ganzfeld* state, it is also possible to perceive information that is not being transmitted mechanically through the headphones, but communicated telepathically by the sender. In a separate experimental session, the sender therefore selects a tape and plays it, not through your headphones, but through *his* – at an audible level. He then tries to visualise the image that the words on the tape create, and proceeds by trying to project them mentally to you.

In the experiment, the two means of transmission – telepathic and subliminal auditory – are varied randomly. The subject therefore does not know how the information is being sent in any one session. Results show that those who are able to receive information that is transmitted subliminally are also sensitive to telepathically transmitted information; while those who find it difficult to pick up information one way generally find it equally difficult to do so in the other way. One objective of the experiments is to pinpoint the kind of psychological state – and the type of people – that make such information-transfer possible.

An analysis of one set of results showed that, out of a total of eight subjects, three consistently succeeded in identifying the target tape, placing it first or second. These three people show an awareness of the information, whether transmitted telepathically or mechanically, that is highly significant.

Transmission of information seems to require a two-stage process. The first stage involves the reception of the information in the subconscious, while the second involves forcing the subconscious knowledge into the conscious mind. Here, it seems that those who have some awareness of the way in which their subconscious minds work have an advantage: it is they who are able to translate the often quite complex and tortuous imagery of their subconscious minds into rational terms.

In order to illustrate the complexities of translation and interpretation, we need to consider an actual example of a *Ganzfeld* session. Here, the target tape carried the five words 'sultan, Aladdin, harem, feasting, and dancing'. While in the *Ganzfeld* state, the subject made the following remarks: 'Seeing something, don't know what it is . . . crib or something – cradle, I mean; definitely a cradle in a sitting room – Middle Ages sitting room – somebody rocking this cradle dressed in Middle Ages clothes – tapestry in the back . . . mineral – either coal or some sort of stone, mineral . . . changing to pool or something . . . flashes of light . . . beansprouts . . . kitchen – copper utensils.'

A successful transmission

The subject, in her own analysis of her impressions, understood the cradle images as being related to the harem; the flashes of light and mineral seemed related to Aladdin and his magic lamp; and the kitchen related to the feasting. Throughout the session, she felt preoccupied with food, and the cradle image occurred again later on. While there is no direct mention of an Arabian nights scene, the subject was able to tie in the thematic content of her image with the target so as to produce what is considered to be a

300

'hit'. Two of the three independent judges, incidentally, agreed with her analysis.

It is, of course, easy enough to see these connections when the person identifies the target. But what if a person 'misses' the target? Such 'misses' are generally not considered to be worthy of attention. But can we really say that telepathic or subliminal perception is operative only on those occasions when a person manages positively to identify the target?

Correct perception of the target, as we have seen, is a two-stage process; and one thing that has become apparent again and again during the experiments is that most 'misses' occur *not* because the information is not getting through to the subconscious, but as a result of incorrect evaluation of impressions gained while in the *Ganzfeld* state. Images that relate to the target are generally present, but the subject is unable to relate them to the words on the target tape.

On some occasions, there appears to be what might be called a low signal-to-noise ratio: the target-related imagery is present, but there is so much extraneous information – 'noise' – from the subconscious that it is extremely hard to identify subliminal or telepathic input. This 'noise' is perhaps one of the mind's principal methods of defending itself against unwanted input. The phenomenon is well-known in psychology, where it is termed 'perceptual defence'. Obvious examples are simply not hearing what you do not want to hear – an ability that makes it possible for you to hold a conversation in a roomful of noisy people, or not to hear a publican calling 'time'. A further clear example was provided by one subject who, in her *Ganzfeld* session, spent 10 minutes talking about how she had given up drinking. The target words were 'tavern, keg, barrel, tankard, goblet'; but she ranked this tape last, simply because, she said, it was 'too much of a coincidence'.

Significant scoring

Most defences, however, are more subtle than this. Take a person who, according to his own estimations, scores only very slightly above chance in both telepathic and subliminal sessions. Yet his session transcripts were scored significantly *above* chance by all three independent judges. In other words. a logical, analytical assessment of his thoughts by independent observers gave statistically significant evidence of target-related imagery. During the sessions, he was 'aware' of the target inasmuch as he thought about things that were related to the target. Yet, on four occasions, he was unable, in the analysis that followed the *Ganzfeld* session, to identify the target, mainly because he chose not to use an analytical judging procedure, instead picking the target that he 'felt' was the right one. Such personal assessment proved inaccurate.

An even clearer example of the defensive process is provided by a subject whose attitude was one of

302

disbelief in ESP. He did not think that the images he saw while in the *Ganzfeld* state could bear any relationship at all to the target; yet, again and again, it did. The relationship was not patently clear, as in the case of the three 'hitters' – but it was very definitely there. Although he was himself unable to pick out the target, independent judges, with some understanding of the symbolic distortions and transformations that occur in the subconscious mind, were generally able to do so.

In another typical session, the target words were 'smugglers, contraband, adventure, horses, moonlight'. In this session, the subject talked several times about ice, icebergs, the Titanic, Alaskan permafrost and so on. After the *Ganzfeld* session, his word association with the target word 'adventure' was 'cold'; his word association with 'smugglers' was 'gallows'; and, during the session, he experienced images of boys in prison, Roman soldiers, Steerpike (a character from Mervyn Peake's Gothic novel *Gormenghast),* with a knife in his hand, cannonballs and, most significant of all, Albert Pierrepoint, England's last state executioner.

Although there is no direct connection between these images and the target words, the word associations do provide a very revealing link. And it is important to remember that in free association work such as this, where a person is attempting to gain access to material from the subconscious, the mind works in distorted and essentially symbolic ways. So, we should not expect to get a direct representation of the target in the *Ganzfeld* images; rather, it is *connections* that we must look for.

Differing signals

Only around 10 per cent of subjects talk directly about the target theme, while transcripts frequently have many rich symbolic and associational connections that are easily recognised by a team of independent judges – even if they are vehemently denied by the subjects, possibly to reduce any distress at the idea of being able to perceive a target using methods not believed in.

Indeed, in the case of a person whose attitude to ESP is negative, distortions and symbolism become even more complex; but the fact that it is more difficult to unravel does not necessarily mean that the subliminal or telepathic information has not been received at a subconscious level. It means merely that the 'noise' level is higher and the 'signal' more distorted. With the 'hitters', the signal is clear and the extraneous noise, very low. Such people are familiar with their own mental processes, and can usually follow the indirect ways in which target words might influence their subconscious.

By examining the differences between those subjects who consistently hit the target and those who consistently miss, we can see that two factors emerge

– factors that may account for these differences. The most important is that of attitude. Thus, someone who does not believe in his or her own capacity to become aware of subliminal and telepathic information and who claims to have had no personal experience of this sort of awareness, is very likely to miss the target. On the other hand, a person who has grown up in an atmosphere in which such things are generally accepted may be able to learn to hit the target much more readily.

Games of telepathy

The following game is intended to reveal whether you can bring to the fore what some believe to be a natural telepathic ability, inherent in all of us, but usually lost following childhood. It requires two players – a 'receiver' and a 'sender' – and an ordinary pack of playing cards. The aim is for the sender to look at each card, without showing it to the other player (the receiver), who has to identify whether the card is red or black. To play, proceed as follows:

1. Sit one behind the other, so that the receiver's back faces the sender.

2. The sender now shuffles the pack of cards and lifts up the top card, looking at its face. The sender should now signal that he or she is ready to transmit information by tapping the card, and then attempt mentally to send either 'red' or 'black' – depending on the colour of the card – to the receiver. One way

of doing this is to close your eyes and imagine the word 'red' or 'black' somewhere around your forehead. Alternatively, try to visualise a red door, a fire engine or a British pillar box.

3. The receiver then calls out the colour that he or she thinks the card is.

4. The sender places a tick (for a correct answer) or a cross (for a wrong one) on a sheet of paper.

A score of 26 correct answers out of 52 – the number of cards in the pack – is what you can expect according to the laws of chance. The player who scores consistently higher then the average 50/50 score is undoubtedly making use of some kind of telepathic power. More advanced games can, of course, be attempted, and will involve the guessing of specific suits.

From experimentation, it appears that we all have certain latent ESP ability. One way of becoming aware of this is to enter a passive and receptive state, such as that induced by the *Ganzfeld,* thereby learning by experience how to interpret the imagery received. In this sense, such experiments can be regarded as a kind of training programme in ESP. Through it, we may eventually come to greater understanding of the processes involved.

THE
UNCONSCIOUS
STOREHOUSE

Many people have a fantastic ability to discuss their past lives in vivid detail – but all too often it turns out they are reciting something once read or heard.

The subconscious mind can be regarded as a vast, muddled storehouse of information. This information comes from books, newspapers and magazines; from lectures, television and radio; from direct observation, and from overheard scraps of conversation. In normal circumstances, most of this knowledge is not subject to recall, but there are times when some of these deeply buried memories are spontaneously revived. And some of these revived memories re-emerge as baffling examples of cryptomnesia – memories with origins that have been completely fogotten.

As a result, material can sometimes seem to have no ancestry and can be mistaken for something newly discovered or created. The late Helen Keller – blind, deaf and mute from infancy – was tragically deceived by such a cryptomnesiac caprice. In 1892, she wrote a charming tale called *The Frost King*. It was published and applauded; but within a few months, it was revealed that the piece was simply a modified version of Margaret Canby's story *The Frost Fairies*, published 29 years earlier. Helen had no conscious memory of ever having heard the story, but it was established that a friend had read a batch of Miss Canby's stories to her in 1888 – and *The Frost Fairies* was among them. Helen Keller was devastated. She wrote: 'Joy deserted my heart... I had disgraced myself.... yet how could it possibly have happened? I racked my brain until I was weary to recall anything about the frost that I had read before I wrote *The Frost King*, but I could remember nothing.'

In the same fashion, a number of cases of automatic writings – allegedly from discarnate spirits – have been traced to published works. For example, the famous 'Oscar Wilde' scripts, produced by two psychics in the 1920s, were shown to be derived from many printed sources, including Wilde's own *De Profundis* and *The Decay of Lying*. One of the writers of the automatic scripts, Dr S.G. Soal, was led to remark: 'The variety of sources from which the script is drawn is as amazing as the adroitness with which the knowledge is worked up into sentences conveying impressions of the different mannerisms of Wilde's literary style.' This is a significant verdict indeed, for very often the cryptomnesic material emerges not in a pure form, but in an edited or paraphrased version. And this may mislead investigators in search of primary sources.

Sound evidence?

Such unconscious plagiarisms are certainly very intriguing, but most baffling of all are surely the vivid memories of 'past lives' that emerge under hypnosis or trance conditions. To some, these have always smacked of cryptomnesia; but to many others, this explanation seems ruled out by the great wealth of detail – often extremely obscure – provided by such 'regressionists'. Here, the use of tape recorders has proved invaluable. Before their introduction, all such research was costly and time-consuming, since everything the subject said had to be taken down in shorthand with the inevitable loss of any accents, nuances and subtleties in the voice. Sound tapes, by contrast, seem to provide lively and more convincing case records than any of those furnished by the pioneer researchers. Even so, there are two classic cases from the turn of the century that still command respect. The most famous involved the Swiss medium, Helene Smith.

Helene was investigated by Theodore Flournoy, professor of psychology at Geneva University. He published his major findings in *From India to the Planet Mars*. In this book, he records that Helene laid claim to a previous existence as the ill-fated Queen of

France, Marie-Antoinette. She also claimed a much earlier reincarnation as the wife of the Hindu prince Sivrouka Nayaka, a 15th-century ruler of Kanara, India. Her Indian memories were enriched with descriptions of ceremonies and palaces, but complicated by her insistence that Flournoy had also been present in Kanara – and as her husband!

Later research seemed to show, however, that Helene's obscure Indian knowledge was drawn from an inaccurate history by De Marles, published in 1823, and that she '... dug down to the very bottom of her memories without discovering the slightest traces of this work'. However, the real proof of her ability to resurrect and restructure unconscious knowledge came with her most extravagant romance – one involving contact with the inhabitants of Mars.

During her Martian episode, Helene produced a small album of highly exotic drawings of Martian landscapes, houses, people and plants. But these were all typically childish pictures with superficial oriental touches. Much more impressive was the emergence of a spoken and written Martian language. Yet an analysis of 'Martian' showed that the sounds were those of the French language; the order of words was absolutely the same as in French, and its crude grammar was simply a parody of that of her mother tongue. The vocabulary alone was her invention. Even so, the whole affair involved a remarkable feat of construction and memory, for Helene was always consistent in her use of what she believed to be 'Martian'. All this was apparently the work of her subconscious.

Although not everyone was satisfied by Flournoy's explanation of the Helene Smith case, the Blanche Poynings case of 1906 was neatly solved within just a few months. Blanche Poynings was a woman who had lived during the reign of Richard II. Ostensibly, she began – in 1906 – to communicate through a clergyman's daughter, known as Miss C., while under hypnosis. Blanche, it seemed, had been a friend of the Countess of Salisbury and proved to be a garrulous gossip. She poured out details of the Countess' affairs, correctly naming her two husbands, children, in-laws and retainers. She also chatted about her own four marriages and her time at court.

Novel experiences

Everyday events were not neglected either, for Blanche tattled away – through Miss C. – about the fashion of the time: 'Men wore shoes with long points which were chained to their knees. They had long hair cut straight across the forehead.' And, apparently, she '... used to wear brocaded velvet, trimmed with ermine, and a high-peaked cap of miniver'.

Among other tit-bits was mention of the three types of bread eaten by the different classes – namely, simnel, wastel and cotchet. In all, she provided a rich and convincing account of life in the late 14th century. By contrast, when out of trance, Miss C. claimed to know nothing at all of this period.

These sessions greatly puzzled Lowes Dickinson of the Society for Psychical Research (SPR). He followed up all the statements of names, relationships and events; and, to his surprise, was able, in almost every case, to verify the truth of Blanche's assertions. This simply increased his puzzlement, for 'some of the facts given were not such as even a student of the period would naturally come across.' Blanche Poynings, for instance, was a relatively unimportant figure, merely referred to by two chroniclers as one of the Queen's attendants. So he concluded that the most likely explanation was that the facts were drawn from an historical novel. Miss C. could recall reading only one novel set in that period: *John Standish*. But this did not feature the material in Blanche's messages.

Further research by Lowes Dickinson only increased his bewilderment. More and more facts came to light that confirmed Blanche's story, but some were drawn from such obscure genealogical data that he began to feel that they would never have been incorporated in a novel. For a while, he came to 'think it possible that Miss C. was really communicating with the departed Blanche Poynings.'

The first stage of a solution to the mystery came at a tea party at Miss C.'s house. Her aunt and brother were present and began talking about the then current craze for planchette readings. (The planchette is a small board supported on castors which is said to spell out messages without conscious direction on the part of those present when fingers are lightly placed on the board.)

Lowes Dickinson was amused by Miss C.'s claim that she could draw faces with the planchette and asked for a demonstration. The faces appeared but he found them uninteresting, so he went on to use the device for the more traditional questions and answers. At one point, he suggested that Blanche should be asked for, and the 14th-century lady immediately obliged.

A string of questions and answers brought out the unexpected name 'E. Holt'. This meant nothing at all to anyone present, but further answers spelled out by the planchette revealed that 'Mrs Holt... wrote a book... all the people are in it... I am there... *Countess Maud* by Emily Holt.'

Once the name of the novel was out in the open, that was it: Miss C. rernembered having read a book with that very title, and her aunt confirmed it. Yet neither of them could remember anything else about the book – not even the period it dealt with !

So a final hypnosis session was arranged, and Miss C. was asked to picture herself when young. When asked about her aunt reading *Countess Maud*, she was now able to describe the cover of the book and its main subjects. She went on to say: 'I used to turn over the pages. I didn't read it, because it was dull. Blanche

Poynings was in the book; not much about her.' Then she confessed that Blanche now seemed to her to have no existence apart from the printed page: 'Nearly all the events [are] from the book, but not her character.'

Lowes Dickinson scrutinized the novel thoroughly and, with trifling exceptions, discovered in it every person and every fact referred to in the hypnotic sessions. But he also noted that Miss C. had exaggerated the importance of the minor character Blanche, and had ignored the order of events in the book and substituted her own plan. In this way, the whole of the borrowed material was skilfully presented in a natural way. He concluded: 'Her subconscious self showed in fact remarkable invention and dramatic power... so that if we had not happened to light upon the source of the information... it might have seemed a plausible view that Miss C. really did visit a real world and hold conversations with real people. As it is, the discovery... throws discredit on everything else, and especially on the elaborate details about her past lives with which Miss C.'s subconscious self favoured us.'

Much of the genealogical information that so impressed Lowes Dickinson occurs not in the main text of *Countess Maud* but in an extremely detailed appendix. Yet when Miss C. was asked under hypnosis whether she had ever read the appendix, she denied this and said that her aunt had never read her this part of the book. Yet it is clear from a comparison of the appendix with the accounts given by Blanche Poynings that it cannot be the case. This confirms the necessity of treating testimony about a past life given under hypnosis with the greatest of caution.

But it is not only hypnosis that may reveal such extraordinary knowledge. Cases of somnambulism, or sleep-walking, fascinated the Victorians. They believed that, when people sleepwalk, information that had long been lost in the subconscious tends to resurface. This interest has provided us with some fascinating case histories.

One, recorded by Dr Dyce of Aberdeen, involved a servant girl who was subject to bouts of 'hypnotic sleep' during the day. In the course of one of these sleeps, she carried out her everyday duties without being in any way aware of what was going on around her. In another, she repeated the entire baptismal service of the Church of England – although she was unable to do so when awake. And, on one occasion, she sat through a church service in a trance-like state and was so moved by the sermon that she burst into tears – although she could not afterwards remember anything about it. However, in her next sleep, she gave an accurate account of that service. The mind is certainly an amazing storehouse.

WORKING WITH DREAMS

We generally attach little importance to our dreams. But, as the Senoi – a Malayan tribe – have long known, dreams may well be channels for extra-sensory perception.

In 1932, British anthropologist, Pat Noone, was exploring a remote area of the highlands of the Malay Peninsula. During his travels, he made a first-hand study of a tribe called the Temiar Senoi. In Noone's view, they were extremely contented – he even called them 'the happy people' in his letters. Their marriages were lasting, and there was no history of crime or violence within the tribe. Their children seemed wonderfully content, too. Noone wondered what it was that made this tribe so different from the superstitious, fearful, and often violent tribes that inhabited the surrounding area. To discover this, he spent the rest of his life studying the Temiar Senoi, and invited an American psychologist, Kilton Stewart, to share this work and contribute his professional expertise.

Noone discovered that the Senoi culture was largely based on the sharing of dreams. Every morning, the extended family would meet over the first meal of the day to tell each other their dreams and then discuss them. As soon as a child was able to speak, he was encouraged to tell his dreams. As a result, he would gradually become more familiar with his own inner world and that of others, too.

Curing nightmares

All children have frightening dreams and nightmares, but the Senoi society is unique, as far as we know, in the way they teach their children to deal with them. If a Senoi child dreams he is being chased by a large animal and wakes up in terror, his father might urge him to turn and face his pursuer in another dream. But if the animal is too large to be confronted by the child himself, he is encouraged to call on his brothers or friends to help him outface the animal in a dream The nightmares will then decrease and eventually stop altogether. The Senoi children also strike up relationships with the figures who have previously frightened them in their dreams, and in time these dream characters become helpful advisers.

The Senoi believe that the inhabitants of their dreams are the spirits of animals, plants, trees, mountains and rivers. Through friendship with these spirits, they believe they can learn things that they could never know by means of the senses.

One man, for example, who had befriended the spirit of the river in his dreams, frequently had dreams telling him where he could catch large fish. When he went to this part of the river the following day, he caught the fish he had dreamed about. On another occasion, he dreamed about the design of a new fish trap. He actually built a trap based on the dream design and found it worked very well indeed. Other men, whose spirit friends were of the animal kingdom, frequently dreamed of the best places to go hunting in the forest. Meanwhile, an aspiring shaman, or healer-priest, Noone found, would acquire a guardian spirit whom he would meet in a dream. He would go into a trance and lead the village in dances taught by the spirit, thereby winning recognition as a shaman.

Stewart also recorded evidence of much more obvious and powerful psychic phenomena in the Senoi's lives. On one occasion, when there was an epidemic in the tribe, a shaman had a dream in which his dead wife visited him. She taught him a dance, which she said would heal those in the tribe who were ill. In the dream, the shaman demanded evidence that she was indeed his wife and not some other spirit impersonating her. She said that if the dance were performed correctly, she would cause a wooden box that was buried with her to appear in the middle of the long hut.

That night, the tribe performed the dream-taught dance: at the end of it, a box appeared in the air and fell to the ground. A cold breeze swept through the hut. Those who were ill quickly recovered.

Stewart and Noone were sceptical of this account, and so decided to hypnotise the shaman in order to discover the underlying truth. Under hypnosis, he recalled the story with only a few minor changes. It therefore seemed to them that he was not guilty of any conscious sleight of hand: indeed, he had been as surprised as anyone else when the box appeared.

Psychic connections

Whether we believe this story or not – and the value of the evidence offered under hypnosis is open to question – it is just one of many from cultures that believe dreams can have a direct healing effect. So can such phenomena also occur in our own society?

In an attempt to discover more about the dynamics of dreams, dream investigator Joe Friedman began to lead groups using the Senoi approach. Each week, a number of London adults, often complete strangers to each other, would meet for one evening to share and discuss their dreams.

Although the main purpose of these meetings was to help members come to understand the content of their dreams, it was found during the very first session that various kinds of psychic phenomena seemed to be facilitated. The most obvious among these was the 'shared dream'.

One group member, Bill, for example, described a dream in which he was standing within a semicircle with a magician, who reminded him of Tom, another member of the group. From the point where Bill stood, lines led to the letters of the alphabet. The magician told Bill that he was an 'H' or a 'K'. On the same night, Tom had a dream in which he was working at a post office, sorting parcels alphabetically into different bags. The correspondence here involved a person in Bill's dream who resembled Tom, assigning letters of the alphabet to Bill.

Precognitive dreams

It appears that, under certain conditions, the kind of extra-sensory perception that emerges in a dream is not linked to the present but to a future event in the life of the dreamer or another member of the group. Such precognitive dreams are often specific and accurate, and foreshadow events that are outside the control of the dreamer.

Yet we are normally unaware of dream ESP. Even when we do remember our dreams, they are rarely recalled in much detail for a long period, we do not usually make a record of them and we rarely discuss them with others. If Bill had not been participating in a dream group, he would not have told the dream to Tom, since they were not close friends, and so he would not have discovered that Tom had experienced a similar dream the same night. There is, it seems, far more to dream content that is immediately apparent, as the Temiar Senoi have clearly long realised.

In a scene from the 1977 film Telefon, *Soviet 'sleepers' in America are activated by a hidden code and blow up a US military base. Read the feature on page 376 and decide for yourself if such 'mind control' is possible.*

What sort of people, it is often asked, make the best hypnotic subjects?
And can someone be hypnotised against his or her will? Find out on
page 342.

Stage hypnotists manage to provide a wealth of entertainment by persuading their subjects to perform in most extraordinary ways. Often a trigger will be used – a snap of the fingers, perhaps – to induce the trance-state at a later stage.

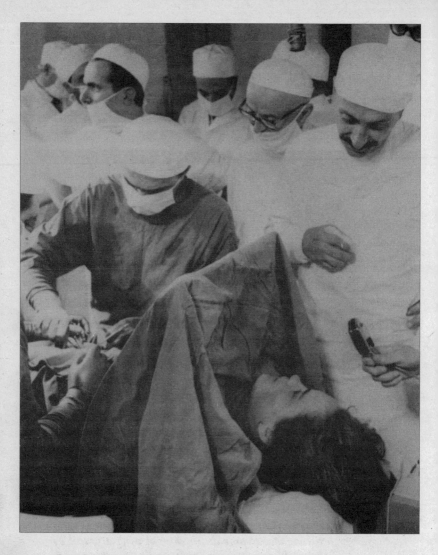

Patient Pierina Menegazzo, above, joked with the surgeon as he removed her appendix. She had been hypnotized to feel no pain and was even able to hold a conversation. On page 334, we take a closer look at the effectiveness of hypnotherapy and the way in which it is regarded by the medical establishment.

SQUATTERS IN THE MIND

Certain individuals seem to possess a host of different selves that come and go continually. What lies behind such cases of fluid and uncertain identity?

The history of Man's advance since the medieval period has been the story of his gradual realisation of how little he seems to matter in the scheme of things. From the pre-Copernican view that he lived at the centre of the Universe – a Universe that was not very much larger than the Earth – he has been forced by modern astronomical discoveries to accept that the Earth is but an insignificant dot in the Galaxy; while the Galaxy, in relation to the visible Universe, is the size of a speck of dust in a cathedral. Man's fond conceit that he was 'Lord of Creation' over the beasts of the field has been swept away by Darwin and his successors: indeed, to many, he seems simply to be an animal species that grew a large brain and is now in serious danger of following both the dinosaur and the dodo to extinction.

During the 19th century, his assumption that he was at least in charge of his mind, overseeing its workings and guiding it according to rational purposes, was also undermined by Freud's theories of the subconscious. Freud discovered that large tracts of Man's thinking processes lay behind a barrier. Often, decisions were taken there and then surfaced: thus, in implementing them, Man was cast more in the role of public relations officer than of managing director.

Notwithstanding such withdrawals to more modest estimates of his position, Man could still console himself with the belief that, at any rate, his mental processes, conscious and unconscious, originated within his skull, woven on the marvellous electrochemical loom of his brain. The raw materials feeding the brain came both through his five senses and the nerves monitoring his body.

The spiritual factor

This view is even held by a large proportion of those who still pay lip service to the religious teachings that there is a non-material factor – the spiritual – capable of influencing and being contacted by human beings. Some believe that their thoughts are their own, and that their dreams, by night or by day, are the products of their mind and brain: they hold that their fantasies, their wishful thinking, belong solely to them. If they are surprised or terrified by the events in their dreams, they attribute this to the fact that the dream-producer, the 'master of ceremonies', is their unconscious, that they have had too much to eat for supper, or that they are worried about something. In

326

their dreams, they are like a person at the cinema who views a film he has had no hand in producing. 'What an imagination I have!' they say in self-admiration.

Unfortunately, not all people can believe this to be the case – among them, multiple personality cases, in which a number of distinct characters dispute the possession of one body. In some such individuals, it seems that the original personality has been shattered by one or more traumatic experience and has given rise to 'secondary' personalities. But others, carefully studied by psychiatrists, demonstrate such bizarre features that the possibility of actual invasion by independent personalities, or parts of personalities, has to be seriously considered. If such a theory seems to the man in the street to be a woeful return to the superstitions of the Dark Ages, its proponents would reply that he is simply ignorant of the facts.

During the last 100 years or so, scores of multiple personality cases have been treated and carefully studied by authorities such as Freud, Jung, William James, Morton Prince, Walter F. Prince and others. Many have common features; but it is rash to assume the same explanation will suffice to cover all of them.

Let us suppose that the personality is a girl. Often she is quiet, reserved, joyless, hyperconscientious. Often she has had a very unhappy upbringing, and is the product of a violent home. She may find herself puzzling over lost stretches of time, the events of which she cannot remember. Strange clothes appear in her wardrobe, and she gradually comes to fear for her sanity. If she consults a psychiatrist, she may be fortunate enough to find one who recognises her condition and encounters one or more secondary personalities that from time to time surface to take control of the body and obliterate the dowdy, everyday personality.

Distinct personalities

In a number of cases, the major secondary personality turns out to be bright and fun-loving, openly contemptuous of the quiet girl with whom she shares a body. Dislike and contempt of the secondary personality may find an outlet in playing tricks upon the bewildered rival, who has no knowledge of the fun-lover's existence, nor memories of the experiences of the other. On the other hand, the fun-lover is often fully aware of everything the dowdy one experiences when the latter is in control. So different are the two characters that the psychiatrist treating the case knows which personality is in control immediately the girl enters the room – a knowledge due not only to different tastes in fashion but also to an almost physical transformation of the patient's face. Truly, Robert Louis Stevenson displayed remarkable insight into the complexities of the human mind when he wrote *Dr Jekyll and Mr Hyde* in the late 19th century.

As many as five or six separate personalities in one body, quite distinct in their beliefs, ethics and mental ages, have been displayed in a number of cases. In that of an American woman, Doris Fischer – studied by Dr Walter F. Prince of Pittsburgh – for instance, there were five personalities: Doris, Margaret, Ariel, Sick Doris and Sleeping Real Doris. Doris was the 'normal' quiet, bewildered personality, while Margaret was the mischievous one who got Doris into trouble. Ariel appeared when Doris was asleep and always claimed to be a spirit who had come to protect her. Sick Doris gave the impression of being a dull, nervous, timid, almost simple-minded person. Sleeping Real Doris seems to have had predominantly the role of guardian of memories: she had no marked separate personality, but could reel off memories of past events, like a living tape-recorder. Dr Prince described her as 'sleeping' because this ability generally lay dormant.

Dr Prince and his wife took the sorely troubled girl to stay with them, almost as a daughter; and thanks to the Princes' care and psychiatric treatment, the girl's mental and physical health improved over the next few years. During that time, the complex relationship among the five personalities inhabiting the body of Doris Fischer altered. At first, Margaret had access to the contents of Doris' and Sick Doris' minds, while Ariel was acquainted with the minds of all three. Sometimes, quarrels would occur for control of the body. As time went on, Doris extended her control, as Sick Doris and then Sleeping Real Doris gradually deteriorated and finally disappeared. It was then the turn of Margaret – the sharp, fun-loving one – who was slowly to recede until she, too, vanished.

There is a touching and thought-provoking account of the last days of Sick Doris. As she began to disintegrate, she seemed to realise that she was going to disappear. She accompanied Dr Prince on a last walk and left a letter for Margaret. (One of the ways by which each entity communicated with the others was by writing letters when in control. These would be read when the appropriate personality took over the body.) In her letter, Sick Doris instructed Margaret as to what to do with her possessions after her demise and tried to leave her sister-personality some helpful advice.

To the end, Ariel maintained her claim that she was a spirit, sent to look after Doris. In his account, Dr Prince admits that, to him, she was the most mature and wise of all the personalities and that he had to consider seriously the hypothesis that her claim was in some way true.

The Christine Beauchamp case displayed many similarities to the Doris Fischer case and is quite often confused with the latter, especially since it was treated by another Dr Prince – this time, Dr Morton Prince, a professor at the Tufts Medical School in Boston, USA. Christine Beauchamp was a student, and was approaching a nervous breakdown when she first consulted him. He tried hypnosis, finding that she was a good subject. But to his surprise, a distinct personality emerged – a relaxed, very much calmer version, whom Prince called *B-2* to distinguish her from the first Christine, *B-1*. But more was to follow. *B-2*, under hypnosis, was always rubbing her closed eyes. Prince discovered that it was a third personality, at first called *B-3*, who did the rubbing in an effort to get them open. *B-3* insisted that she had a right to see; and on a subsequent occasion, she at last managed to open Christine's eyes. From then on, she insisted on being known as Sally.

Practical joker

Sally was a bright, mischievous person, not nearly so well-educated as Christine, but exhibiting perfect health in contrast to Christine's debilitated and nervous state. She seemed to hate Christine and claimed that she never slept, but stayed awake while the other personality was asleep. She also continually tormented Christine with practical jokes. According to Dr Prince, Sally went out into the country where she collected in a box some snakes and spiders. She packed them up and addressed the package to Christine, who opened the box in due time and went into screaming hysterics – not surprisingly, since she had a horror of such creatures.

B-3, or Sally, would also force the strait-laced Christine into embarrassing situations in which she would have to tell lies. In spite of Dr Prince's efforts, this feud continued until, quite suddenly, a fourth personality, *B-4,* surfaced. *B-4* was a mature, responsible, firm personality who defended the luckless Christine from Sally's torments by giving Sally as good – or as bad – as she gave Christine.

Dr Prince decided that, if he could merge *B-1* and *B-4* and suppress Sally, he might get in tune with the true Christine. Using his hypnotic skills, he attempted to achieve this goal. It is not surprising to learn that Sally resisted to the end, claiming that she had every right to live and enjoy life. But Dr Prince succeeded in producing a more complete personality for Christine, though never quite eliminating Sally.

Of more than one mind

It has been suggested that the population figures for the United States should be increased – so many of its citizens seem to be afflicted, or even favoured, by extra personalities. William Milligan, for instance, was found guilty of raping four young women in Columbus, Ohio, in 1976. He was diagnosed as having ten personalities – of whom the guilty one was an 18-year-old lesbian. One of the psychiatrists who hastened to interview Milligan was Dr Cornelia Wilbur. She had previously treated 'Sybil', the subject of a book and a film, who is said to have had as many as 16 personalities.

But these cases are surely excelled by that of 'Charles' – the pseudonym given by a psychiatrist to what he hoped was the core personality of one of his patients, Eric, who had been found wandering in a daze in Daytona Beach, Florida, in February 1982. Eric immediately 'split' into two selves – 'young Eric' and 'older Eric'.

'Young Eric' told a (fictitious) tale of how he had been brought up by drug dealers, of having been raped, and of having witnessed murders committed by his stepfather.

Further personalities emerged over a period of weeks. These included violent 'Mark', arrogant 'Michael', and blind and mute 'Jeffrey'. Finally, the psychiatrist identified no fewer than 27.

Many of the selves were in conflict and created problems for each other. 'Michael', for example, was athletic and once went on a long jog that left 'Eric' – and all the other occupants of his body – physically aching for days. 'Charles', supposedly the true personality, said afterwards of his existence: 'I've lived through hell. I'm surprised I didn't go crazy.'

If a personality under shock can shatter into fragments, so that each fragment is made up of a fraction of all those moods, emotions, beliefs, prejudices, and desires that contribute to the 'normal' person, then – even though, in the Doris Fischer case, Ariel claimed to be a spirit – we can still cling to the belief that no outside influences are at work. But there are a number of cases that, to certain investigators, stretch this hypothesis almost to breaking point.

THE HEALING TRANCE

*In the 1850s, a man had
a leg amputated while under hypnosis, but
eminent doctors accused him of pretending to feel
no pain. How much faith, then, does modern
medicine put in use of hypnotherapy?*

The story of hypnotherapy is one of the most disturbing, as well as one of the saddest, in the history of medicine. It offers us what is potentially an immensely valuable therapeutic weapon but one never been properly exploited – and it is still generally neglected, in spite of much evidence in its favour.

Hypnosis has a long history. There are indications, for instance, that a hypnotic element entered into ancient tribal medicine, and that it was used in the Aesculapian temples of healing in ancient Greece. But the first clear demonstration of its powers in modern times came as a result of experiments conducted by some of Franz Mesmer's disciples, two centuries ago. They found that they could relieve, and often remove, the symptoms of illness in mesmerized subjects. In particular, they could banish pain.

As there were no anaesthetics available at the time, this ought to be a boon for patients undergoing surgery. Surgeons, however, would have none of it. When, in 1829, a Commission appointed by the French Academy of Medicine to investigate mesmerism watched an operation in which a tumour was painlessly removed, its members were impressed, but the medical establishment simply refused to accept that the case could have been genuine.

To Sir Benjamin Brodie, a fashionable London surgeon of the 1850s, mesmerism was nothing more than 'a debasing superstition'. And after watching a man having a leg amputated while in a mesmeric trance, the eminent physiologist Marshall Hall explained that the man must have been only pretending not to feel pain; if he had really been unconscious, his other leg surely would have been seen to twitch in sympathy.

Anybody who has read contemporary accounts of what surgery was like in those days will appreciate just what it would have meant to thousands of agonized patients to have a mesmerist on hand. The coolies in the service of the East India Company in Calcutta were fortunate; they had James Esdaile as their surgeon. In the 1840s, he performed hundreds of operations while his patients were entranced. But the medical journals in England would not credit his accounts; and by that time, in any case, ether and chloroform were at last becoming available.

James Braid, who coined the term 'hypnotism' to describe his method of inducing the mesmeric trance state, did not make much use of it as a therapy, but his work on it led a French country doctor, A. A. Liébeault, to try out hypnotherapy on patients in the late 1870s. If they wanted drugs, they could have them, he would say, but they would have to pay. Hypnotism would cost them nothing. Being thrifty (and poor), most opted for hypnotism.

A converted sceptic

So successful was Liébeault's form of treatment – having hypnotized the patients, he simply suggested to them that their symptoms would go away – that it attracted the attention of Hippolyte Bernheim, professor of medicine at the nearby town of Nancy. At first sceptical, he became a convert after a visit to Liébeault, in 1882; and for the first – and, as things turned out, last – time, hypnotherapy established itself as a routine form of hospital treatment.

Considering what the alternatives were – bleeding, cupping, purging, and useless drugs – the patients must be considered to have been exceptionally lucky.

All this time, the medical establishment had refused to accept that hypnotism even existed, let alone that it could be used as a therapy; but in the 1880s, Jean-Martin Charcot managed to convince a committee of the Academy of Medicine that it was genuine – that people really could be put into a state of hypnotic trance. He did so, however, only by persuading them that the state of trance was linked with hysteria, so that it need not be taken seriously as a therapy. And in spite of Bernheim's continuing demonstrations that hypnotherapy was a simple and effective way of dealing with everyday disorders, doctors still shied away from it.

A committee appointed by the British Medical Association went to Nancy and returned in 1892 to report that Bernheim's methods did indeed work. Hypnotherapy, they could confirm, would be an asset in Britain. Their verdict was ignored, however; and by the turn of the century, hypnotherapy had faded out of the picture. It was not repudiated, the French psychiatrist Pierre Janet was later to recall; it simply fell into disuse.

Unquestionably, the main reason was that, in this period, the theory established itself that physical, 'organic' diseases could only be treated successfully by physical means – drugs or surgery. Hypnotherapy might be all right for people suffering from neuroses or hysteria, but not for people suffering from coughs and colds, let alone from more serious disorders. So, although a few individual doctors continued to use it, along with dentists who found it useful when patients reacted badly to 'jabs', little was heard of hypnotherapy for about half-a-century.

The first reminder of just how unwise the British medical profession was to ignore hypnotherapy came in the *British Medical Journal* in 1952. This was a report on the case of a boy suffering from congenital ichthyosis – a condition that caused a warty layer, with a foul odour, to cover most of his body. After all the standard forms of treatment had failed, he had been taken to the hospital at East Grinstead in Surrey, where remarkable feats of plastic surgery had been achieved during the Second World War, to see if skin from parts of his body that were unaffected could be grafted to replace the affected areas; but that was equally ineffective.

Last resort

One of the doctors at the hospital suggested that, as a last resort, they should try hypnotism. The boy was put into a trance and told that the condition of his left arm would clear. (They decided to proceed in this way so that if the warty layer disappeared only from his arm, it would be related to the suggestion, and could not be dismissed as coincidence). After a few days, the scaly layer on the arm softened, and fell off, with the skin underneath being entirely normal. And, in time, the condition disappeared altogether.

Not merely was the 'rhino boy' – as press reports called him – healed, he was able to return to live the full social life that his appearance (and repulsive smell) had previously denied him. The report on his case concluded that although, formerly, he had been a lonely and solitary character, he had become, a year after the treatment, 'a happy, normal boy' and had also found a job.

338

It would be gratifying to be able to record that this case caused a change of heart in the medical establishment. But, in fact, it made very little perceptible difference. The fact is that most doctors had for so long been conditioned to assume that organic diseases can be treated only by organic methods that they could not think in any other terms. Even today, when the medical profession is widely aware that this dogma has been discredited, most doctors continue to diagnose disorders, and prescribe for them, as though it were still gospel.

A minority of doctors and dentists do use hypnotism; but the chief impetus behind what appears to be a current revival has come from practitioners who are not qualified members of the medical profession. Some of them have no qualifications at all; some have had training courses, often of doubtful value; and some are qualified psychologists who have decided to enter this territory.

What, then, is *good* hypnotherapy? For simplicity, hypnotherapy can be divided into two main categories. It can be used as Liébeault used it, simply as a means of getting rid of unwanted symptoms – in particular, pain. In this capacity, it is on a par with chemical analgesics such as aspirin; but, although rapport has to be established first between therapist and patient, which takes time (and not all patients are susceptible), there are no adverse side effects, and no prescription charges.

Most hypnotherapists, however, regard their work as being a branch of psychotherapy; and this means that they use hypnosis as an aid in whatever type of psychotherapy – Freudian, behaviourist or pragmatic – they favour. A plate on the door, or an entry in the classified telephone directory, saying simply 'Hypnotherapist' consequently affords no clue whatsoever to the kind of treatment patients – or 'clients', as many hypnotherapists refer to them – may expect to undergo.

Speedy analysis

Freud himself used hypnosis for a time, to regress his patients to the age at which their emotional conflicts had first been repressed, but he came to the conclusion that it did not disclose repressed material satisfactorily, and replaced it with the technique of free association that came to be known as psychoanalysis. Some of his disciples, however, decided that, for all its possible disadvantages, the use of hypnosis could enormously speed up the process of analysis. In the USA, particularly, it is now extensively used for this purpose.

Hypnotherapy might appear to have been just what the behaviourists needed, providing them with an easy way to implant ideas in patients' minds. But establishing the rapport with patients that is needed for successful hypnosis irked some behaviourists. Others were disappointed to find that the effects of suggestion soon wear off, like the effects of a drug. They were also, as Professor Hans Eysenck observed in *Sense and Nonsense in Psychology,* put off by the 'unfortunate associations which the term hypnosis arouses in so many people' – associations with occultism, quackery, and music hall performance.

However, hypnotherapy is gradually shedding this image. A great deal of research is now being undertaken, most of it in the USA. Indeed, the survey in *Hypnosis at its Bicentennial,* edited by Fred H. Frankel of the Harvard Medical School, describes interesting results from trials of hypnosis in the treatment of, among other conditions, burns, migraine, asthma and impotence.

Hypnotherapists today totally reject the Svengali image. Their aim, rather, is use of hypnosis to reveal to the patient what his own mind is capable of accomplishing – for hypnotic suggestion, however effective in the short term, is not lasting. For maximum results, the patient must learn how to play his own part in the therapy, as you will discover when we delve further into hypnosis in the chapter that follows.

THE POWER OF SUGGESTION

Hypnosis is a highly popular form of stage entertainment. No one is quite sure how the trance-state comes about; but the technique can also be helpful as a form of medical treatment, in crime detection and in exploring possible evidence for past lives.

Some people still think of hypnotists as slightly shady characters, practising a highly dubious craft. They see in their mind's eye the evil Svengali, the character in George du Maurier's novel who lived off the unfortunate Trilby, by hypnotising her so that she became an internationally acclaimed concert artist, though her ordinary voice was truly terrible. Today's stage hypnotist, however, is no longer the seedy villain of such a story – merely an entertainer.

Performances tend to follow a standard formula. Volunteers are called for; and one by one, the hypnotist addresses soothing words to them, like a mother putting her child to sleep. Those who respond remain on stage: the rest are sent back into the audience. Then, in groups or individually, those still on stage are told that they are very hot or very cold, very thirsty or very drunk; and they behave and feel just as they are told to do, even if they make themselves look ridiculous.

Altered consciousness

There is not, as yet, any clear explanation of the nature of hypnotism. It is generally defined as a trance – that is, an altered state of consciousness, the extent of the alteration depending on the individual. In any group, some volunteers will remember everything that has been done while they are on stage, but others may recall nothing. Nevertheless, they all will have come under the hypnotist's influence.

What this means is that each of them has shed some of his or her controls, or thrown off certain inhibitions that training and habit normally impose. If somebody said to any of them, in ordinary conversation, 'You are a watchdog and you hear a burglar', it would raise only a laugh. On stage, however, the hypnotised subject gets down on hands and knees, and barks. The hypnotist is he-who-must-be-obeyed; and commands from other people are ignored, unless the hypnotist has given instructions that they should be obeyed, too.

Even more impressively, the accomplished hypnotist can give commands that will be obeyed after subjects have come out of their trances and returned to their seats in the audience. If he gives them a 'post-hypnotic suggestion' that they should stand up and shout 'hip-hip-hooray' whenever the orchestra plays a certain tune, for instance, they will do so, without knowing why.

Hypnosis appears to switch off some part of our minds that ordinarily monitors our behaviour, instructing us what to do in any given set of circumstances without thought on our part. We hand this control system over to the hypnotist, much as an airline pilot may hand over the controls of his aircraft to somebody on the ground, who then guides it in by radar with the help of an automatic pilot.

Hypnosis has been exploited by tribal witch doctors and by priests in the temples of ancient Greece. But we owe the form in which it is practised today to Franz Mesmer and his disciples. Two hundred years ago, they realised that subjects in the trance state could be made to obey every command. But more importantly, in the course of their experiments, they made two discoveries of great potential significance.

For a start, they found that if they told a subject that he would feel no pain, he could be struck, pricked and even burned without giving out so much as a yelp – and this was before the invention of anaesthetic drugs. Mesmerists further proceeded to demonstrate that pain-free surgical operations could be performed under hypnosis.

The second discovery was that some hypnotised subjects suddenly found themselves enjoying talents they did not know they had in their ordinary lives.

One might draw well under hypnosis; another, sing melodiously. A few even appeared to become clairvoyant, describing events or places that they could not have seen. This, too, was dismissed as occultism. And to this day, hypnotism has never quite rid itself of its reputation of lying beyond the boundaries of orthodox science.

Justified claims

Yet we know now that the Mesmerists' claims were largely justified. Endless demonstrations have shown that a subject under hypnosis can put his finger into a candle flame and, if told he will feel no pain, will indeed feel no pain. Even more remarkable, if told he will have no blister, no blister appears.

Certain researchers have taken this even further. If a hypnotised subject is told he is going to be touched with a red-hot skewer, not only will he cry out in pain even if the skewer is stone cold, its touch will actually raise a blister.

Scepticism about the possibility that some subjects become clairvoyant under hypnosis has also been shaken by recent research into hypnotic regression. It has long been known that hypnotised subjects can be escorted back in time to earlier occasions in their lives. Asked to recall what they were doing on, say, New Year's Day ten or twenty years ago, they will describe in detail episodes long since consciously forgotten. Where it has been possible to check such accounts, they have been found to be accurate. In the United States, the police have exploited this faculty by asking witnesses of crimes and accidents to allow themselves to be hypnotised to find out whether they can recall, say, the number of a stolen car.

Hypnotic regression

A hundred years ago, researchers in Europe even found that some hypnotised subjects appeared ro be able to recall events from past centuries. Recently, this line of investigation has been taken up again, and the results are described in detail in works like Jeremy Iverson's *More Lives Than One*, an account of Arnall Bloxham's investigations, and Joe Keeton's *Encounters With The Past*.

It remains to be established whether such hypnotised subjects are regressing to their own past lives, or tuning into what might be described as a 'videotape from the collective unconscious', but it seems clear they are genuine. The material, even if not accurate in details, is certainly being picked up from somewhere.

Hypnosis, then, involves a trance or altered state of consciousness, (some people prefer to describe it as a state of altered awareness of consciousness), in which certain faculties and abilities can be liberated. Clearly, the potential benefits, for anybody prepared to master the art of auto-hypnosis, can be considerable. Why, then, is more use not made of it?

Fear is, of course, partly responsible – the lingering suspicion that hypnosis is in the occult category and not scientifically resepctable, or that to undergo it is to put oneself into the hands of a Svengali. Yet the fact that a stage hypnotist can so easily manipulate volunteers is somewhat misleading. The volunteers know it is a game. They choose to play it, presumably out of curiosity in most cases, and would not volunteer if they thought they might be made to do something dangerous, criminal, or even immoral, by their standards.

A celebrated occasion demonstrated this a century ago. A girl taking part in an experiment in Paris, who had been told to kill one of the students, appeared to try to do so and had to be restrained. Yet when asked to take off her clothes, she blushed, came out of the trance and ran from the room.

Presumably, she must have sensed in some way that she would be prevented from doing anything dangerous or criminal, and so agreed to join in. But actually to have undressed would almost certainly have compromised her own moral code to a marked degree – something unacceptable.

The implications of hypnosis for medicine are striking too; yet, until very recently, they have been largely ignored. It is only in the last 20 years or so that the results of research into hypnosis have been confirmed and amplified with the help of investigation involving biofeedback. These have shown how individuals can actually learn to control many bodily functions – heartbeat, blood pressure and gastric secretions, for instance – by auto-suggestion or self-hypnosis.

New horizons

Hypnosis, or auto-suggestion, can also accomplish much more. Individuals, like the American Jack Schwartz, have even demonstrated how they are able to control bleeding, staunching blood flow as if turning off a tap. Similarly, it has been shown that much the simplest way to remove warts and other skin blemishes is by suggestion under hypnosis. It can also help in curing allergies and in getting a subject to stop smoking (though good hypnotherapists emphasize that they can only help those who want to help themselves).

The distinguished Australian psychiatrist, Ainslie Meares, and Americans Carl and Stephanie Simonton, have shown how hypnosis and auto-hypnosis can also be used to help terminal cancer patients in particular, not merely by enabling them to control pain, but also by giving them a welcome distraction from their worries. In some cases, this has prolonged survival; and in others, X-rays have revealed actual regression of tumours. No false hopes of miracle cures are raised, as has so often happened with other forms of cancer treatment. Rather, patients are told that it is how they react to their own voyages of discovery in altered states of consciousness that counts.

Self-hypnosis has two major advantages. It can be taught, so that patients can learn to control, for instance, their own headaches and sometimes even prevent them. And it costs nothing – except, of course, for the practitioner's initial time in passing on the technique.

Post-hypnotic suggestion can also help in other spheres, such as golf. It will, for instance, send a golfer out on to the course in an utterly relaxed frame of mind – which, in golf, is said to be half the battle. Outside the medical field, too, it seems the possibilities for hypnosis are only just beginning to be appreciated.

CURSES OF WRATH

Curses have always been feared – with justice it seems, for disease and death have often befallen victims of such invocations.

Invocations of destruction or evil are part of the accustomed armoury of the magician, shaman or ill-wisher. But do curses actually work and, if so, how? Swearing at someone gives vent to pent-up feelings; and most psychologists would say that curses do nothing more – unless, that is, the victim is expecting trouble. Sandford Cohen, a psychologist at Boston University, USA, became convinced from field research, however, that curses *can* be lethal, because of the feeling of utter helplessness they can inspire. Indeed, he saw a similarity between western Man dying from a fear of some disease believed to be fatal and primitive Man dying from a witch doctor's curse.

Another explanation involves the 'tape recording' theory – that a thought can imprint itself on an object or person, and also be transferred to others. If the thought is malevolent, so is the effect. There are certainly numerous cases of victims who were totally sceptical of supernatural 'mumbo-jumbo', but this did nothing to save them from the effects.

Take the case of Robert Heinl Junior, a retired colonel in the US Marine Corps. From 1958 to 1963, he served in Haiti as chief of the US naval mission, while his wife studied the voodoo religion. Afterwards, back in the United States, they wrote *Written in Blood,* a history of Haiti that was openly critical of the ruling dynasty of François 'Papa Doc' Duvalier. Then they learned from a newspaper published by Haitian exiles that a curse had been placed on the book, probably after Papa Doc's death in 1971, by his widow, Simone.

Initially, the Heinls were flattered that their book was thought to be worth cursing, but amusement soon turned to fear. First, the manuscript was lost on the way to the publishers, then it turned up four months later in a room that the publishers never used. Meanwhile, the Heinls prepared another copy of the manuscript and sent it off for binding and stitching, but the machine immediately broke down. Next, a reporter who was preparing to interview the authors was struck down with appendicitis. The colonel then fell through a stage when he was delivering a speech, injuring his leg. And while walking near his home, he was suddenly – and severely – bitten by a dog.

Accidents continued, two involving the number 22, which Papa Doc considered magical. Finally, on 5 May 1979, the Heinls were on holiday on St Barthélémy Island, east of Haiti, when the colonel dropped dead from a heart attack. His widow mused: 'There is a belief that the closer you get to Haiti, the more powerful the magic becomes'.

Curses, precisely laid down in many rituals, are still cast by priests in many of the world's major religions. In September 1981, for example, Rabbi Moshe Hirsch, leader of the Neturei Karta, an orthodox Jewish sect, threatened to invoke the 'Rod of Light' against the Israeli archaeologist Yigal Shilo if he persisted in excavating the biblical city of David. This, the rabbi maintained, involved desecrating a medieval Jewish burial ground. Archaeologists, meanwhile, denied the very existence of such a cemetery.

The ceremony involves the reading of a text based on Kabbalistic writings. The participants burn black candles, sound a ram's horn and invoke the name of the cursed man's mother. 'This ceremony is an absolute last resort', said the rabbi. 'It has only been invoked twice in 30 years, both times with horrible consequences. There are many ways of dying, some that are less pleasant than others.' Interestingly, the rabbi claims he failed to discover Shilo's mother's name.

In the Church of England, too, spiritual contracts are occasionally put out on church thieves. Since the 1970s, in Gloucestershire alone, at least two vicars have performed the commination (or divine threat) service – the Reverend Harold Cheales of Wych Rissington in 1973, and the Reverend Robert Nesham of Down Ampney in 1981. The commination service contains 12 curses and leaves room for more. It first appeared in the 1662 *Book of Common Prayer;* but in the 1928 revision, the word 'curse' was replaced by 'God's anger and judgement'. It was traditionally used against enemies of the Church on the first day of Lent, or whenever a church or churchyard had been desecrated. Christian curses seem to be, on occasions, just as effective as demonic ones: the old abbeys that Henry VIII seized from the monks after the dissolution of the monasteries in the early 16th century, for instance, often bedevilled their new owners over generations with the dreadful curses laid by angry monks.

A heart of stone

There is a widespread ancient belief that no good will come from disturbing old stones or buried treasure: folklore worldwide is full of such tales, and the theme continues in the enduring popularity of the idea of a mummy's curse. Some researchers even believe that such deep-seated and widespread beliefs, as part of the collective unconscious, can exert a material influence, bringing old myths to life and also reinforcing them.

The old castle of Syrie in Aberdeenshire, Scotland, is one such building plagued by a legendary curse. A group of stones in the local river is known as the Weeping Stones, one of which is missing. It is said that no heir to Syrie will ever succeed until that stone is found. And in 1944, when a 2-tonne 'Witch's Stone' was shifted from a crossroads at Scrapfaggot

Green, Great Leighs, Essex, England, in order to widen the road, psychic havoc broke out. A great boulder appeared outside the local pub, chickens were found locked up in rabbit hutches, rabbits ran loose in the garden, the church bells chimed irregularly, 30 sheep and two horses were found dead in a field, and a village builder's scaffolding poles tumbled about 'like matchsticks'. The 'Witch's Stone' was replaced and peace duly restored.

More recently, in 1980, a 30-tonne boulder was removed from the Devil's Marbles to a park in Tennant Creek, an isolated mining town in the Australian outback. Aborigines of the Warramungu tribe believe the Marbles are a relic from the so-called 'Dream Time' – when ancestral spirits created the world – and that any interference with such relics will lead to sickness and death. After the boulder's removal, a number of Aboriginal children fell ill with sores on their legs, and a tribal elder, Mick Taylor, warned that 'someone would get killed' if the stone was not returned. In March 1981, Mick Taylor died from meningitis at the age of 50. The town then agreed to return the boulder.

Curses that are inflicted as result of moving sacred stones are found in the New World, too. During the summer of 1977, airline vice-president Ralph Loffert, of Buffalo, New York state, USA, his wife and four children visited the Hawaiian volcano, Mauna Loa. While there, they collected some stones from the volcano despite a warning from the locals that this would anger the volcano goddess, Pele. Some claim to have seen Pele, who traditionally appears to warn of imminent eruptions. Shortly after they returned home, Mauna Loa erupted, and Pele certainly seems to have been angered for, within a few months, one of the Loffert boys, Todd, developed appendicitis, had knee surgery and broke his wrist; another son, Mark, sprained an ankle and broke his arm; his brother, Dan, caught an eye infection; and the daughter, Rebecca, lost two front teeth in a fall.

In July 1978, the Lofferts sent the stones to a friend in Hawaii who was asked to return them to the volcano. But the disasters continued: Mark then hurt his knee, Rebecca broke three more teeth, Dan fractured a hand bone, while Todd dislocated an elbow and fractured his wrist again. Mark then confessed that he still had three stones. They were returned – and the trouble ceased.

The notion of a curse affecting a whole family is as old as civilisation. The ancient Greeks were firm believers in the efficacy of curses – the most celebrated affecting the house of Atreus. Atreus himself had killed the son of the god Hermes in a love contest, and as a result the deity put a curse on the murderer 'and all his house'. Atreus killed his own son by mistake; another son, the hero Agamemnon, was killed by his wife's lover; and she in turn was murdered by her son.

In Britain, several aristocratic families are believed to be afflicted by family curses. In the 18th century, for instance, the Scottish Earl of Breadalbane moved a graveyard to build the castle of Taymouth. According to tradition, a lady whose grave was disturbed laid a curse on the family whereby no two earls of this line would succeed each other. The prophecy apparently came true.

Even researching the subject of curses might be considered hazardous. In 1928, the occultist and magician Aleister Crowley ('The Beast'), met the young radio producer, Lance Sieveking, on the French Riviera. They spent many hours in conversation, and Crowley subsequently cast Sieveking's horoscope. It contained a number of predictions that were later fulfilled. One, however, was not. Crowley wrote: 'By the way, you will oblige me personally by dying at the age of forty-five'. Sieveking was then 32, but he disobligingly lived to be 75.

Crowley's curses, however, often claimed victims. The last was Dr William Brown Thompson, who withheld the addicted Beast's supply of morphia. In a rage, Crowley put a curse on him, saying that when he died he would take the doctor with him. Crowley died on 1 December 1947, aged 72. Thompson was dead within 24 hours.

THE FANTASY-PRONE

Most of us dream only while we are asleep. But there are also some whose minds seem to revel in a curious world of fantasy most of their waking time.

For years on end, a young American woman called Ruth, living in London, was afflicted by hostile hallucinations of her father, who lived on the other side of the Atlantic at the time. These hallucinations affected her senses of sight, hearing, smell and touch. Indeed, it was almost as if her father had been constantly physically present. Ruth thought she was going mad; but, through the treatment of a wise psychiatrist, she learned that her ability to fantasize was, in its way, a gift that she could – and did – develop for positive use. She was, unwittingly, what is known as a fantasy-prone personality, and the late developer of a talent that some people, perhaps 3 or 4 per cent of the population, possess all their lives.

There have been several studies into the nature of such personalities. Dr Sheryl C. Wilson and Dr Theodore X. Barber, both of Cushing Hospital, Framingham, Massachusetts, USA, for instance, tested 27 female, fantasy-prone personalities together with a control group of 25 'normal' women. The fantasy-prone women were selected on the grounds of their extremely positive responses to certain standard psychological tests in guided imagining, hypnosis and suggestibility, and to other tests devised by the experimenters. With two exceptions, every member of the group was university educated. Their ages ranged from 19 to 63 years, with a mean of 28.

All but four, in the experimenters' estimation, were either socially normal or exceptionally well-adjusted: the remainder, one of whom had been through a nervous breakdown, faced difficulties such as depression. Twenty-four had husbands or relationships with one or more boyfriends. It cannot be over-emphasized that, aside from their genius for fantasizing, the fantasy-prone women were perfectly normal people. They were, so to speak, at one extreme end of a curve representing a certain kind of ability. Otherwise, they were quite ordinary – just as a mathematician, artist or musician, exceptionally talented in his or her field, may be entirely ordinary in everything else.

The abilities of fantasy-prone people, Wilson and Barber found, generally begin in childhood. Many of them – like many sensitives – had childhood playmates who, to them, were as real as flesh-and-blood companions but whom, as they sometimes learned through bitter experience, adults could not see. Not only this, they often 'became' characters from books that they read, ceasing to be themselves in a way that is perhaps similar to that in which a great actor loses himself completely in the character he portrays. But childhood fantasies are not without danger: a child who believed she was leading a lamb through a meadow, for instance, suddenly 'awoke' to find herself alone, surrounded by traffic in a city street.

A consciously developed ability to fantasize can also continue into adult life for a number of reasons. Adults significant to the child may provide encouragement through accepting the child's viewpoint supportively, and convincingly, as their own. A child may also use his fantasy world to escape from isolation, loneliness, a deprived or distressing environment or a particular activity that he dislikes, such as intensive piano practice.

Secret talents

In adulthood, realisation that they are not like others in their fantasizing ability frequently makes fantasy-prone individuals somewhat secretive about their talents. Consequently, they share their secrets with no one, not even their marital partners. Some, however, actually find relief in fantasizing during contact with strangers, pretending to be characters other than themselves.

Interestingly, fantasy-prone people often have psychic abilities above the average; and the 27 women in the Massachusetts experiment were found to be

359

gifted in telepathy, precognition (waking and in dreams), premonitions (one subject forecast the Kentucky Derby winners for 10 years in succession but did not back them because she considered this a misuse of her faculty), psychometry, mediumistic trances, perception of the presence of spirits, encounters with apparitions (one apparition revealed to one of the subjects the existence of a missing will), 'seeing' people's thoughts in images above their heads, dowsing, automatic writing (felt to come from an entity outside the subject), and the capacity to affect the working of electrical appliances. Twenty-two subjects reported out-of-the-body experiences, while two claimed to carry out healing, and a third to minister to the dying during astral travel.

Home movies

Like other psychics, fantasy-prone people have vivid imaginations. They do not merely recall events but relive them with the sights, smells, sounds, tactile impressions and emotions of the original experiences. Many of them also have a perfect auditory memory. Their recollections, like their fantasies, are in many ways similar to films – but films that they not only watch, but in which they also play a part. Some fantasy-prone people are also able to eliminate unpleasant memories through amnesia. However, they have a marked tendency to confuse fantasy recollections with memories of actual events.

Fantasy-prone people live an outwardly normal life – but many of them admit to spending more than half their lives in a fantasy existence. In social contacts, for example, they can fantasize about what is being discussed or described by their companions, or use fantasy to escape from boredom. They often react intensely to stimuli – a passing mention of Egypt, for example, can transport them to a pharaoh's court or to modern Alexandria. They can fly from routine or unpleasant experiences into a holiday world, a 'previous life', a trip into the future, travel to other galaxies or enjoy a sexual experience with a fantastic lover, who can give them greater orgasmic satisfaction than any live human being.

In idle moments, or while preparing for sleep, they can surrender to fantasy, set the stage, create the plot and characters and then sit back, as it were, to watch the play unfold. One third of subjects found it better to watch their 'home movies' with closed eyes; but to two-thirds, it did not matter whether their eyes were open or shut. All the subjects, however, reported that they experienced their fantasies with all their senses as real events. To all fantasy-prone people, 'real' life is a shadow of their fantasy existence. To be deprived of the latter would, to them, be a living death too terrible to contemplate.

But there are dangers and inconveniences associated with fantasies for adults, too. The fantasy of a child running on to a road from behind a parked car, for example, may make a driver brake suddenly and actually cause an accident. Physical symptoms, even actual illnesses, may result from fantasies. Thirteen out of 22 women questioned in the Massachusetts project admitted having had at least one false pregnancy. Two had even sought abortions.

The experiences of such fantasy-prone people are certainly significant for psychical research. Study of their characteristics may throw light on mediums, for example. Indeed, it is possible that some spirit guides and communications are actually created by subconscious fantasizing. Their experiences also challenge the nature of our very perception of reality, which we assume communicates itself, by stimulation of the senses, in approximately the same way to everyone experiencing it.

So perhaps there is indeed another, inner or 'mirror' reality that communicates in a different way. And just as the average person is ordinarily unaware of psychical phenomena, yet has perhaps one or two experiences of them during the course of his life, so perhaps he may have, very rarely, a momentary revelation of the fantasy-prone person's 'inner' reality, in which he experiences an hallucination as real. The knowledge that there are personalities who constantly have such experiences may thus help the ordinary man or woman to come to terms with such a one-off event.

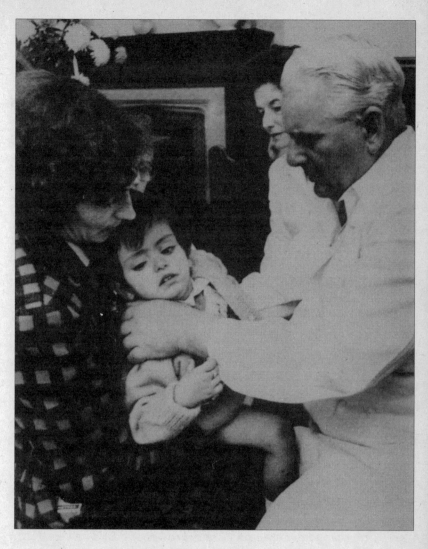

Although miracle healer Linda Martel, above, died aged five, she is still credited with healing powers – as are her clothes. Explanations for such apparent miracles are considered on page 287.

American psychic dentist Willard Fuller, a former Baptist minister who cured dental ailments by purely spiritual means, is seen above. After an initial inspection of the patient's mouth, Fuller would pray and, within minutes, fillings – and sometimes even new teeth – would appear.

Curses, as discussed on page 350, seem to exert a very real effect on all those who believe in them. In the picture above, *a 788-year-old curse is seen being ritually lifted by the former British Chief Rabbi at the consecration of Clifford's Tower in York, in 1978.*

Many may claim to have exceptional mindpower; but for the Christian, the greatest miracle-worker of all was Jesus Christ, seen depicted in G.P. Jacomb Hood's picture The Raising of Jairus's Daughter.

REMOTE VIEWING

Can the mind somehow travel many miles, tour a target location and report back with an accurate description? There are many controversial claims made for the bizarre phenomenon of remote viewing.

When two researchers, Russell Targ and Harold Puthoff, published their book *Mind-reach* in 1977, they were not modest about its claims: they had, they asserted, made the final breakthrough and established scientifically that the phenomenon known as remote viewing was fact. What was more, they considered it to be 'probably a latent and widely distributed perceptual ability.'

Remote viewing – a form of ESP – was not a new subject for discussion and experiment. Papers covering aspects of the phenomenon had appeared in the early 1970s in the British science journal *Nature*, as well as in other highly respected publications. Although controversial, it was believed to be a subject to be taken seriously, Targ and Puthoff's work in this field especially so, for they were both established physicists on the academic staff of California's Stanford Research Institute (SRI).

Their standing as reputable scientists and the confident way in which they presented their case made it impossible to ignore their claims. Nevertheless, their research was subjected to intense scrutiny – and the reaction they received was little short of savage.

Targ and Puthoff were accused of everything – from deliberately misreading the results and prompting the subjects to unscientific methodology. Even so, they invited other scientists to try to reproduce their results. But to many psychical researchers, it seemed that remote viewing, like so many other similar 'breakthroughs', was a kind of mirage. Was it possible that the researchers trying to reproduce the results of Targ and Puthoff's work had missed some element in the experiments? Or was it that the two physicists had, in their enthusiasm, pushed their conclusions too far?

Targ and Puthoff began their experiments with a series of remarkable successes, using as subjects a New York artist and psychic, Ingo Swann, and a retired police commissioner, Pat Price. Both showed remarkable aptitude for remote viewing: in some cases, they even named the target location instead of merely describing it. Sometimes they were given only map co-ordinates and then asked to describe in detail what they 'saw'.

These and other successes inspired Targ and Puthoff to mount several more tightly controlled experiments in order to validate beyond doubt the phenomenon of remote viewing.

Altogether, there were nine experiments using Pat Price, which were duly written up and published in *Nature* in October 1974. In these papers, a high proportion of the transcript description is very specific – some might have thought suspiciously so. Perhaps it was for this very reason that the series provoked a most hostile reaction.

On target

Nine specific locations in the Stanford area were chosen. Before the experiment began, these were noted down, and each was sealed in an envelope before being locked away in a safe. Pat Price and an experimenter – usually Russell Targ – stationed themselves in a room about 30 minutes before remote viewing was due to begin. Meanwhile, Harold Puthoff, together with at least one other member of the target team, selected an envelope at random from the safe, opened it, and set off for the specified location. Neither Price nor Targ had any communication with the rest of the team from the beginning of the test.

The first site was a well-known landmark on the Stanford campus, the Hoover Tower. Not only did Price immediately describe a tower-like structure, but actually specified it as the 'Hoover Tower'.

This seemed almost too good to be true. The protocol of the experiments was then tightened to prevent security leaks. The divisional director, whose function it was to open the target envelope, now drove the team to the site before revealing its identity to them. The first time they did this, the target was Redwood City Marina, south of San Francisco. Price's first taped words were: 'What I'm looking at is a little boat jetty or... dock along the bay.'

Another bull's eye description was given for the seventh target on the list – an arts and crafts plaza with shops, flowers, ceramic ornaments, fountains, paths and vine-hung arbors. In the report, Price's unedited transcript is quoted verbatim, and contained much that was specifically relevant to the arts and crafts plaza.

Price said, for example: 'I'm looking at something that looks like an arbor... Seems to be cool, shaded. Doesn't seem to me that they're [i.e. the target team] out in the direct sunlight... there's lots of trees, in an arbor area.'

Startlingly accurate though much of this was, many of Price's transcripts also included much that was incorrect. The researchers began to see a pattern in his remote viewing, noting 'the occurrence of essentially correct descriptions of basic elements and patterns, coupled with incomplete or erroneous analysis of function, was to be a continuing thread throughout the remote viewing work.' In other words, he was often muddled or wrong.

The scientists noted, too, that Price drew target locations or objects as mirror images, which proved –

to them – that the right hemisphere of the brain was somehow involved in the process, for the right side of the brain is believed to control holistic, pattern-making and intuitive thinking.

But perhaps the most fascinating aspect of Price's involvement was that he, although obviously a successful 'viewer', did not claim to possess any special gift for it: he merely said that he was willing to give the experiments a try. If it were true that he had no special 'talent' and yet was so strikingly successful, the researchers now wondered if *anyone* could do it.

The team found a suitable guinea-pig for the next stage in the series in Hella Hammid, a professional photographer. Another nine experiment series was mounted, along similar lines to that using Price. The only difference was that Hammid's remote viewing time was cut from 30 to 15 minutes.

Drawing conclusions

Hammid preferred to make drawings of her mental impressions, rather than describe them verbally, as Price had done. Some of these 'doodles' were remarkably accurate.

Again, an independent judge was brought in to repeat the matching process, and the results were just as impressive: five direct hits and four second ranks. The odds against this were given as 500,000:1.

Such results should, indeed, as the book *Mindreach* claimed, have proved beyond a shadow of doubt

371

that remote viewing is fact. So why did critics attack Targ and Puthoff so fiercely?

Two of the sceptics were David Marks and Richard Kamman, both psychologists at New Zealand's Otago University. Their students, reading of Puthoff and Targ's conclusions, had begun to bombard them with questions about remote viewing and parapsychology in general. The Stanford Research Institute (SRI) had suddenly become the centre of attention.

Neither Marks nor Kamman had, until that point in the late 1970s, any special interest in ESP, and they admitted their relative ignorance about parapsychology. But pressure from their students was so intense that they realised they would have to give it attention. They were interested in the SRI experiments particularly, because Targ and Puthoff had claimed that almost anyone, psychically gifted or not, could be successful in remote viewing tests. It was also claimed that the results of the experiments were easy to reproduce.

So, between 1976 and 1978, Marks and Kamman ran 35 trials that were similar to the SRI sessions. They used five subjects: a graduate psychologist, a hypnotist, a housewife, an arts student and a medical undergraduate. All of them expressed the belief that they had some psychic ability.

Marks and Kamman followed the SRI routines as faithfully as possible. The target team was given 20 minutes to reach its specified destination, then the subject – back at the laboratory – noted down any feelings or impressions about the unknown target for 15 minutes. The team returned, collected the subject, and all then went to the target site to check the subject's transcript against the location.

Marks and Kamman were pleased to find encouraging correspondences at the early stages of their project. Indeed, one of their subjects was so confident that he said: 'If the judges can't match my descriptions accurately, there will be something wrong with them.'

Unfortunately, this confidence was misplaced – the independent judges, brought in to try to match transcripts with actual target locations, failed to do so in every case that they were asked to consider.

Willing success

Up to this stage, everyone at Otago had felt very positive about the outcome of the experiments; so what had gone wrong? Marks and Kamman decided to accompany one subject and the target group on one of their joint trips to the target location after the remote viewing had taken place. This was to reveal serious flaws in the nature of the experiment – and, by implication, the experiments of Puthoff and Targ, whose methodology they had followed.

The New Zealanders labelled the problem 'subjective validation': put simply, this means that if you want an experiment to work, it will – because you will tend to select the results you were seeking and reject the rest. Since all the subjects had been strongly motivated to succeed, they had tended to grasp at correspondences – between their impressions and the target – that, according to the judges, did not exist.

The Otago team then asked the question: if we have had this difficulty, then how did Targ and Puthoff manage to achieve so many direct hits? They began to investigate the SRI findings in closer detail and came up with some provocative discoveries about the way the transcripts had been judged.

Their conclusion, as published in *Nature,* says: 'Our investigation of the SRI remote viewing experiment with Pat Price forces the conclusion that the successful identification of target sites by judges is impossible unless multiple extraneous cues, which were available in the original unedited transcripts, are utilized. Investigators of remote viewing should take more care to ensure that such cues are not available. Furthermore, the listing of targets given to judges should be randomized and not presented in the same sequence as that which occurred in the experiments.'

Their final, damning verdict, published in their book *The Psychology of the Psychic,* was that: 'It appears to us that the remote viewing effect is, at present, nothing more than a massive artifact of poor methodology and wishful thinking.' But they did admit that they had been working with incomplete data and, of course, they had not been present during the SRI tests.

However, Professor Robert Morris, currently researching into parapsychology at Edinburgh University, who reviewed *The Psychology of the Psychic* in the *Journal of the American Society for Psychical Research* (ASPR), investigated the New Zealanders' criticisms and, in turn, found much to criticize. They had, he asserted, jumped to as many conclusions as, in their opinion, had Puthoff and Targ. Marks and Kamman, said Morris, had overstepped the mark by juggling with incomplete or improperly understood data, reaching the wrong conclusions.

Indeed, nothing to date seems totally to invalidate the basic premise that different people, in different places, can somehow 'see' with each other's eyes, telepathically.

PSYCHIC WARFARE

One of the most disturbing rumours to arise in the late 20th century was that the Soviets had mastered the art of mind control – and that they had used it.

Astral espionage; subliminal propaganda by telepathy; thought-moulding of western leaders; bioenergy as an anti-personnel weapon; knocking out military equipment and space vehicles with psychokinesis – these are not jottings from a science-fiction writer's notebook but some of the techniques solemnly discussed in two reports compiled in 1972 and 1975 for the US Defense Intelligence Agency (DIA) under the titles *Controlled Offensive Behavior – USSR* and *Soviet and Czechoslovak Parapsychology Research.*

The former, scheduled for declassification only in 1990, was obtained earlier under the Freedom of Information Act; and while parts of the documents may strain the credulity of the most avid science fiction fan, a study of them in conjunction with other published information points to the possibility that the Third World War was well under way by the mid 1970s – and that the West was losing it.

According to the DIA reports, the Soviets had a start of several decades over the West in officially funded research into psychic phenomena, especially telepathy, and their top priority has always been practical application. In other words, while the West was holding psychical research at arm's length, or even arguing it out of existence, the Soviets were looking for – and finding – ways of making telepathy and psychokinesis (PK) work for them.

However, a 1976 report (allegedly funded by one of the US intelligence agencies) was more cautious. This study concluded that, although most published material was 'confusing, inaccurate and of little value from a scientific point of view', there was good reason to suppose that secret research was indeed going on in the Soviet Union, the results of which were intended to be used by the military and secret police. One of the authors of the report was later quoted as saying: 'I believe the Soviets are actually building prototype equipment for psychic warfare.'

It became known in 1980, thanks to successful use of the Freedom of Information Act by US journalist Randy Fitzgerald, that the Central Intelligence Agency's involvement in psychic matters could be traced back at least to 1952. In a CIA document dated 7 January of that year, the remarkable claim was made that 'it looks as if... the problem of getting and maintaining control over the ESP function has been solved,' and it was recommended that 'suitable subjects' should be trained and put to work as psychic spies. An American psychic, Shawn Robbins, later revealed that she had been invited to take part in a US Navy project along the lines of the remote viewing experiments carried out at Stanford Research Institute (SRI) with Ingo Swann and Pat Price.

Voodoo warriors

Finally early in 1981, psychic warfare made headlines in the USA when columnist Jack Anderson announced that the Pentagon had been maintaining a secret 'psychic task force' since 1976. 'The brass hats,' he said, 'are indeed dabbling in the dark arts.' Anderson does not seem to have taken the activities of what he calls 'the voodoo warriors' very seriously; yet by a curious coincidence, the first of his two columns appeared just after a much more thoroughly researched piece on psychotronic warfare in *Military Review* (December 1980), the professional journal of the US Army.

The article, on 'The New Mental Battlefield', was humorously subtitled 'Beam me up, Spock'. But there was nothing funny in the eight-page text, written by Lieutenant-Colonel J.B. Alexander, a holder of three university degrees who had clearly done his homework. Psychotronic research had been under way for years, he wrote, and its potential use in weaponry had been explored. 'To be more specific,' he went on, 'there are weapons systems that operate on the power of the mind and whose lethal capacity has already been demonstrated.'

After a candid and open-minded survey of his subject, he admitted that some would find it ridiculous 'since it does not conform to their view of reality'. However, he added, 'some people still believe the world is flat', and he called for more co-ordinated research into the paranormal, recommending that leaders at all levels should be provided with a basic understanding of weapons systems they may encounter in the not-too-distant future.

Weapons of the mind

But before the psychotronic scenario gets even more bizarre, two questions must be asked: who is winning the psychic arms race, and is there any real evidence that such mental weaponry has ever been used?

According to Richard Deacon, author of several studies of international espionage, the first country to take the lead in psi warfare techniques could achieve 'something like total superiority'. And, he says, the country with the most active interest in and best information on the subject is neither of the superpowers, but Israel. Quoting intelligence sources, Deacon states that the Israelis have first-hand knowledge of military psi research in seven Russian cities and at least four Eastern European countries. One of the Israelis' most alarming claims is that the Soviets were working in the mid 1970s on 'subliminal conditioning' by telepathy, through 'transference of behaviour impulses'. According to Deacon's source, telepathic mind control had already been put into practice.

One possible means by which this could be done has become public knowledge. In 1976, a number of new Soviet radio stations went on the air, mystifying listeners around the world by confining their programme content to a loud and steady rattle. One of these stations, at Gomel (near Minsk), was believed to have 20 times the peak output of any previously known transmitter, and the Soviet 'woodpecker' (which is what it sounded like) was splashing across several frequencies on the short-wave band and even interfering with telephones.

Telecommunications companies, amateur radio societies and several governments complained to the Soviet Union. The Soviets apologised, said they were carrying out 'experiments' and promised to minimise disruption. But they never explained what they were doing, and early guesses were that they were working on a new form of over-the-horizon radar.

Then, in November 1977, the American psychical investigator Andrija Puharich startled a London audience with a detailed account of what he believed was really going on. 'It isn't that they are interfering with radio and telephone systems,' he said. 'They are actually interfering with your heads. Somebody, far away, is playing with your minds.'

The Soviets, he said, had put into practice an idea originally thought up by Nikola Tesla (1857-1943) around the turn of the century, and were using their transmitters to set up a colossal stationary wave passing through the core of the earth and carrying a signal tuned to resonate with the earth-atmosphere system. This signal was being pulsed at frequencies in the extremely low frequency (ELF) band, of 4 to 15 pulses per second, a range of special importance to the human brain, comprising the theta and alpha bands.

Sinister sounds

In laboratory experiments, Puharich found that brain rhythms fell into step with whatever frequency in these bands was being beamed at them, even when the subject was in a shielded metal Faraday cage. Fine tuning of the pulse rate could produce a wide range of symptoms, from tension headaches to nausea and drowsiness, and this sinister process of 'bioentrainment' was being tried out on the country selected for the Soviet 'experiment' – Canada.

This was not all. Puharich reckoned that ways had been found to get the psychotronic effect, in the form of a telepathic signal, on to the woodpecker signal. Fantastic as it may seem, it is an idea that has occurred to others besides Puharich. The physicist Dr Ippolit M. Kogan, for example, put forward a hypothesis in the 1960s on the use of ELF waves as carriers of telepathy, and after 1969 Kogan's name completely disappeared from the published literature, nobody in the West heard any more from him. Western parascientists also noticed that any accounts of psychical research published by the Soviets after 1970 described old, well-known experiments, as if their real work in this field were suddenly deemed top secret.

A pawn in their game

But psychic espionage has been used in other ways, too. Indeed, researchers have questioned who really won the 1978 World Chess Championship – Soviet grand master Anatoli Karpov, Soviet defector Viktor Korchnoi, or a mysterious man named Dr Vladimir Zukhar? According to the record books, it was the seemingly unflappable Karpov who retained his title after winning five games out of the first six, losing the next four, and finally returning to form and sweeping the board.

The more volatile Korchnoi thought otherwise. Dr Zukhar, he alleged, was a psychic saboteur who had been sent to Baguio City in the Philippines to make sure that Karpov avoided losing to a defector.

Korchnoi obviously believed that psychic powers could affect his game, for he took countermeasures of his own, in the form of training in yoga and meditation from a couple of American members of the Anand Marg sect who happened to be in town. They also taught him a Sanskrit mantra to ward off evil, which he claimed to have used against Zukhar with devastating effect.

This was not the first time psychic matters had

been raised at a world chess tournament. Interestingly, it was the Soviets who cried foul play at a confrontation between Bobby Fischer and Boris Spassky, suggesting not only that Fischer's chair was wired to receive messages from accomplices, but that Fischer, or at any rate somebody, was actually trying to cast an evil spell over Spassky. And at a later world title elimination bout, Spassky had part of the stage screened off, so that he could hide from both Korchnoi and the audience. The former was paralysing his mind, he said, while the latter were beaming rays at him.

So could Dr Zukhar have helped Karpov win in 1978? By then, the Soviets had more than 50 years of state-backed research into telepathy to draw on; and if it is true that scientists in the 1920s had successfully broadcast suggestions that subjects should scratch their noses, it seems possible that Zukhar could indeed have made Korchnoi move the wrong pawn at the wrong time.

INCREDIBLE PHENOMENA

Spontaneous human combustion,
spirit photography and other
spell-binding enigmas

Contents

Introduction

When we hear about some bizarre occurrence – the appearance of a corn circle, a series of extraordinary coincidences, or the creation of a thought form, for instance – there are several possible reactions. We can, of course, choose to dismiss the event outright, putting it down to hysteria, wanderings of the mind, or trickery. Alternatively, we may accept that it could indeed have happened but opt to leave it there. Then again, we may take what is surely a far more rational approach, accepting that anything is possible and seeking to identify likely (or even unlikely) explanations. We may even be brave enough to take a leap of faith and declare that some things are simply way beyond human understandings but happen nevertheless.

So how will you react when you read about 67-year-old Mary Reeser, reportedly a victim of spontaneous human combustion, whose only remains were a pile of ashes and one velvet-slippered foot, while the rest of her room escaped undamaged? Can someone actually conjure up a creature merely through imagination? Will you accept that ghostly 'extras' can somehow appear on a photograph and that they are indeed images of spirits in the world beyond? And can you credit that time travel is indeed feasible?

These are just some of the incredible phenomena described throughout the pages that follow. We hope that you will find them compelling reading and that you will enjoy considering the numerous fascinating theories put forward as a result of extensive research. Many of the events recounted, however, still defy any sort of explanation according to the laws of nature as we know them, and for the present can only be marvelled at.

FIRE OF UNKNOWN ORIGIN

Of all the strange and inexplicable fates that may befall someone, perhaps the most bizarre is spontaneous human combustion. It is a fatal phenomenon that occurs without warning and without apparent cause.

People have long believed that, in certain circumstances, the human body can burst into flames of its own accord – flames, furthermore, of such ferocity that within minutes the victim is reduced to a heap of carbonised ashes. This idea – some would call it a superstition – has been around for centuries, smouldering in a belief in divine retribution. 'By the blast of God they perish,' says the author of the biblical book of *Job*, 'and by the breath of his nostrils are they consumed.'

Such Gothic horrors were hugely popular in the 18th and 19th centuries, and their literary use has been extensively discussed in the pages of the magazine, *The Dickensian,* stimulated by author Charles Dickens' own fascination with the subject. Dickens had examined the case for spontaneous human combustion (SHC) thoroughly, and knew most of the early authorities and collections of cases.

Indeed, he probably based his description of Krook's death in *Bleak House* (1852-3) upon the real-life case of Countess Bandi.

The death of 62 year-old Countess Cornelia Bandi, near Verona, is certainly one of the first more reliable reports of SHC. According to one statement, dated 4 April 1731, the Countess had been put to bed after supper, and fell asleep after several hours' conversation with her maid. In the morning, the maid returned to wake her and found a grisly scene. As the *Gentleman's Magazine* reported shortly afterwards: 'The floor of the chamber was thick smear'd with gluish moisture, not easily got off... and from the lower part of the window trickl'd down a greasy, loathsome yellowish liquor with an unusual stink.'

Heaps of ashes

Specks of soot hung in the air, covering all the surfaces of the furniture, and the smell had also penetrated adjoining rooms. The bed was undamaged, and the sheets were turned back, indicating that the Countess had got out of bed.

'Four feet (1.3 metres) from the bed was a heap of ashes, two legs untouch'd, stockings on, between which lay the head, the brains, half of the back-part of the skull and the whole chin burn'd to ashes, among which were found three fingers blacken'd. All the rest was ashes which had this quality, that they left in the hand a greasy and stinking moisture.'

Due primarily to the efforts of Charles Fort, pioneer collector of accounts of strange phenomena, and the people and journals who continue his work, a fair number of reports of SHC right up to the present have been accumulated from newspaper and medical journal sources.

Very few of the accounts actually refer to SHC as such, however, simply because, officially, it does not exist as a phenomenon. Coroners and their advisers therefore have the unenviable task of dealing with evidence that seems to contradict both accepted physical laws and medical opinion. Inevitably, suppositions are made about knocked-over heaters, flying sparks, careless smoking and, in the case of child victims, playing with matches. Faced with the alternative – a terrifying mystery – it is not really surprising that these causes of death by fire are more readily accepted.

There are occasional exceptions, though, and these are, of course, far more useful to those who wish to solve the enigma. In *Lloyds Weekly News* for 5 February 1905, for instance, it was reported that a woman asleep by a fireplace woke to find herself in flames and later died. The honest coroner said he could not understand the data with which he was presented. Apparently, the woman had gone to sleep facing the fire, so any cinder that shot out of the grate would presumably have ignited the front of her clothes. Yet it was her back that bore severe burns.

At worst, a story may be rejected out of fear or disbelief, as in the case of the elderly British spinster, Wilhelmina Dewar, who combusted near midnight on 22 March 1908, in the Northumberland town of Whitley Bay. Wilhelmina was found by her sister Margaret who, although in a state of shock, managed to summon her neighbours. Inside the house, they found the severely charred body of Wilhelmina in an upstairs bed. Yet the bedclothes were unscorched and there was no sign of fire anywhere else in the house.

Fear of the truth

When Margaret told this story at the inquest, the coroner thought her evidence preposterous and asked her to think again. But she repeatedly said she was telling the truth and did not change her story – even after a policeman had testified that Margaret was so drunk that she could not have known what she was saying. As Fort pointed out, however, the policeman was not called upon to state how he distinguished between signs of excitement and terror, and intoxication. The coroner finally adjourned the inquest to give Margaret more time to think; and when it was re-convened a few days later, it was obvious that a great deal of pressure had been placed upon poor Margaret.

Both sisters were retired school teachers and, until then, had lived respectably. Now the coroner was calling her a liar, the papers labelled her a drunk, and friends and neighbours had turned away, leaving her to face a hostile court. It was hardly surprising, therefore, that Margaret gave in and said she had been inaccurate. This time, she said she had found her sister burned, but alive, in the lower part of the house. She then went on to say that she had helped her upstairs to bed, where Wilhelmina died.

Superficially more plausible, this story was accepted, and the proceedings promptly closed. The court was not interested in how Wilhelmina had been transformed into the cindered corpse with charred abdomen and legs; nor how, if she had continued to smoulder after being helped into the bed, there was no other sign of fire. 'But the coroner was satisfied', Fort wrote sarcastically. 'The proper testimony had been recorded.'

Yet, ironically enough, it is actually medico-legal interest that has kept alive the notion of SHC, with pathologists endorsing the phenomenon and then rejecting it. There is, of course, also the possibility that a murderer might simulate a case of SHC to hide a crime. One of the earliest test cases along these lines occurred in Rheims, France, in 1725, when an innkeeper, Jean Millet, was accused of having an affair with a pretty servant girl and killing his wife. The wife, who was often drunk, was found one morning, about a foot (30 centimetres) away from the hearth.

'A part of the head only, with a portion of the

lower extremities, and a few of the vertebrae, had escaped combustion. A foot-and-a-half (45 centimetres) of the flooring under the body had been consumed, but a kneading-trough and a powdering tub very near the body sustained no injury.'

A young assistant doctor, named Le Cat, was staying at the inn and managed to convince the court that this was no ordinary death by fire but a 'visitation of God' upon the drunken woman, and an obvious result of soaking one's innards with spirits. Millet was vindicated, and Le Cat went on to qualify with distinction, and to publish a treatise on SHC.

Eyewitnesses sought

Spontaneous human combustion subsequently received what has perhaps been its severest criticism from a great pioneering chemist, Baron Justus von Liebig, who wrote a spirited refutation on the grounds that no one had actually seen it happen. As a scientist, he regarded historical evidence as an unsupported record of the belief in SHC rather than an actual proof of it. He also lamented the lack of expert witnesses, and dismissed most accounts because, in his opinion, they 'proceed from ignorant persons, unpractised in observation, and bear in themselves the stamp of untrustworthiness'.

Despite Liebig's assertion, however, there is plenty of evidence from both medical and police sources. Many of these bear witness to the ferocity of SHC, as in the case investigated by Merille, a surgeon in Caen, France, recorded in Trotter's *Essay on Drunkenness,* 1804. Merille was asked, on 3 June 1782, by the king's officers to report on the death of Mademoiselle Thaurs, a lady of over 60 who had been observed, that day, to have drunk three bottles of wine and one of brandy. Merille wrote:

'The body lay with the crown of the head resting against one of the hand-irons... 18 inches (45 centimetres) from the fire, the remainder of the body was placed obliquely before the chimney, the whole being nothing but a mass of ashes. Even the most solid bones had lost their form and consistence. The right foot was found entire and scorched at its upper junction; the left was more burnt. The day was cold but there was nothing in the grate except two or three bits of wood about an inch (2.5 centimetres) in diameter, burnt in the middle.'

Dr W. Krogman, who had experimented with sophisticated crematorium equipment, stated: 'Only at 3000° F (1500° C) plus have I seen bone fuse or melt so that it ran and became volatile.' Such a heat would certainly char everything within a considerable radius and set the house ablaze, yet the meticulous Merille wrote: 'None of the furniture in the apartment was damaged. The chair on which she was sitting was found at the distance of a foot (30 centimetres) from her, and absolutely untouched... the consumption of the body had taken place in less than 7 hours, though according to appearance, nothing around the body was burnt but the clothes.'

The following two cases also come from the USA. On the night of 24 November 1979, Mrs Beatrice Oczki was watching television in her home in Bolingbrook, Illinois. The next day, her charred remains were discovered in front of the television set, which was still on. Amazingly, a newspaper lying only a few feet from her body was untouched by any flames. However, heat had peeled paint off the ceiling above the chair which caused a beer can to explode and used up all the oxygen in the rooms, causing both of her dogs to asphyxiate.

Mrs Ona Smith was a 23-year-old invalid from Alva, Oklahoma. According to a newspaper report of 14 March 1922, blue flames bursting out at intervals from her bedclothes, the bed itself and, in fact, any inflammable material in the room. The fires began without any apparent reason, and were witnessed by several people in the room. Presumably, she needed a permanent fire-fighter in her bedroom to stop the flames from engulfing her.

An officially rejected theory, current until the end of the 18th century, held that a substance known as Phlogiston was the principle or element of heat inherent in all matter. When latent, it was said to be imperceptible; but when operative, it was believed to produce all the effects of combustion.

As any student of elementary chemistry will be

aware, bring metallic sodium into contact with ordinary tap water, and the sodium will explode into violent flames. Expose phosphorous to the air, and it, too, will burst into flame. It is not impossible, therefore, that some human beings may have within them a fatal inherent response to the force that lies behind SHC.

Horrific evidence

No one has yet been able to offer an explanation for all the various forms of SHC that have been reported, and the phenomenon still occurs.

Dr J. Irving Bentley, a retired physician, lived on the ground floor of an apartment building in Coudersport, northern Pennsylvania, USA. On the rather cold morning of 5 December 1966, Don Gosnell entered the building's basement to read the meter for the North Penn Gas Company. In the basement, a light-blue smoke of unusual odour hung in the air. Scattering an unfamiliar heap in the corner with his boot, Gosnell found it was ashes. There had been no answer to his greeting on the way in, so he decided to look in on the old man. There was more strange smoke in the bedroom but no sign of Bentley. Gosnell peered into the bathroom and was confronted with a sight he would never forget.

A large hole had burned through the floor, exposing the joists and pipework below. On the edge of the hole, he saw '... a brown leg from the knee down, like that of a mannequin. I didn't look further!' The coroner's verdict of asphyxiation was thought unsatisfactory by many.

A few years later, the *Washington Post* of 29 May 1990, also reported the following rather curious death by fire: 'Los Angeles – Sheets covering a patient caught fire during surgery at UCLA Medical Center, filling the operating room with smoke so thick that staff members could not extinguish the flames. The patient, 26 year-old Angela Hernandez, died. "The sheets just caught fire", Fire Department Chief Pat Marek said.'

Today, researchers into SHC readily quash the idea that the phenomenon does not exist, and a growing number of cases has also been authenticated by doctors and pathologists. Indeed, this number would most probably be far higher, some say, if fear of ridicule for belief in the phenomenon could be completely removed.

American physician Dr B.H Hartwell was sufficiently confident, however, about what he once personally witnessed to report it to the Massachusetts Medico-Legal Society.

He had been driving through Ayer in Massachusetts when he was stopped and called into a wood. There he saw a most horrible sight: in a clearing, a woman was crouching in flames at the shoulders, both sides of the abdomen, and both legs. Neither he nor any of the other witnesses to this bizarre and terrifying event could think of an obvious rational cause for the fire.

This doctor's experience was not unique; and support for the suspicion that many a physician would be able to tell of similar mysterious deaths by fire has come from a number of forthright members of the medical profession. Some have even admitted to coming across the phenomenon several times in the course of their career; and a certain Dr David Price stated that, on average, he met with it approximately once every four years. SHC may indeed be a far more common occurrence than we have previously been led to believe.

THOUGHTS MADE FLESH

Apparitions, many people believe, exist only in the human mind. But what of the art allegedly practised by Tibetan adepts – that of making their thought forms materialise so strongly that they can actually be seen by other people?

Conditions on the road from China to Lhasa, the forbidden capital city of Tibet, were even worse than usual in the winter of 1923-1924. Nevertheless, small numbers of travellers, mostly pilgrims wishing to obtain spiritual merit by visiting the holy city and its semi-divine ruler, the Dalai Lama, continued to struggle onwards through the bitter winds and heavy snow. Among them was an elderly woman who appeared to be a peasant from some distant province of the god-king's empire.

The woman was poorly dressed and equipped. Her red woollen skirt and waistcoat, her quilted jacket, and her cap with its lambskin earflaps, were worn and full of holes. From her shoulder hung an ancient leather bag, black with dirt. In this were the provisions for her journey: barley meal, a piece of dried bacon, a brick of compressed tea, a tube of rancid butter, and a little salt and soda.

With her black hair coated with grease and her dark brown face, she looked like a typical peasant woman. But her hair was really white, dyed with Chinese ink, and her complexion took its colour from oil mixed with cocoa and crushed charcoal. For this Tibetan peasant woman was in reality Alexandra David-Neel, a French woman who, 30 years before, had been an opera singer of note, warmly congratulated by Jules Massenet for her performance in the title role of his opera *Manon*.

In the intervening years, Mme David-Neel had travelled to many strange places and had undergone even stranger experiences. These included meeting a magician with the ability to cast spells to hurl flying rice cakes at his enemies, and learning the techniques of *tumo,* an occult art that enables its adepts to sit naked, without freezing, amid the Himalayan snows.

Most extraordinary of all, she had constructed, by means of mental and psychic exercises, a *tulpa* – a phantom form born solely from the imagination, and yet so strongly vitalised by the adept's will that it actually becomes visible to other people. A *tulpa* is, to put it another way, an extremely powerful example of what occultists term a thought form.

To understand the nature of the *tulpa,* one has to appreciate that, as far as Tibetan Buddhists (and most occultists) are concerned, thought is far more than an intellectual function. Every thought, they believe, affects the 'mind-stuff' that permeates the world of matter, in very much the same way as a stone thrown into a lake makes ripples upon the water's surface. A thought, in other words, produces a 'thought ripple'.

Lasting ripples

Usually, thought ripples have only a short life. They decay almost as soon as they are created and make no lasting impression. If, however, the thought is particularly intense, the product of deep passion or fear, or if it is of long duration, the subject of much brooding and meditation, the thought ripple builds into a more permanent thought form, and becomes one that has a longer and more intense life.

Tulpas and other thought forms are not considered by Tibetan Buddhists to be 'real' – but neither, according to them, is the world of matter that seemingly surrounds us and appears to be solid enough. Both are illusory. A Buddhist classic from the first century AD expresses this firm belief: 'All phenomena are originally in the mind and have really no outward form; therefore, as there is no form, it is an error to think that anything is there. All phenomena merely arise from false notions in the mind. If the mind is independent of these false ideas, then all phenomena disappear.'

If the beliefs about thought forms held by Tibetan Buddhists, mystics and magicians are justified, then many ghostly happenings, hauntings, and cases of localities endowed with a strong 'psychic atmosphere' are easily explained. It seems plausible, for example, that the thought forms created by the violent and passionate mental processes of a murderer, supplemented by the terror stricken emotions of a victim, could linger around the scene of a crime for months, years or even centuries. This could produce intense depression and anxiety in those who visited the 'haunted' spot; and, if the thought forms were sufficiently powerful, 'apparitions', such as a re-enactment of the crime, might at times be witnessed by people possessed of psychic sensitivity.

Sometimes, it is even claimed by students of the occult, that those 'spirits' that haunt a particular spot are in fact *tulpas*, thought forms that have been deliberately created by a sorcerer for his or her own specific purposes.

The existence of extremely potent thought forms that re-enact the past would, of course, also explain the worldwide reports of visitors to old battlefields 'witnessing' military encounters that took place long before. The sites of the battle of Naseby, which took place during England's Civil War, for instance, and of the 1942 commando raid on Dieppe, are among battlefields that enjoy such ghostly reputations.

A *tulpa* is no more than an extremely powerful thought form, no different in its essential nature from many other ghostly apparitions. Where, however, it does differ from a normal thought form is that it has come into existence, not as a result of an accident, or as a side-effect of a mental process, but as the result of a deliberate act of will.

The word *tulpa* is a Tibetan one, but there are adepts in almost every part of the world who believe they are able to manufacture these beings by first drawing together and coagulating some of the mind-stuff of the Universe, and then transferring to it some of their own vitality.

Creative power

In Bengal, home of much Indian occultism, the technique is called *kriya shakti* ('creative power'), and is studied and practised by the adepts of Tantrism, a religious magical system concerned with the spiritual aspects of sexuality and numbering both Hindus and Buddhists among its devotees. Initiates of so-called 'left-handed' Tantric cults – that is to say, cults in which men and woman engage in ritual sexual intercourse for mystical and magical purposes – are considered particularly skilled in *kriya shakti*. This is because it is thought that the intense physical and cerebral excitement of the orgasm engenders quite exceptionally vigorous thought forms.

Many Tibetan mystical techniques originated in Bengal, particularly in Bengali Tantrism, and there is a very strong resemblance between the physical, mental and spiritual exercises used by the Tantric yogis of Bengal and the secret inner disciplines of Tibetan Buddhism. It thus seems likely that Tibetans originally derived their theories about *tulpas,* and their methods of creating these strange beings, from Bengali practitioners of *kriya shakti.*

Students of *tulpa* magic begin their training in the art of creating these 'thought beings' by adopting one of the many gods or goddesses of the Tibetan pantheon as a 'tutelary deity' – a sort of patron saint. But while Tibetan initiates regard the gods respectfully, they do not look upon them with any great admiration. For, according to Buddhist belief, although the gods have great powers and are, in a sense 'supernatural', they are just as much slaves of illusion, and just as much trapped in the wheel of birth, death, and rebirth as the humble peasant.

The student retires to a hermitage or other secluded place and meditates on his tutelary deity, known as a *yidam,* for many hours. Here, he combines a contemplation of the spiritual attributes traditionally associated with the *yidam* with visualisation exercises. These are designed to build up in the mind's eye an image of the *yidam* as portrayed in paintings and statues. To ensure that every waking moment is dedicated to concentrating on the *yidam,* the student continually chants traditional mystic phrases associated with the deity he serves.

He also constructs the *kyilkhors* – literally circles, but actually symbolic diagrams that may be of any shape and believed sacred to his god. Sometimes he will draw these with coloured inks on paper or wood;

sometimes he will engrave them on copper or silver; sometimes he will outline them on his floor with coloured powders.

The preparation of the *kyilkhors* must be undertaken with care, for the slightest deviation from the traditional pattern associated with a particular *yidam* is believed to be extremely dangerous, putting the unwary student in peril of obsession, madness, death, or a stay of thousands of years in one of the hells of Tibetan cosmology.

It is interesting to compare this belief with the idea, strongly held by many Western occultists, that if a magician engaged in evoking a spirit to visible appearance draws his protective magical circle incorrectly, he will be torn in pieces.

Thoughts made visible

Eventually, if the student has persisted with the prescribed exercises, he 'sees' his *yidam,* at first nebulously and briefly, but then persistently and with complete – and sometimes terrifying – clarity.

But this is only the first stage of the process. Meditation, visualisation of the *yidam,* the repetition of spells and contemplation of mystic diagrams is continued until the *tulpa* actually materialises. The devotee can feel the touch of the *tulpa's* feet when he lays his head upon them; he can see the creature's eyes following him as he moves about; he can even conduct conversations with it.

Finally, the *tulpa* may be prepared to leave the vicinity of the *kyilkhors* and accompany the devotee on journeys. If the *tulpa* has been fully vitalised, it will by now often be visible to others besides its creator.

Alexandra David-Neel tells how she 'saw' a phantom of this sort which, curiously enough, had not yet become visible to its creator. At the time, Mme David-Neel had developed a great interest in Buddhist art. One afternoon, she was visited by a Tibetan painter who specialised in portraying the 'wrathful deities'. As he approached, she was astonished to see behind him the misty form of one of these much feared and rather unpleasant beings. As she approached, she stretched out an arm towards it and felt as if she were 'touching a soft object whose substance gave way under the slight push'.

The painter told her that he had for some weeks been engaged in magical rites, calling on the god whose form she had seen, and that he had spent the entire morning painting its picture.

Intrigued by this experience, Mme David-Neel set about making a *tulpa* for herself. To avoid being influenced by the many Tibetan paintings and images she had seen on her travels, she decided to 'make' not a god or goddess, but a fat, jolly-looking monk whom she could visualise very clearly, and began to concentrate her mind.

She retired to a hermitage, and for some months devoted every waking minute to exercises in concentration and visualisation. Soon she began to get brief glimpses of the monk out of the corner of her eye. He became more solid and lifelike in appearance; and eventually, when she left her hermitage and started on a caravan journey, he included himself in the party, becoming clearly visible and performing actions that she had neither commanded nor consciously expected him to do. He would, for instance, walk and stop to look around him as a traveller might do. Sometimes Mme David-Neel even felt his robe brush against her, and once a hand seemed to touch her shoulder.

Mme David-Neel's *tulpa* eventually began to develop in an unexpected and unwished-for manner. He grew leaner, his expression became malignant, and he was 'troublesome and bold'. One day, a herdsman, who brought Mme David-Neel a present of some butter, saw the *tulpa* in her tent, and mistook it for a real monk. It had got out of control. Indeed, her creation turned into what she called a 'day-nightmare' and she decided to get rid of it. Eventually it took her six months of concentrated effort and meditation to succeed.

Wolf at the door

In her book *Psychic Self Defence*, the occultist Dion Fortune, related how she once formulated a were-wolf accidentally. She had this alarming experience while brooding about her feelings of resentment against someone who had hurt her. Lying on her bed, she was thinking of the terrifying wolf-monster of Norse mythology, Fenrir, when suddenly she felt a large grey wolf materialise beside her, and was aware of its body pressing against hers.

From her reading about thought forms, Fortune knew she must gain control of the beast immediately. So she dug her elbow into its hairy ribs and pushed the creature off the bed. The animal disappeared through the wall.

The story was not yet over, however, for another member of the household said she had seen the eyes of the wolf in the corner of her room. Dion Fortune realised she must destroy the creature. Summoning the beast, she saw a thin thread joining it to her and began to imagine she was drawing the life out of the beast along this thread. The wolf faded to a formless grey mass, and ceased to exist.

If this, and many similar stories, are to be believed, the creation of a *tulpa* is not a matter to be undertaken lightly. It is, in fact, yet another fascinating example of the remarkable powers of the human mind.

UNEXPECTED DEVELOPMENTS

If spectral figures appear on a photograph when nothing of the kind was visible at the time it was taken, psychic investigation is clearly called for. Who might such ghostly 'extras' be?

The ease with which 'extras' may be imposed upon photographs has led most people to believe that many, if not all spirit photographs are in some way fraudulent. However, while the greater number of so-called psychic pictures are indeed intended to amuse or defraud, a few have been made in circumstances that place them on a level beyond ordinary understanding.

The strangest spirit photographs of all have been made during seances, often under rigid test conditions; but a few interesting ones have also been made quite unexpectedly, and by amateurs. Someone takes a snapshot of a friend, of an interior, or of a pet, and afterwards finds, to his astonishment, the image of a face or figure – sometimes recognisably that of a deceased relative or friend. This occurs rarely, but it does happen; and many examples with written accounts have been preserved by archivists and librarians interested in psychic phenomena. The earliest preserved examples of spirit photographs were of this order: they were taken by amateur photographers who had no specialist interest in psychic effects and who were disappointed at their portraits and landscapes being spoiled by the mysterious 'extras'.

It is generally accepted that spirit photography as such began in Boston, Massachusetts, USA, on 5 October 1861, when William Mumler accidentally produced his first spirit picture. But this date may not be entirely accurate. For, according to an early pioneer of Spiritualism in Boston, Dr H.F. Gardner, a few portraits exhibiting a second figure that was definitely not present when the photograph was taken had been made previously at nearby Roxbury. The Roxbury photographer was an orthodox Christian who, after hearing about Mumler's pictures, refused to print any negatives containing 'spirits' on the grounds that, if these pictures had anything to do with Spiritualism, they were the work of the Devil.

The fact is that, well over a century later, we still do not know what it is that causes 'spirits' to appear on prints. The majority of psychical researchers involved with spirit photography claim it occurs by the direct intervention of the spirits themselves. If one accepts such a theory, the phenomena may be viewed not so much as 'spirit photography', as 'photography by spirits'.

The famous English journalist W.T. Stead was an

411

early champion of spirit photography, and many portraits of him show images of recognised 'extras' alongside. After he died in the *Titanic* disaster in April 1912, he continued to converse from the spirit world with his daughter, Estelle, as she reported. And then the matter went further, for his image began to appear as an 'extra' alongside her in pictures. When Estelle asked him to say something about the actual production of such images, Stead insisted that the spirits were themselves involved with them, in order to convince us of the reality of life after death.

The spirit photographs made by professionals and participants in seances are fascinating enough. But it is an element of the unexpected that permeates the accidental spirit photographs of amateurs that intrigue the investigator of the genre most.

One such example is a photograph taken in 1964 inside the English church of St Mary the Virgin, in Woodford, Northamptonshire. It was taken by 16-year-old Gordon Carroll who, with a friend, had been on a cycling tour. They had decided to visit the church because of its historic value – it is mentioned in the *Domesday Book*. After checking that the church was empty, Gordon took two pictures of the interior – one looking towards the altar, and another photograph of the rear of the interior.

After the pictures had been processed, the young photographer filed them away and only took them out a year later in preparation for a Christmas slide show. On examining the pictures, he and his friend saw that one of them featured a ghostly figure, apparently kneeling in front of the altar: its head was not visible since it was bowed down as if in prayer. The figure appeared to be wearing a monk's robes. Both Gordon and his friend at the time were convinced there had been no one at the altar when the photograph was taken, nor – according to a film processing expert – had any fraud been involved.

Ghostly portraits

Only rarely do amateur photographers take pictures in the knowledge that they are recording psychic phenomena. One of the few exceptions is the case of the *Watertown* pictures, which contain images of drowned seamen. These were deliberately taken by one of the passengers on board a vessel, the *Watertown*, from which two seamen had been swept overboard and drowned during the course of the journey. For several days afterwards, passengers and crew alike insisted that the seamen's spectral heads could be seen in the waves and spray.

Much more typical is the account of the curious extras on a snapshot taken by a certain Mrs Wickstead in 1928. The snapshot – now quite faded but never of first-rate quality – was one of two taken at the church in the village of Hollybush, not far from Hereford. Mrs Wickstead was on a car tour with friends and had stopped to see the church. She decided to take a photograph of her friend, Mrs Laurie, who in the event can barely be seen in the photograph. After the picture had been taken, Mrs Laurie drew Mrs Wickstead's attention to the grave of a soldier who had died on active service. Alongside this grave was another of a girl who had died shortly afterwards. 'I wonder if they were lovers?' Mrs Laurie had remarked to her companion.

In a letter to Sir Oliver Lodge, later President of the Society for Psychical Research (SPR), Mrs Wickstead wrote that Mrs Laurie had seemed impressed by the two graves and had made a point of showing them to her husband. 'We thought no more about it until about six weeks later when the film was developed and came out as you see, with these two figures on the path in the shadow of the yew tree,' Mrs Wickstead wrote. The two figures were in an embrace. The picture was investigated by the SPR, but the mystery of the 'extras' was never solved by the research group.

There have also been cases of sensitives both seeing and photographing spirits that have remained invisible to others present – but these are rare. One of the most famous examples has become known as the 'Weston' photograph.

The Reverend Charles Tweedale and his family lived in Weston vicarage, a much haunted house in the town of Otley in West Yorkshire. While having lunch on 20 December 1915, Mrs Margaret Tweedale saw the apparition of a bearded man to the left of her son. The others around the table could see nothing. However, Margaret's husband immediately fetched the camera and took a picture of the area indicated by his wife. When the negative was developed, a portrait of the apparition appeared on the print.

Spiritual instruction

An extraordinary picture session that took place in Belgium seems to support the belief that the spirits intervene directly in psychic photography. In this instance, a spirit actually instructed an amateur photographer in the most precise manner as to how and when to take a picture in which the spirit would manifest itself. The picture was taken by Emile le Roux in 1909 and is one of the very few stereoscopic spirit photographs that exist.

The instructions apparently came from a spirit who claimed to be the uncle of le Roux's wife. The spirit made contact through her while she was practising automatic writing in le Roux's presence. Through the automatic script, the 'uncle' said that he could be photographed at a later point in the day and gave instructions as to the time and necessary exposure. Le Roux, a keen amateur photographer, considered the exposure to be far too long; but he followed instructions and took the picture with his stereoscopic camera at the time indicated. The image of the deceased uncle not only appeared, but was quite recognisable. In its day, the plate became very famous – but time after time, le Roux had to defend himself against the usual charges of fraud. His own simple words echo the recurrent story of the amateur caught up in a mysterious process:

'In reality, this photograph was made under the most simple circumstances, and I would say that except for the strangeness of the spirit head, there were so few difficulties both before and after its execution that, in spite of the scepticism which arose within me and which has not yet quite vanished, I am forced to admit that in order to explain this negative, it is necessary to look in another direction than fraud or the double exposure of the plate.'

The subject of spirit photography greatly excited psychical investigators in the 1870s and 1880s, but no organised and sustained study seems to have been made. There are many references to the phenomenon in the *British Journal of Photography*, and a number of articles in the *Journal* of the SPR. But the issue was clouded by the controversy over Spiritualism, and no undistorted and full treatment of psychic photography itself has come down to us.

The faking of spirit photographs seems to have begun almost as soon as the genuine product appeared in the mid-19th century. One of the most common faking techniques was the double exposure – not a problem with the large plates then in use. But a more cunning method involved the painting of a background screen with a special chemical, invisible to ordinary sight, which would show up on photographic film. This screen was pre-painted and placed behind the sitter. Other complex techniques were also devised by unscrupulous photographers.

Fraudulent exposure

The case now known as the 'Moss photographic fiasco' is among the most interesting of the proven frauds. During the early 1920s, G.H. Moss was employed as a chauffeur by a man who was interested in the paranormal. Moss was a keen amateur photographer, and one day brought a print with a ghostly 'extra' to his employer. The employer showed interest and, after some experiments on his own, introduced Moss to the British College of Psychic Science. Around 1924, Moss was given a year's contract to work under test conditions at the College, on a fixed salary. His work there was impressive and very well-received – until, that is, he was found to be a fraud.

Moss produced a number of spirit images that were recognised as the likenesses of dead relatives and friends by sitters. In one of these, the sitter was a trance medium. She recognised the 'extra' as her dead sister. A cut-out photograph of that sister was mounted alongside the 'extra' to illustrate the resemblance. In another, the image was recognised by a person observing the photographic session, though it was not clear whether the recognised individual was dead or alive.

A third example of Moss's work, was made in a seance with the well-known medium Mrs Osborne Leonard on 5 January 1925. The sitter was informed by 'a voice from beyond' that he would be sitting for a photograph in eight days. The invisible speaker promised that she would reveal herself then.

That sitting, which had already been arranged without Mrs Leonard's knowledge, did indeed produce an 'extra' – and some of the sitter's friends insisted that the image bore a strong likeness to his recently deceased wife. A portrait of her was then pasted alongside so that a comparison could be made.

Moss was finally unmasked by the astute F. Barlow, at that time the Honorary Secretary for the now defunct Society for the Study of Supernormal Pictures. While Barlow was examining a group of Moss's negatives containing 'extras', he noticed a peculiar roughness on the edges of certain plates. Closer examination showed that each negative bearing a spirit image had one edge that was filed. Detailed examination of the plate wrappings revealed that they had been skilfully opened by steaming and subsequently resealed.

Moss vehemently denied fraud and even signed a statement declaring his innocence. However, when faced with the filed plates, he made a confession. He had secretly opened certain plates and superimposed an image on them, marking them for later use by filing the edges.

In any event, psychic photography did not end with the unexplained appearance of spirit forms on prints. One new form that has emerged in recent times is the manifestation of UFOs. What is more, since the main question is whether images on film can he produced without optical processes, thoughtography is of relevance too.

By thought alone

The term 'thoughtography' first came into use in Japan in 1910, following a series of tests by Tomokichi Fukurai of a clairvoyant who accidentally imprinted a calligraphic character on a photographic plate by psychic means. Later, the sensitive found he was able to do this by concentrated effort. Fukurai's work was published in English 20 years later, and experiments similar to his were then undertaken in Europe and the United States. But it was not until 1962 that interest in thoughtography was activated by Pauline Oehler, of the Illinois Society for Psychic Research, through her work with the American psychic Ted Serios.

Serios was much investigated under strictly controlled conditions, particularly by Dr Jule Eisenbud, a psychical researcher working mainly in Denver, Colorado, USA. In many experiments planned by Eisenbud over a period of two years,

Serios could produce, at will, pictures of what he was thinking about – an old hotel, cars, a corner of a room, and many other mental images. He could also produce an image of a target set by himself or others. For example, one day he glanced casually at a travel magazine in Eisenbud's waiting room. The next day, he decided to produce a picture of London's Westminster Abbey, which he had noticed in the publication – and succeeded in doing so.

Thoughtography has continued to be subjected to psychical research; and although Ted Serios' ability to transfer his thoughts on to film has never been fully explained, neither has it ever been proved to be fraudulent.

Among the professional spirit photographers of the late 19th century, however, there were undoubtedly frauds – and a number of them were eventually exposed. But that, of course, does not negate the important fact that many 'spirit' images may well have been produced by paranormal means: indeed, it could still be the case today.

The engraving above *shows a group of peasants, utterly terrified by the ball lightning that appeared at Salagnac, France, in 1845. As the feature on page 432 explains, the phenomenon is now acknowledged but its origins continue to baffle us to this very day.*

These three pictures seem to feature portraits from the spirit world; but could they be the work of unscrupulous photographers? The picture, top, *is said to be of the spirit of William T. Stead who died in the* Titanic *disaster, beside his daughter Estelle. Another spirit 'extra' can also be seen* above *in a photograph taken at a seance with the medium Mrs Osborne Leonard.*

The ghost of a medium, dead for a week, appears in a picture taken by her daughter. She is apparently sitting in the back seat of the car. Experts have confirmed that this photograph has in no way been tampered with, however. You can assess such spirit images for yourself on page 410.

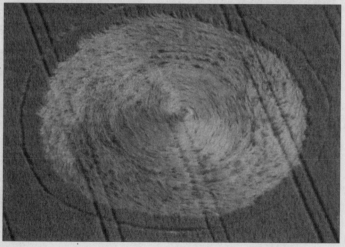

Crop circles have been appearing since 1678, when they were first found in a Hertfordshire field and blamed on the Devil, who is depicted, top, at his task. Today, as you will discover on page 470, some still believe them to have an extra-terrestrial origin.

TONGUES OF MEN, OR OF ANGELS?

Few expressions of religious ecstasy are as dramatic or as bewildering as 'speaking in tongues' – a bizarre, yet surprisingly common phenomenon.

The scene is set for an extraordinary – but by no means rare – phenomenon. A Pentecostalist minister's prayers grow more fervent; and the congregation's responses correspondingly increase in enthusiasm. Cries of 'Glory be to God!', 'Jesus, blessed Jesus!', and 'Hallelujah!' resound through the church. A woman rises from her seat. Her voice then swells until it drowns all the others, which sink into a chorus of soft murmurings. Now she begins to pour out a stream of completely unintelligible sounds – yet it is clearly passionate praise for the Lord. Minister and congregation then join in exalting the Holy Spirit of God who has granted their sister the gift of 'speaking in tongues'.

This phenomenon can be witnessed by anyone who visits a Pentecostalist church – although you may have to attend more than once in order to be present when it takes place as it does not automatically occur at every service.

Nowadays, 'speaking in tongues' implies *unidentified* tongues (or *glossolalia*). But before they could be recorded on tape, such sounds were often considered to belong to real, if unrecognised, human languages, both ancient and modern (such as Incan and Eskimo), or even to be the 'tongues of angels'.

But since the advent of tape recorders and computers, not a single case of *xenolalia* (paranormal speaking in real languages) has been recorded; and the sounds that pour out so fervently at Pentecostalist services have been proved not to be languages but, rather, language-types.

A linguistics expert can tell the difference by analysing the structure of the 'tongues' spoken. A personal knowledge of every language is not required; for the rule, to the expert, is quite simple – languages follow set laws and language-types do not. 'Tongues' have neither vocabulary nor syntax, and so it must be concluded that they are neither the language of men nor, it has been assumed, of angels.

Although speaking in 'tongues' has been called 'refined gobbledygook', it is nevertheless a genuine form of worship. Indeed, it seems that this bizarre phenomenon enables people, who normally lack the ability to express themselves in public, to give vent to their religious emotions in such a way as to convince themselves and their fellow worshippers that the Holy Spirit is among them. It seems somehow to uplift the congregation and to give the speaker a sense of euphoric psychological release. But this form of communication, by its very nature, is emotional rather than educational – a sharing of mood rather than a conveying of information.

However, in almost every such congregation there is at least one 'interpreter of tongues' who sincerely believes that he or she is translating the 'tongues' into the vernacular. What is more, although the interpretation itself can help to reinforce the ecstatic mood of the congregation, it of course cannot be a direct translation or even a paraphrase of a language that does not exist.

Miracle conversions

Many Pentecostalists would affirm that *xenolalia* has been known in their churches, rightly pointing out that only a tiny percentage of all 'tongues' has ever been recorded or analysed. They also tell stories of numerous occasions when a foreign unbeliever, who is a casual visitor to the church, has been converted – by being preached to in his own language. Such a 'miracle' convinces the foreign sinner of the need to repent and join the Lord's church. Sometimes such a tale is told by the convert himself, sometimes by those who witnessed the alleged conversion. And since religious people are supposedly truthful, such reports are widely taken to be genuine.

Speaking in tongues among Christians first happened, so the New Testament tells us, when the disciples gathered in Jerusalem for the annual Jewish feast of Pentecost. This occasion was just seven weeks after Christ's crucifixion. The story is told by Luke (also author of one of the Gospels) in *Acts 2*.

The disciples were worshipping at the Temple in Jerusalem, mingling with Jews from all over the known world, when suddenly they were seized by an extraordinary ecstasy, said to have been caused by the conviction that Christ had risen from the dead. The Holy Ghost is said to have descended on them, bestowing the 'gift of tongues' so that they shouted aloud their praise of God in all the various languages of the visiting worshippers, to the great astonishment of the crowd.

Objectively, however, the source of such *xenolalia* is not hard to pinpoint. Jewish religious law made attendance at certain festivals compulsory for every male adult Jew, but made allowances for great parts of the services to be spoken in the various vernaculars of the visitors present. So the disciples would often have heard what was recognisably praise of God in many languages, which they did not understand but which they probably stored deep down in their subconscious minds. Moreover, Christ had promised to send them his 'Comforter' – whoever or whatever that might be – specifically at the feast of Pentecost. This heightened sense of expectation, together with their conviction that Christ had risen, could have resulted in the first Christian 'tongues'. (Interestingly, the official account does not claim that the disciples understood a word of what they were saying, nor does it mention that their utterances contained any specifically Christian message – it simply states that it happened, and that it astonished fellow worshippers.)

Sacred mandate?

The disciples' experience at Pentecost might have been considered unique in the annals of the Christian Church had it not been for St Paul's statement (in *1 Corinthians* 12-14) that it was considered part of the normal worship of the Church at Corinth and that he himself spoke in 'tongues'. Whether the Corinthian mode of worship was typical of that of the early church is debatable, but – despite Paul's warnings against abuses of 'the gifts of the Spirit' (especially the misuse of 'tongues') and his stress on the 'more excellent way' of Christian love – these references to Corinthian *glossolalia* have been taken by some sects as a sacred mandate to use 'tongues' as proof of 'baptism by the Holy Spirit'.

However since the early days of the Church, the use of 'tongues' has not always found favour among Christians. The Roman Catholics banned it from about the end of the first century, and later regarded speaking in 'tongues' as a sign of possession (except in the case of certain saints). Mainstream Protestantism has also found no place for it. However, it was kept alive down the centuries through fringe movements and heretical sects until, in the 20th century, it became the focal point for Pentecostalism.

This movement started humbly, its members mainly drawn from ethnic minorities and poor people, and it was tainted at first – as its own historians admit – by hysterical behaviour and fanaticism. But it was a fast-growing movement, and quickly spread throughout the world, soon becoming by far the strongest Protestant group throughout predominantly Catholic South America, and surprisingly numerous even in countries such as Italy and Portugal, as well as in Protestant lands like Sweden.

Expressing the inexpressible

Today, however, Pentecostal conduct and beliefs are more moderate; and in some of their churches, the emphasis on 'tongues' is not as great as it was originally. 'Tongues' now tend to be used more in private than in public worship. But possibly a much more important development in the use of *glossolalia* than the spread of Pentecostalism is the Charismatic Movement, which has affected almost every Christian denomination today.

Small groups in individual Anglican, Baptist, Methodist, Presbyterian and even Catholic churches now meet to worship God in private, using 'the gift of tongues'. Unlike the humble members of the original Pentecostal Church, the members of the Charismatic Movement tend to belong to the professional middle-classes, and they use 'tongues' in private, in quiet, unemotional prayer. Such people do not regard 'tongues' as being real foreign languages, but take them as a sign of the Holy Spirit's revitalising effect upon the Church, often enabling members to express in sounds the otherwise inexpressible.

The use of strange 'languages' is not exclusive to the Pentecostalists nor the Charismatic Movement, however. Since the foundation of modern Spiritualism about 130 years ago, hundreds of claims of spoken and written *xenolalia* by sensitives and psychics have also been made, and continue to mystify researchers in this field.

GREAT BALLS OF FIRE!

For centuries, scientists refused to believe that ball lightning even existed. The phenomenon is now acknowledged, but what lies behind these remarkably powerful glowing spheres?

Flying towards Elko, Nevada, USA on a routine mission to refuel B47 bombers in flight on 16 June 1960, a USAF KG97 tanker aircraft suddenly ran into a layer of cloud at 18,000 feet (5,500 metres). The pilot was concentrating on the instrument panel, when he was surprised to see a yellow-white ball of light, 18 inches (45 centimetres) in diameter, emerge silently through the windshield. It passed at a fast running pace between his seat and the co-pilot's, and travelled down the cabin passageway, past the navigator and engineer.

The pilot had been struck by lightning twice on previous flights and knew that an explosion was imminent. His immediate reaction, as an experienced airman, was to concentrate on flying rather than to turn round and watch the ball as it drifted towards the back of the aircraft.

After a few seconds of shocked silence, the four

men in the flight compartment heard over the intercom the excited voice of the boom operator, who was sitting in the rear of the aircraft. A ball of fire had come rolling through the cargo compartment, and then danced out over the right wing, before rolling off harmlessly into the night.

This remarkable report concerns ball lightning – one of the many natural phenomena for which science has no explanation. In fact, the properties of ball lightning are so hard to explain that, for years, scientists doubted its very existence. Their principle was that what cannot be explained cannot exist.

This attitude, unfortunately, is by no means rare among scientists. The fall of meteors to Earth was for many years considered a superstition of ignorant peasants, for instance. Indeed, despite many well-documented observations of these fiery bodies, sceptics were at one point so sure of their case that rare meteorite specimens were removed from museum collections and destroyed on the grounds that stories of meteorites falling from the sky were mere superstition.

The ball lightning controversy has divided the scientific community since the early 19th century, when comprehensive reports were first prepared on the subject. Then, in 1890, a large number of luminous globes resembling ball lightning appeared in a tornado and were the subject of a meeting of the French Academy of Sciences. The glowing spheres entered houses through the chimneys, and bored circular holes in the windows as they departed.

A member of the Academy stood up at the end of the account and commented that the extraordinary properties supposedly attributed to ball lightning should be taken with a liberal pinch of salt, since the observers must have been suffering from hallucinations. In the heated discussion that followed, it was agreed that the observations made by uneducated peasants were valueless. At this point, the former Emperor of Brazil, a foreign member of the Academy, silenced the meeting by remarking that he himself had actually seen ball lightning!

Colourful effects

Even today, many such reports still have a certain medieval aura of witchcraft and magic about them, which scarcely serves to endear the subject to sceptics. Yet over the centuries, literally hundreds of sightings have been made, so that the evidence for ball lightning now seems to be irrefutable.

One observation reported in great detail was made by a Russian chemist, M.T. Dmitriev, in 1967. He was camping on the banks of the River Onega in western Russia when there was an intense flash of lightning. A ball of fire appeared, hovering over the water. It took the form of an oval mass of light with a yellow-white core, surrounded by layers of dark violet and blue.

Apparently unaffected by the wind, it hovered across the water at a height of about one foot (30 centimetres). Dmitriev heard it crackling and hissing as it flew across his head and on to the river bank, where it hung motionless for about 30 seconds.

It left a trail of acrid, bluish smoke as it passed into a group of trees. Then it bounced like a billiard ball from tree to tree, emitting burst after burst of sparks. After a minute, it disappeared from view.

From this and many similar reports, it is possible to sketch out the properties typical of ball lightning. Firstly, it usually occurs at the same time as cloud-to-ground lightning. The balls are generally spherical or pear-shaped with somewhat fuzzy edges, and they range from half-an-inch to a yard (1-100 centimetres) across. They shine as brightly as a domestic electric lamp; they vary in colour, but are often red, orange or yellow; and they last for anything from just a second to over a minute. The disappearance of a lightning ball may either be silent or accompanied by an explosion.

Probably the best known report of a lightning ball causing material damage was reported in 1936 by a correspondent to the *Daily Mail*. He wrote that, during a thunderstorm, he saw a large 'red hot' ball, later described as the 'size of an orange', come down from the sky. It struck the house, cut the telephone wire, burnt the window frame and then buried itself in a tub of water underneath the window. The water boiled for some minutes; but when cool enough to search, nothing could be found.

Surprisingly, perhaps, ball lightning may not be that rare. In one survey, for instance, 4,000 NASA employees were asked whether they had seen ball lightning, and their answers indicated that it might occur more commonly than had previously been thought. As the report states: 'A comparison of the frequency of observation of ordinary lightning impact points [with appearances of ball lightning] reveals that ball lightning is not a particularly rare phenomenon. Contrary to widely accepted ideas, the occurrence of ball lightning may be nearly as frequent as that of ordinary cloud-to-ground strokes.'

All in the imagination?

The Canadian scientist Edward Argyll, however, claimed that ball lightning is merely an optical illusion. When lightning strikes the ground, he said, it creates such a bright flash that an observer will see a persistent after-image that can easily be mistaken for ball lightning.

By embracing this theory, Dr Argyll finally made sense of the extraordinary properties of ball lightning that were the despair of theoreticians who had attempted identification of a plausible physical cause.

'Passage through physical surfaces, such as metal screens, is possible for after-images and is reported for lightning balls. After-images last for 2-10 seconds, and most lightning balls are reported to have a duration in the same range,' he explained, linking the two phenomena.

Unlike lightning balls, after-images generate no sound. But this is no problem for the sceptical scientist. The typical observer finds it easy to imagine 'suitable accompanying sounds'. But what did Dr Argyll make of cases where the lightning ball leaves behind actual physical signs of its presence? He simply rejected the evidence that contradicted his theory.

Yet there can be little doubt that, however imperfect the observations and in spite of the outlandish behaviour of ball lightning, it does occur. No one will deny the existence of after-images, and most of us have experienced them. But how could they possibly explain fireballs that appear to more than one observer, on the same occasion, and that have precisely the same form and travel along the same path?

One early theory suggested that the balls were burning puffs of inflammable gas, released by the impact of lightning on the ground. But if this were so, how could a puff of gas rise to the height of an aeroplane? And could it pass through solid walls, as so many lightning balls reportedly do?

According to one report, a red lightning ball about two feet (60 centimetres) in diameter dug a trench a full 100 yards (91 metres) long and over three feet (one metre) deep in soft soil near a stream, and then literally tore away another 75 feet (23 metres) of the stream bed. To dig this trench, the ball would have had to have an enormous amount of power; and to account for this, it has been suggested that some sort of atomic reaction would have had to be involved.

Flaming sphere

However, ball lightning has been observed by some people at close quarters and does not appear to involve any nuclear effects. A characteristic incident was reported by a housewife after a violent thunderstorm in Staffordshire, England, on 8 August 1975. She was in the kitchen when a flaming sphere of light suddenly appeared over the cooker. It came towards her, making a strange rattling sound and moving far too quickly for her to be able to dodge out of the way.

'The ball seemed to hit me below the belt and I automatically brushed it away. Where I had touched it, there was a redness and swelling on my hand. It seemed as if the gold wedding ring was burning into my finger.'

The ball exploded with a bang and scorched a small hole in her skirt, but she was otherwise unharmed.

An even more bizarre suggestion is that ball lightning may be due to minute particles of meteoric anti-matter that fall to Earth from the upper atmosphere. It is suggested that thunderstorms act as giant vacuum cleaners that suck up anti-matter dust particles. As the anti-matter then comes into contact with normal matter, it is gradually annihilated, releasing the energy that produces the glowing ball.

Yet another theory is that ball lightning is generated by currents flowing from thunder clouds to the ground. By postulating an external energy source for the ball, this theory elegantly accounts for the long life of lightning balls; but unfortunately it does not explain how a ball could enter the metallic skin of an aircraft, in the way that it did with the USAF tanker aircraft, and as witnessed by the crew.

Ball lightning is as much a puzzle today as when it was first reported some 1,500 years ago. In the sixth century, St Gregory of Tours is said to have watched in absolute horror as a fireball of blinding brightness appeared in the air above a procession of religious and civil dignitaries during a ceremony marking the dedication of a chapel. The sight was so terrifying that everyone in the procession immediately threw themselves to the ground. Since there was no reasonable explanation for the ball, he concluded that it was a miracle.

THE MAKING OF A MIRAGE

Gigantic shadows that haunt mountain ranges; cities and armies that appear in the skies – some are at times perfectly natural phenomena that have a scientific explanation, but others are not.

A climber is feeling his way along a precipice high on the Brocken, a 3,747-foot (1,142-metre) peak in the Harz Mountains of Germany, treacherous to all but the most experienced mountaineers. As he moves cautiously from one precarious foothold to another, he suddenly sees an immense human figure loom out of the mist towards him. In his fright, the climber loses his footing and falls to his death.

It is the classic story of the Brocken spectre. This particular version may be no more than folklore, but it is undoubtedly true that such spectres of the mind exist – and not only on the Brocken. A vivid example of the same phenomenon was reported to *Nature* magazine in 1880. It occurred on Clifton Down, near the Avon gorge, in south-west England. The time was around 10.30 a.m., and the gorge was filled with mist. The witness was standing on the top of nearby Observatory Hill, when he was startled to observe 'a dim gigantic figure apparently standing out through the mist upon one of the lower slopes of Clifton Down'. He soon realised, however, that the figure was not as solid as it seemed. 'A moment's glance sufficed to show me that it was my own shadow on the mist; and as I waved my arms about, the gaunt spectre followed every movement.'

The physical explanation of the Brocken spectre given by the anonymous observer is correct. Such spectres can be seen anywhere that shadows are cast on dense mist and water droplets. While this may be understandable, the suddenness with which these natural phenomena occur can make them startling and even frightening.

The observer on Clifton Down also happened to note a curious feature of the phenomenon. 'A gentleman who stood beside me likewise saw his spectre, but not mine, as we ascertained by the movements executed; nor could I see his, unless we stood so close together that the spectres seemed combined into one.'

But it is not only human figures that cast these strange and dramatic shadows. Adam's Peak, a 7,360-foot (2,243-metre) mountain in Sri Lanka, regularly produces its own spectre. The mountain stands isolated, rising around 1,000 feet (305 metres) above the ridge of which it is a part. The phenomenon, for which the mountain is famous, occurs just after sunrise. To an observer standing on the mountain, the shadow of the peak appears to rise in front of the observer, while the summit is surrounded by a rainbow-hued halo and two dark streamers leading off into the sky. Suddenly, the shadow either disappears or falls down to the ground.

Sunrise spectre

This mystified scientists for many years. It was assumed that it must be some kind of mirage, but these are caused by layers of hot and cold air, superimposed on each other, and scientists could not measure any atmospheric temperature differences in this particular phenomenon. Then, in 1886, a scientist named Ralph Abercromby made the brave decision to spend the night on Adam's Peak in order to see what would actually transpire at sunrise. He and his companions were evidently in low spirits by the time dawn came. According to his journal:

'The morning broke in a very unpromising manner. Heavy clouds lay all about, lightning flickered over a dark bank to the right of the rising Sun, and at frequent intervals masses of light vapour blew up from the valley and enveloped the summit in their mist.'

Then, at around 6.30 a.m., the Sun appeared briefly from behind clouds, and the observers saw the weird shadow of the mountain. It disappeared and then appeared again – and 'seemed to rise up and stand in front of us in the air, with rainbow and spectral arms, and then to fall down suddenly to the

442

earth'. This was the feature of the phenomenon that had mystified scientists for so long. From his vantage point, however, Abercromby could see what had eluded observers on the ground. 'As a mass of vapour drove across the shadow, the condensed particles caught the shadow... As the vapour blew past, the shadow fell to its natural level – the surface of the Earth.' Abercromby added that, as a good scientist, he had conducted a fair number of temperature measurements, and the results were enough to confirm his belief that the phenomenon could not have been due to a mirage.

Phantom city

A mirage, however, is the explanation for another extraordinary natural oddity – the *Fata Morgana* (Italian for 'Fairy Morgan'). This often impressive phenomenon takes its name from Morgan le Fay, King Arthur's enchantress sister, who could make cities or ports appear anywhere on the open seas – a talent that she apparently found useful when luring sailors to a watery death. Strictly speaking, the *Fata Morgana* is the name of one particular manifestation of this phenomenon – a magnificent city that appears over the Strait of Messina, between Italy and the island of Sicily. As a Dominican friar, Antonio Minasi, described it, in 1773:

'When the rising sun shines from that point whence its incident ray forms an angle of about 45 degrees on the sea of Reggio [the Strait of Messina], and the bright surface of the water is not disturbed either by the wind or the current, the spectator... with his back to the sun and his face to the sea... he sees appear in the water... various multiplied objects, such as numberless series of pilasters, arches, castles well delineated, regular columns, lofty towers, superb palaces with balconies and windows, extended alleys of trees, delightful plains with herds and flocks, armies of men on foot and horseback, and many other strange figures, all in their natural colours and proper action... if the air be slightly hazy and opaque... then the objects will appear... vividly coloured or fringed with red, green, blue and the other prismatic colours.'

Refracted light

Antonio Minasi believed that the image was a direct reflection of the mainland coast in the water of the Strait of Messina. It appeared where it did, he explained, because the strong currents that exist in the Strait caused the surface of the water to tilt slightly. Today, however, the phenomenon of the mirage is much better understood: differences in temperature can cause patches of air to act in much the same way as lenses, refracting light rays in unpredictable directions. This causes magnified images to appear with great clarity, even at a considerable distance from the original object. The most frequent example is the mirage of the sky seen in the hot air above a hot road, which gives the impression of shimmering water. At sea, mirages of ships or land, seen while either is still over the horizon, have been familiar to sailors the world over for centuries.

In some parts of the world, such mirages are commonplace. For example, the mirage of Tallinn in Estonia, a former Soviet republic, is regularly seen in Helsinki in Finland, 50 miles (80 kilometres) to the north, across the Gulf of Finland. It is said to be so distinct that individual buildings can be recognised. The sky above Alaska in North America is also said to be strangely receptive to impressions of the city of Bristol, 6,000 miles (9,500 kilometres) away in south-west England.

Visions of Bristol

In his book *New Lands*, published in the 1920, Charles Fort mentions the tradition that Bristol is visible over Alaska between 21 June and 10 July every year. He notes that, remarkably, the image is said to have been seen regularly by the Alaskan Indians long before Europeans settled there and identified the city of the mirage. In 1887, a certain Mr Willoughby took a photograph of the mirage, in which several of the buildings of Bristol could be recognised. Indeed, many people protested that the likeness was so good that the photograph had to be of Bristol itself.

But what of cases involving action and movement?

The following extraordinary example was reported in the German newspaper *Allgemeine Zeitung* of 13 February 1854. Three weeks earlier, on 22 January 1854, an extraordinary phenomenon had been witnessed by the inhabitants of the village of Büderich, in north-west Germany.

'Shortly before sunset, an army, of boundless extent, and consisting of infantry-cavalry, and an enormous number of wagons, was observed to proceed across the country in marching order. So distinctly seen were all these appearances that even the flashing of the firelocks, and the colour of the cavalry uniform, which was white, could be distinguished. This whole array advanced in the direction of the wood of Schafhauser, and as the infantry neared the thicket, and the cavalry drew near, they were hid all at once, with the trees, in a thick smoke. Two houses, also, in flames, were seen with the same distinctness. At sunset, the whole phenomenon vanished.'

Such armies in the sky have been reported with reasonable regularity, and are often believed to be re-enactments of battles that have taken place at that spot in the past. The repeat performances, on four successive Saturday and Sunday nights in 1642, of the English Civil War battle of Edgehill is a particularly well-known example. It seems likely, however, that the Büderich case was a mirage of military manoeuvres that were actually taking place elsewhere at the time.

Gravity – that is, the force that pulls objects towards Earth – is still only imperfectly understood but may also play a part in what are recognised as optical illusions. Scientists explain gravity as a force of attraction between masses, but one that varies according to the size of the masses and the distance between them. Mathematically formulated, this law has become the basis of a complex theory that allows the effects of gravity to be calculated with minute accuracy. The nature of the force, however – the way in which it is transmitted – is still a mystery.

Coasting uphill

It is agreed among scientists that the force of gravity is not constant on the Earth's surface; indeed, it varies according to the alignments of the heavenly bodies. Alignments of the Sun and Moon, for example, are responsible for spring and neap tides. There also appear to be certain purely local variations that are not connected with the movements of the planets: the lines of prehistoric stones at Carnac in Brittany, France, for instance, mark subtle changes in the magnitude of the gravitational force.

These subtle changes in gravity are discernible only by sensitive instruments. But, occasionally, gravitational anomalies can cause dramatic effects.

The Electric Brae, or Croy Brae, is a gentle slope overlooking the south side of Culzean Bay, near Ayr in the Strathclyde region of Scotland. Motorists

447

driving down it find that, if they park in a layby, and release the handbrake, the car appears to run backwards, uphill, even though this would seem to be an impossibility.

Another example occurs in Belo Horizonte in Brazil. Peanuts Street is a narrow and unpretentious suburban road that runs slightly uphill for around a quarter of a mile (350 metres). But switch off your engine and release your handbrake, and your car will move, slowly but steadily, uphill. The reason for this strange phenomenon is thought to have something to do with magnetic forces induced by surrounding rocks that are rich in iron.

In cases such as these, the normal and the paranormal come very close. Science can certainly explain some – but not all – of these bizarre phenomena, and then only partially.

The prodigious feats performed by devotees of François de Paris, as shown here, were all utterly repulsive. Women were beaten with sticks and stabbed with spears and swords. Yet they emerged from their ordeals unharmed, as revealed on page 487.

One of the best-known of all simulacra – images that can be seen in fire, water, clouds or other surfaces – is of the face of Christ and is alleged to have appeared as a shadow in the snow, as shown above. *As the chapter starting on page 494 outlines, nature continues to produce many such oddities that science cannot yet explain.*

Turn to page 400 and marvel at how certain Tibetan adepts attempt to make their thoughts and their gods, such as the representations above, materialise merely by means of sustained effort of concentration.

This Christian convert emerges from baptism by total emersion, crying aloud with joy. Often, such religious ecstasy results in 'tongues' being spoken by one or more of the participants. You can find out more about this bizarre form of religious fervour on page 425.

WHAT A COINCIDENCE!

Every one of us has, at some time, experienced a coincidence. Mathematicians explain them away as mere chance events – but there are those who seek deeper reasons.

Shortly after British actor Anthony Hopkins had been chosen for a part in the film *The Girl from Petrovka*, he decided he ought to read the novel by George Feifer, from which the screenplay was taken. He could not find it in a single London bookshop, however. Then, while waiting for a train at Leicester Square underground station, he caught sight of a volume lying on a seat. Amazingly, it was that same novel. What is more, it had scribbled notes in the margin. As Hopkins later found out, a friend had lost Feifer's own annotated copy, and it was this very one that Hopkins had come across.

Coincidences such as this certainly take one aback. Yet most of us actually have an intriguing coincidence of some sort or other to relate: bumping into a long-lost friend in some unexpected situation; suddenly thinking of someone who immediately telephones; humming a tune, and then hearing it on the radio seconds later; or even, perhaps, coming across an individual with your very own name whose life seems to run in parallel to your own.

One such occurrence involved King Umberto I of Italy who was dining with his aide in a restaurant in Monza, where he was due to attend an athletics meeting the next day. With astonishment, he suddenly noticed that the proprietor looked exactly like him. Speaking to him, he discovered that there were other similarities, too.

The restaurateur was also called Umberto; like the King, he had been born in Turin – on the same day in fact; and he had married a girl called Margherita on the day that the King had married Queen Margherita. He had also opened his restaurant on the day that Umberto I was crowned.

The King was intrigued, and invited his 'double' to attend the athletics meeting with him. But the next day, the King's aide informed him that the restaurateur had died that morning in a mysterious shooting. Even as the King expressed his regret, he himself was shot dead by an anarchist in the crowd.

Another strange coincidence connected with a death occurred on Sunday 6 August 1978, when the little alarm clock that Pope Paul VI had bought in 1923 – and that for 55 years had woken him at six every morning – rang suddenly and shrilly. But it was not six o'clock: the time was 9.40 p.m. For no explicable reason, the clock had started ringing as the Pope lay dying. Later, Father Romeo Panciroli, a

Vatican spokesman, commented: 'It was most strange. The Pope was very fond of the clock. He bought it in Poland and always took it with him on his trips'.

Many such examples of coincidences seem to defy all logic, luck or reason. It is not surprising, therefore, that the 'theory of coincidence' has excited scientists, philosophers and mathematicians alike for more than 2,000 years. Running like a thread through all their theories and speculations is one theme. Could coincidences have a hidden message for us? But only in this century have any real answers been suggested, answers that strike at the very roots of established science and prompt the question as to whether there are powers in the Universe of which we are still only dimly aware.

Hidden affinities

Early cosmologists believed that the world was held together by a principle of wholeness. Hippocrates, known as the father of medicine, who lived at some time between 460 and 375 BC, believed the Universe was joined together by 'hidden affinities' and wrote: 'There is one common flow, one common breathing, all things are in sympathy'. According to this theory, coincidence could be explained by 'sympathetic' elements seeking each other out.

Similar beliefs have continued, in barely altered forms. The philosopher Arthur Schopenhauer (1788-1860), for instance, defined coincidence as 'the simultaneous occurrence of causally unconnected events'; and he went on to suggest that simultaneous events run in parallel lines. These events, although links in totally different chains, nevertheless fall into place in both, he said, so that the fate of one individual invariably fits the fate of another.

Probing the future

The idea of a 'collective unconscious' – an underground storehouse of memories through which minds can communicate – has been debated by several thinkers. One of the more extreme theories to explain coincidence was put forward by the British mathematician Adrian Dobbs in the 1960s. Dobbs coined the word 'psitron' to describe an unknown force probing, like radar, a second time dimension that was probabilistic rather than deterministic. The psitron, he claimed, was capable of absorbing future probabilities and could relay them back to the present, bypassing the normal human senses and somehow conveying information directly to the brain.

But the first person actually to study the laws of coincidence scientifically was Dr Paul Kammerer, Director of the Institute of Experimental Biology in Vienna. From the age of 20, he had kept a logbook of coincidences. Many were essentially trivial: names that kept cropping up in separate conversations, successive concert or cloakroom tickets with the same number, or a phrase in a book that kept recurring in real life. For hours, Kammerer also sat on park benches, recording people who wandered past, and noting their sex, age, dress, and whether they carried walking sticks or umbrellas. After making the necessary allowances for factors like the rush-hour, weather and time of year, he found the results broke down into 'clusters of numbers' of a kind familiar to statisticians, gamblers, insurance companies and opinion pollsters.

Curious clusterings

Kammerer called the phenomenon 'seriality', and in 1919 he published his conclusions in a book called *Das Gesetz der Serie* (*The Law of Seriality*). Coincidences, he claimed, come in series – or 'a recurrence or clustering in time or space whereby the individual numbers in the sequence are not connected by the same active cause'. Coincidence, suggested Kammerer, is merely the tip of the iceberg in a larger cosmic principle that mankind, as yet, hardly recognises.

Like gravity, it is a mystery; but unlike gravity, it acts selectively to bring together in space and time things that possess some affinity. 'We thus arrive,' he concluded, 'at the image of a world mosaic or cosmic kaleidoscope which, in spite of constant shufflings and rearrangements, also takes care of bringing like and like together.'

But the great leap forward happened when two of

Europe's most brilliant minds collaborated to produce a most searching book on the powers of coincidence – one that was to provoke both controversy and attack from rival theorists working in this area. These two men were Wolfgang Pauli – whose daringly conceived exclusion principle earned him the Nobel Prize for Physics – and the Swiss psychologist-philosopher, Carl Gustav Jung. Their treatise bore the unexciting title *Synchronicity, An Acausal Connecting Principle*; but it was described by one American reviewer as 'the paranormal equivalent of a nuclear explosion'.

Order out of chaos

According to Pauli, coincidences are 'the visible traces of untraceable principles'. Coincidences, elaborated Jung, whether they come singly or in series, are manifestations of a barely understood universal principle that operates quite independently of the known laws of physics. Interpreters of the Pauli-Jung theory have even concluded that telepathy and precognition are also manifestations of a single mysterious force at work in the Universe that is trying to impose its own kind of discipline on the utter confusion of human life.

But of all recent investigators, none wrote more extensively about the theory of coincidence than Arthur Koestler, who summed up the phenomenon in the vivid phrase 'puns of destiny'.

One particularly striking 'pun' was related to

Koestler by a 12-year-old English schoolboy named Nigel Parker: 'Many years ago, the American horror-story writer, Edgar Allan Poe, wrote a book called *The Narrative of Arthur Gordon Pym*. In it, Mr Pym was travelling in a ship that wrecked. The four survivors were in an open boat for many days before they decided to kill and eat the cabin boy, whose name was Richard Parker.

'Some years *later*, in the summer of 1884, my great-grandfather's cousin was cabin boy in the yawl *Mignonette* when she foundered, and the four survivors were in an open boat for many days. Eventually, the three senior members of the crew killed and ate the cabin boy. His name was Richard Parker.'

The most striking coincidences often involve the most commonplace of objects or occasions. One such bizarre incident was experienced by the Chicago newspaper columnist Irv Kupcinet. As he recounted:

'I had just checked into the Savoy Hotel in London. Opening a drawer in my room, I found, to my astonishment, that it contained some personal things belonging to a friend of mine, Harry Hannin, then with the Harlem Globetrotters basketball team.

'Two days later, I received a letter from Harry, posted in the Hotel Meurice, in Paris, which began "You'll never believe this." Apparently, Harry had opened a drawer in his room and found a tie which had my name on it. It was a room I had stayed in a few months earlier.'

459

In his book *Homo Faber*, Swiss writer Max Frisch told the extraordinary story of a man who, through a most amazing series of coincidences, meets the daughter he never knew he had, falls in love with her and sets in motion a sequence of events that result in her death. But Faber, a rational man, refused to see anything more than the laws of chance in his bizarre story.

'The occasional occurrence of the improbable does not imply the intervention of a higher power... The term probability includes improbability at the extreme limits of probability, and when the improbable does occur this is no cause for surprise, bewilderment or mystification.'

Few people could be so matter-of-fact in the face of the events that Frisch described – but Faber may be right. Every mathematician knows that a random distribution of events produces a clustering effect, just as cherries randomly distributed in a cake will tend to be found in groups, rather than in the orderly arrangement one might expect.

But even sceptics must have been stunned by the news announced on 5 January 1996 that tenor Richard Versalle died on stage at the Metropolitan Opera, New York, after delivering the line 'Too bad you can only live so long' in a performance of Janacek's *The Makropulos Case*.

An extraordinary number of people also report amazing coincidences when searching out information in libraries, so much so that Arthur Koestler coined the term 'library angel' to describe the mysterious force that somehow leads individuals straight to the right book.

Journalist Bernard Levin had a similar experience. He had been looking for a very long while for reference to a story about a statue of Alexander the Great. This statue was said to be so large that it could hold an entire city in its hand. He happened to be looking up another reference entirely in Plutarch's *Lives*, turned by mistake to the wrong page due to a misprint, and there found the story of the statue.

Sir Arthur Conan Doyle, creator of Sherlock Holmes, was also astonished to come across a story by de Maupassant, entitled *L'Auberge*, which was almost identical in every respect to a plot which he had been developing for a book of his own. It was even set in the very same inn at the Gemmi Pass in Switzerland.

More recently, astrologer and writer Derek Walters was assisted by the library angel when researching in the Chinese section of a university library. The information he sought was not readily available; what is more, his knowledge of Chinese was somewhat limited at the time, and there was no one to assist him. Suddenly, however, a volume fell from a shelf at his feet. Picking it up, he found it contained precisely the information required.

In his book *Coincidence, A Matter of Chance – or Synchronicity*, Brian Inglis, writer and researcher into the paranormal, describes broadcaster Alistair Cooke's experience with the library angel. Pulling down a volume from a shelf, he noticed he had unfortunately picked the wrong one. In fact, it was on a different subject altogether: the *Good Food Guide* for 1972. However, he immediately realised that it would be just what he needed for a programme on the subject of inflation that he had to record in a few days' time, and he was able to find reference to a meal costing £3-4, thought to be rather expensive at the time.

Some investigators have utterly dismissed such reports, pointing out that we ought to consider the frequency with which significant events of this kind do *not* occur. But most people surely experience several such seemingly meaningful events in the course of a lifetime? Can there really be no more to them than mere coincidence?

TIME-TRAVEL

The general belief is that time flows along steadily 'like an ever-rolling stream'. But modern science is discovering that the reality may in fact be far more complex. Indeed, the enduring fantasy of time-travel may well be physically possible after all.

We are all time-travellers, moving a certain distance in time with every full rotation of the Earth – a distance that is shared by everyone else. That is the reality of our everyday lives. But who has not speculated on the possibility of varying this steady progress, so that either we speed up while everything around us seems to move more slowly, or we somehow drag our feet so that everything hurries by as we are left behind? And what of the possibility of travelling backwards down that same road, to visit the past and, perhaps, to alter it? Even if physical time-travel is an impossibility, could we maybe communicate across time, through our dreams and visions?

Surprisingly, science actually acknowledges the possibility of physical time-travel in certain circumstances. This, however, demands a new way of looking at reality. To provide a bridge between our everyday experience of time and the bizarre possibilities that stem from abandoning this view, it is best to look first at some of the paradoxes inherent in the very concept of time-travel. The discovery of a paradox, to the unimaginative, demonstrates impossibility. To the truly imaginative, however, a paradox is actually a challenge for us to find a more radical solution.

Space-time theories

The idea of a steady flow of time is already outmoded by experiments involving particles that travel at speeds close to that of light, under conditions where Einstein's theory of relativity, far removed from our usual perception of the world, provides the best description of how the Universe works. Time, like space, is elastic, not rigid; and Einstein's description involves a blending together in which time and space are seen as two sides of the same coin – a coin dubbed 'space-time'. Both time and space can be stretched and squeezed, depending on circumstances, and time can be traded for space as long as the total balance is maintained. This is all solid, sober scientific fact.

Relativity theory is confirmed by the direct measurement of what happens to sub-atomic particles that are whirled at huge speeds inside modern 'atom-smasher' machines – accelerators. It is fact, not mere speculation, that such a particle has a longer lifetime than a stationary counterpart; and it is fact that an astronaut travelling at a speed that is a sizeable fraction of the speed of light – 186,000 miles per second (300,000 kilometres per second) – ages less rapidly than the rest of us left behind on Earth.

Another way in which we can stretch time, entirely within accepted modern scientific thinking, involves sitting in a strong gravitational field – the sort of gravitational field you might find near a sizeable black hole. This does not necessitate travelling through the back hole, just sitting in its gravitational field and watching the Universe go by, seemingly at a speeded-up rate. Both tricks are forms of time-travel, and they get the intrepid astronaut into the future 'faster' than the usual rate. If, however, the astronaut does not like what he finds there, he faces a problem for there may be no way home. Whether or not time is a steadily flowing stream, within the framework of modern science, it is usually regarded as a one-way street. Hurrying forward may, just, be possible; bucking the stream and swimming back into the past is probably not, at least that is what scientists have thought until recently.

The key to the discussion is causality – the assumption that events always follow their causes in an orderly procession. A bullet leaves the gun *after* the trigger is pulled, not before; the results of the 3.15 at Ascot reach us only *after* the race is run, not in time for us to be able to rush round to the betting shop and make a killing. The logical implication is therefore that, if time-travel involves violation of causality, it must be impossible. Logically, a theory that tells us we can commit suicide, and *then* go to a restaurant and enjoy a good dinner, must be suspect. But the Universe may yet hold a few surprises for logicians.

Science-fiction writers have their own answers to this paradox and highlight two possibilities – branches and loops in time. The hoariest example of a time-travel paradox concerns a traveller who goes back in time and, wittingly or unwittingly, prevents the birth of the person who would have been his grandfather. But if so, he could never have been born himself. So how could he go back in time if he had never been born? The very existence of the paradox is seen by many people as proof that time-travel is impossible.

Loops in time

Michael Moorcock developed the theme in his novel *Behold the Man*. In this, the time-traveller is a disturbed individual with a tendency to religious mania, who journeys back to the time of Jesus to view the crucifixion. His time machine is destroyed beyond repair, and he finds no trace of the Jesus described in the Bible. Inexorably, as he attempts to tell people about the Jesus he came to see, he is drawn into the role of Jesus, playing out events he remembers from the Bible, up to and including the crucifixion. So history is created, and in 2,000 years time a certain individual travels back in time to close the loop, like the snake that eats its own tail.

This resolution of the paradox sees time as fixed in some greater fabric, with ourselves merely actors who are playing out predetermined roles on the stage of space-time. The alternative resolution of the paradox sees space-time as infinitely variable. It also sees each of us master of his or her own destiny to an extent few people ever realise. Again, an example from science fiction makes the point. In *Lest Darkness Fall,* L. Sprague de Camp's hero is a 20th-century man who is mysteriously deposited in sixth-century Italy and averts the Dark Ages single-handed. The story is hokum but the author's explanation is that, having 'slipped down the trunk' of the tree of history, the hero has created a new branch, a new line of history growing out as a result of his introduction of 20th-century ideas into a sixth-century environment.

With only slight modifications, this idea becomes a respectable philosophical concept, whereby there may exist parallel universes, worlds running alongside one another in some sense, with an infinite number of variations.

Taken to its logical conclusion, this view of reality argues that we have complete control over our destiny, because literally anything is possible, and also actually happens somewhere among the infinite array of parallel universes. All we have to do is find a way to travel across the time barrier, not forwards or backwards but *sideways* in time. It is, of course, much easier said than done; but if physical time-travel remains at the very least an unlikely prospect for us, there remains the intriguing possibility that dreams, ghosts and other mysterious phenomena generally classified as paranormal experiences could be just as well explained in terms of information somehow leaking into our world from parallel worlds.

The pigeon hole paradox

One of the most startling philosophical theories sees everything as being in the mind. Sir Fred Hoyle, an eminent astronomer who had a penchant for speculation and science fiction, mentioned this idea in a serious scientific book, *Ten Faces of the Universe*, and elaborated on the theme in his science-fiction novel, *October the First is Too Late*. In these, he suggests that all the events that we imagine making up the flow of time exist in a kind of infinite sorting office, with each event, or state, in its own pigeon hole.

Hoyle explains: 'Suppose that in each of these states your own consciousness is included. As soon as a particular state is chosen, as soon as an imaginary office worker takes a look at the contents of a particular pigeon hole, you have the subjective consciousness of a particular moment, of what you call the present. Think of the clerk in an office taking a look, first at the contents of one pigeon hole, then at the contents of another. Suppose he does this, not in sequence, but in any old order. What is the effect on your subjective consciousness? So far as the clerk

468

himself is concerned, he's jumping about all over the place among the pigeon holes. So your consciousness jumps all over the place. But the strange thing is that your subjective impression is quite different. You have the impression of time as an ever-rolling stream.'

We may all, in fact, be experiencing time-travel, as well as travel between different possible universes; but, because one of the rules of the game is that the clerk in the office can look at only one pigeon hole at a time, we never know it.

True or not, theories such as these show that there is more to time than we may suppose; and that there are, philosophically speaking, a number of possible ways round the paradoxes of time-travel. And if there are ways round the paradoxes, there seems to be no logical reason why it should not be possible one day for us to build an actual time machine. Indeed, in the foreword to a new book, *The Physics of Star Trek*, by American astronomer Lawrence Krauss, Britain's leading cosmic physicist Professor Stephen Hawking has pointed out that: 'One of the consequences of rapid interstellar travel would be that one could also travel *back* in time.'

THE CROP CIRCLE CONTROVERSY

Appearing out of the blue each year, crop circles are as baffling as ever. Could they be unearthly? Or are they nothing more than elaborate hoaxes?

The most popular current enigma; an intellectual challenge strong enough to baffle the entire planet; a continually changing phenomenon: all these phrases, and many more, have been used to describe the bizarre – even beautiful – circular designs that over recent years have regularly appeared in British cereal fields – and elsewhere, too – during the high summer months.

They come in swirls: they come in rings: they come as singles, doubles, triples, and even complex formations like dials, and have manifested in ever-increasing profusion since August 1980 when research began at White Horse Hill, near Westbury in Wiltshire.

We have not seen the likes of it for a long time in the world of unexplained phenomena: and, certainly, the nature of these mysterious formations still eludes us. Are they always created by intrepid hoaxers? Is there a natural solution, possibly triggered by changes in our atmosphere or even the controversial greenhouse effect? Or, could it be, as some researchers insist, that we are the subject of alien visitations? Is someone, somewhere, trying to tell us something?

Powerful vibrations

Probably the most remarkable formation to date appeared right on cue on Friday, 13 July 1990. It arrived just after a scientific conference in Oxford had gathered physicists and meteorologists from three continents to dismiss corn circles as a novel weather phenomenon, and the day before a UFO conference in Sheffield met in order to support the same conclusion.

The scene of this timely wonder was Alton Barnes in the Vale of Pewsey, Wiltshire. This is an area where circles had appeared, like a rash of extra-terrestrial pimples each May, June, July and August. It is an evocative place, scattered with ancient sites, such as the stone circle at Avebury and the imposing mound of Silbury Hill. The esoteric community loves this region: if you are psychically in tune, they say, then you sense its powerful vibrations.

The Alton Barnes formation attracted tremendous global interest because it had a series of six interlocking rings, circles, straight lines and arms with spokes emanating from them – by far the most elaborate grouping ever seen, almost impossible not to accept as intelligently designed, and also perhaps highly symbolic in content. Researchers soon found that this kind of mark bears a curious resemblance to ancient picture writing from the Sumerian culture – to such an extent that, within just a few days, the formations became known as 'pictograms' rather than crop marks.

The farmers who owned the land were insistent that a hoax was impossible because the pattern was so complex that it would have taken a very long time to fabricate. Noted circle researcher Colin Andrews agreed that it was far too elaborate, adding that it seemed to have been created by some sort of intelligent life force as an attempt to communicate with us.

Officially, the crop circle mystery was born in a field in August 1980. There was sporadic local interest and an immediate suggestion that its very regular edges (it seemed a giant cookie-cutter might have descended from the sky) indicated an intelligence, rather than a natural phenomenon. What is more, it seemed that the most likely candidate for that intelligence was located in outer space, especially as UFO phenomena had apparently centred on nearby Warminster some 20 years earlier.

Tourists from all over the world started skywatching from local hills to look out for 'the thing', as the UFO was quaintly nicknamed. Crop circles had become a centre of attention.

More circles then appeared in 1981 and 1982 at other sites in the counties of Hampshire and

Wiltshire; and subsequently local media regenerated the story every year, eagerly awaiting the first circle of summer with as much enthusiasm as nature-watchers traditionally anticipate the first cuckoo of spring.

Diffusing the myth

By 1983, the phenomenon was still little more than a local enigma, but it was debated in various UFO societies, and some fascinating investigations were conducted by the research group PROBE, the British UFO Research Association (BUFORA) and Dr Terence Meaden, a physicist specialising in unusual vortex mechanisms within the atmosphere and who operated TORRO (the Tornado and Storm Research Organisation). The general conclusion was that a natural phenomenon was to blame, and researchers did a fine job of defusing the 'alien myth' that some UFO spotters, sometimes displaying more imagination than common sense, had tended automatically to read into such matters.

However, this was not the end of the mystery, merely the beginning. The main proponent of an 'alien intelligence' interpretation of the phenomenon was *Flying Saucer Review* consultant Pat Delgado, later to be joined by colleague Colin Andrews. Their approach – that crop circles were some sort of warning from another intelligence – was the most popular with the media, and Delgado was successful in interesting the national press in the first 'quintuplets' (a formation of five circles, with a large one at the centre and four smaller satellites). This latest development ensured escalation of the subject to a nationwide level.

Cosmic joker?

A hoax, however, occurred in July 1983, when one national newspaper paid a farmer for a quintuplet to be 'created' on his land, right alongside an identical and allegedly 'real' pattern that had achieved great publicity in a rival daily. The hoax would probably have gone unrecognised but for some diligent investigation by serious researchers blamed in *New Scientist* magazine for actually fanning the flames of mystery.

Over the next few summers, there was occasional interest in the subject, especially when another new type of formation (a ring) appeared in 1986. Rings differ from circles in that only a narrow band of crop is laid down, whereas circles contain a whole area of flattened cereal. Ringed circles also began to appear; but simple circles still predominated in the British countryside.

It was from a mixture of gradually escalating activity, and claim and counter-claim between rival researchers, that the first signs of the possibility of a 'cosmic joker' – some sort of force emanating from somewhere beyond that could be playing tricks on us – began to appear.

Various strange things were now being discovered in the centre of some circles. Columnist Jean Rook visited a circle and found a single lone poppy staring up at her from the corn. In July 1989, this was reproduced at Mansfield and hailed as the first circle in Nottinghamshire. However, after careful investigation, the circle was found to be a hoax, a diagnosis supported by full confession on the part of the hoaxers. But the presence of another lone poppy at the centre of a circle was seemingly a coincidence – or was it?

A white 'goo' then turned up inside another formation, and speculation resulted about litter-bugging aliens who had visited our planet. Analysis, however, revealed the most likely source to be Earth-based confectionery that had 'gone off', then interacting in some strange way with the soil. Much jovial commentary about Martians dumping a 'Mars bar' as a cosmic signal resulted.

Name games were another feature of the increasingly perplexing phenomenon. Circles (a quintuplet formation) also appeared for the first time in Sussex. Remarkably, the pattern was astride Cradle Hill, which bears the same name as the famous UFO-watching location at Warminster in Wiltshire, where circles continued to appear.

Researchers have also looked for some sort of logic in the placement of circles. Some of the earliest, at Warminster and Westbury in Wiltshire, and Wantage in Oxfordshire, were at places with names starting with the letter 'W', forming the so-called 'Wessex Triangle', but this lost meaning when circles began to dot the map all over the UK.

Particularly intriguing was the message 'We are not alone', which was found cut into crop at one site. Other circle researchers, meanwhile, have chosen to cover up this particular story because they believe it could well damage the credibility of all their investigations to date.

Many have also had fun trying to align the circle locations with ancient monuments, stone circles, ley lines, and the like; but such theories are now generally disputed.

Mounting operations

In 1989, Operation Whitecrow was mounted, and watch was kept for several days on a field where circles were expected to appear. Hundreds took part, with cameras permanently trained on the suspect zone. Nothing was spotted; but as the operation shut down, new circles appeared in a field right behind the observers' backs.

Then, in the early summer of 1990, a group of meteorologists led another expedition, armed with sophisticated equipment. No circles were seen to form, although several did appear in a nearby field, out of line of sight as the investigators sat and waited.

Operation Blackbird followed. A sequel to Operation Whitecrow, this had backing from the BBC and Nippon TV in Japan. It involved expensive cameras with thermal imaging equipment, necessary because most circles are known to form during pre-dawn hours.

Yet again, however, the observers fell victim to a joker. Cameras at the Nippon site detected orange lights shortly after 4 a.m. on 25 July (only hours after major national press coverage for the mission, and three days after one tabloid newspaper had offered £10,000 to the first person who could solve the mystery). As the sun rose, there was a brand new formation of circles in the field. Were 10 years of research about to be rewarded?

The dramatic news immediately spread around the world, and there was talk of a major scientific breakthrough. Journalists then flocked to the scene, only to find the complex formation crudely trampled into the corn and very obviously a hoax. At the centre of each circle, they also found two strange objects – a ouija board and a wooden cross: researchers had been foiled again.

Crop circles also occur elsewhere in the world. On 18 February 1977, at 4 a.m., for example, a Uruguayan rancher, together with his family and several farmhands, suffered a nasty shock while herding cattle. The generator that provided the farm with light suddenly cut out as a rotating shape with a central bulge and glowing bright orange descended on to the farmland. Cows ran away and dogs barked in panic; but Topo, the family guard dog, large and police-trained, rushed immediately towards the 'thing' as it rocked from side to side, giving out terrific blasts of strong wind that tore off branches from adjacent trees.

When almost on top of the terrifying 'object', Topo froze in his tracks and began to howl in pain. Streaks of white 'lightning' emerged from the beneath the shape and were earthed when they made contact with the ground. The farmer, who had been chasing his dog, felt a wave of heat strike him from some distance, and his skin tingled in response to an electrical charge. He stood paralysed, his muscles convulsing.

As the glow shot upwards and vanished, the generator immediately began to work again. However, all the wiring to the lights had been burnt right through by a power surge.

When their fear had been somewhat allayed, the farmworkers approached the spot and discovered that the ground beneath where the rotating sphere had hovered was a classic swirled crop circle, some 36 feet (11 metres) in diameter.

The farmer had a severe skin rash that lasted several days, felt unwell, but thankfully recovered; not so the dog. Topo was found dead at the very spot where he had confronted the unbelievably powerful force. An autopsy by the local vet revealed that the animal had been 'cooked' from within by a mysterious powerful electro-magnetic force that had generated intense energy.

Fortunately, most other cases of a close encounter with the cause of a crop circle are far less traumatic; but the force that is generating these marks is clearly powerful and, at times, perhaps even a killer.

Atmospheric forces

At first, one of the most derided, but least understood, explanations for crop circles was that they are the product of some sort of atmospheric force, usually dismissed as a 'whirlwind' or 'tornado'. Dr Terence Meaden, of the Tornado and Storm Research Organisation (TORRO), involved in circle studies far longer than anybody else, developed an extensive and complex set of ideas that have won growing support. Indeed, in a survey of 50 meteorologists conducted in 1990 by Paul Fuller, almost all were now willing to accept the theory, or believed it worthy of further research.

Essentially, Dr Meaden suggested that spinning columns of air above the surface during certain weather conditions and at key geographical sites (gentle hill slopes being prime examples) produce an electrical field by ionizing the surrounding air. This can, in some circumstances, drop to Earth like a curtain of electric rain. It is very short-lived but interacts with the resistive properties of cereal fields to leave geometric marks. The 'curtain' (or plasma vortex to give it its technical name) is confined to a well-defined shape by surface tension: floating soap bubbles retain their precise and seemingly 'artificial' design in the same way. Critics of Dr Meaden's theory, however, suggest that it fails to take into account the highly complex pattern of some circles.

All in a night's work

But some circles are merely the result of elaborate hoaxes – if, that is, the confessions of supposed perpetrators are genuine. On 9 September 1991, *Today* newspaper led with an article on its front page entitled: 'The men who conned the world'. The paper claimed that the crop circle debate was over. Doug Bower and David Chorley, both in their 60s, demonstrated how they first designed a circle at home and then, using 4 ft (1.2 m) wooden plinths, a ball of string and a baseball cap with a piece of wire threaded through its visor, executed their designs in the middle of the night at a preselected site. They also offered to create a circle for the paper which would fool the experts.

Having shown their design to the *Today* reporter, the two men set off at 1.30 a.m. First, they tied string to each end of a plinth to form a pair of reins. Chorley then placed his foot on one end of the plinth while Bower worked it round; this gave them the basic circle. From then on, each man took turns at holding the reins and walking round with his foot on the plinth – always with the plinth half way up the corn. In this way, the corn was flattened, but never trampled. The men kept walking around until they were satisfied that the circle was big enough.

Then, wearing the baseball hat with the wire fed into its visor, Bower lined up a point on the horizon and started to walk in a straight line, backward and forward, until he had formed what was to become the corridor between two circles. Once this was completed, another circle was created at the other end using the same technique. When the men had finished, they left the way they had come in – along a tramline made by the farmer's tractor.

The following day, the newspaper called in Pat Delgado, best-selling author and crop circle expert, who examined and then 'authenticated' the circles, describing them as '... the greatest of modern mysteries'. It must have been a highly embarrassing moment when the hoax was revealed.

Bower and Chorley went on to describe how they had first learned about crop circles in Australia. They had become drinking partners in England, had found the idea highly amusing and decided to try them out here. The publicity that the circles received only increased their desire to make them more and more intricate.

Despite the men's claims, however, most scientists

are by no means convinced that all circles are the work of hoaxers. And so the debate continues.

But if you think that the appearance of crop circles is purely a modern phenomenon, you are quite wrong. As we know from engravings produced at the time, they have been appearing since 1678, when they were found in a field in Hertfordshire, southern England, and blamed on the Devil.

Carl Jung, the Swiss psychologist who developed a theory of archetypal images that are buried deep inside us, would probably have loved to tangle with the crop circle mystery, just as he theorised about the true nature of UFOs. Indeed, perhaps the full solution will not require a cereal specialist, UFO enthusiast or even a meteorologist after all. Instead, it may take a psychologist to unravel the innermost secrets of crop circles.

In the engraving, above, *an army is seen advancing through the sky. Such images have been reported as occurring long after the events they depict and may therefore be mirages in time, a most mysterious phenomenon described on page 440.*

How could part of this body have burned so thoroughly without the rest of the room having been affected in any way? The death of this victim of what seems to be spontaneous human combustion remains an intriguing mystery.

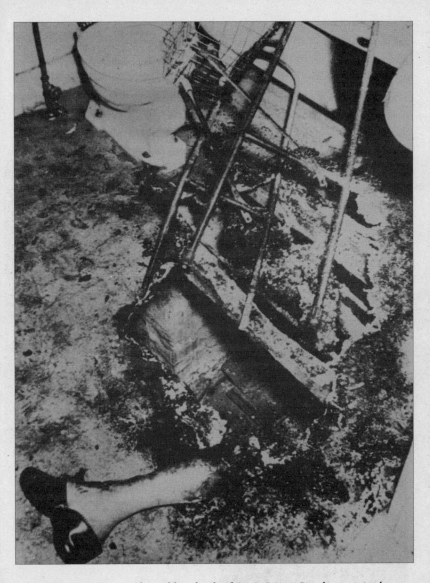

Strange, too, was the sudden death of Dr J. Irving Bentley, a retired physician from Pennsylvania. All that remained was the single, charred limb, above. *You can read about several such cases of SHC in the chapter beginning on page 389.*

The back panel of one of *Tutankhamun's thrones,* above, depicts the young King being anointed by his Queen. It is a most beautiful work of art: yet the tomb in which it was discovered by Howard Carter and his assistant A. C. Mace, left, together with Lord Carnarvon, is said to have carried a curse for whoever disturbed the Kingdom of the Dead, as you will discover on page 502.

HEALING THROUGH HORROR

In 18th-century France, certain women underwent tortures that should have been more than flesh could bear — yet, mysteriously, they flourished on them and went on to heal the sick and crippled poor by miraculous means.

The strange events that took place in the little Paris churchyard of St Medard between 1727 and 1732 sound so incredible that the modern reader is tempted to dismiss them as pure invention. This would be a mistake, however, for an impressive mass of documents, including accounts by doctors, magistrates and other respectable public figures, attests to their genuineness.

They began with the burial of Francois de Paris, the Deacon of Paris, in May 1727. Francois was only 37 years old, yet he was revered as a holy man, and was said to be blessed with powers of healing. He was a follower of Bishop Cornelius Jansen, who taught that men can be saved only by divine grace. The Deacon had no doubt whatever that his own healing powers came from God.

Great crowds followed his coffin, many weeping. It was laid in a tomb behind the high altar of St Medard. Then the congregation filed past, laying their flowers on the corpse. A father supported his son, a cripple, as he leaned over the coffin. Suddenly, the child went into convulsions and seemed to be having a fit. Several people helped to drag him, writhing, to a quiet corner of the church. Then the convulsions stopped. The boy opened his eyes, looked around in bewilderment, and slowly stood up. An expression of incredulous joy crossed his face as, to the astonishment of the spectators, he began to dance up and down, singing and laughing. His father found it impossible to believe, for the boy was using his withered right leg, which had virtually no muscles. Later it was claimed that this limb had become as strong and normal as the other.

The news spread. Within hours cripples, lepers, hunchbacks and blind men were rushing to the church. At first, few believed the stories of miraculous cures. But it soon became clear that ignorance and credulity could not be used as a blanket explanation for all the stories of marvels. Deformed limbs, it was said, were being straightened; hideous growths and cancers were disappearing without trace; horrible sores and wounds were healing instantly.

One of those who investigated the happenings was a lawyer named Louis Adrien de Paige. The first thing he saw when he entered the churchyard was a number of women writhing on the ground, twisting themselves into the most startling shapes, sometimes bending backwards until the backs of their heads touched their heels. These ladies were all wearing a long cloth undergarment that fastened around the ankles. M. Paige ascertained that this was now obligatory for all women who wished to avail themselves of the Deacon's miraculous powers. In the early days, when women had stood on their heads or bent their bodies convulsively, prurient young men had begun to frequent the churchyard in order to view the spectacle.

Mysterious masochism

Some of the women and girls were also being sadistically beaten – at least, that is what at first appeared to be going on. Men were striking them with heavy pieces of wood and iron. Other women lay on the ground, apparently crushed under immensely heavy weights. One girl was naked to the waist: a man was gripping her nipples with a pair of iron tongs and twisting them violently. None of these women seemed to feel any pain, however; on the contrary, many begged for more blows. And an incredible number of them were cured of deformities or diseases by this violent treatment.

In another part of the churchyard, an attractive, pink-cheeked girl of about 19 was sitting at a trestle table and eating. That seemed normal enough until one looked more closely at the food on the plate, and realised from its appearance – as well as from the smell – that it was human excrement.

In between mouthfuls of this sickening fare, she drank a yellow liquid, which was urine. This girl had come to the churchyard to be cured of what we would now call a neurosis: she had to wash her hands hundreds of times a day, and was so fastidious about her food that she would taste nothing that had been touched by another human hand. The Deacon had indeed cured her: within days, she was eating excrement and drinking urine, and did so with every sign of enjoyment.

Such cases might not be remarkable in asylums; but what was quite extraordinary was that after one of these meals, she opened her mouth as if to be sick, and milk came pouring out. It was apparently perfectly ordinary cow's milk.

Overcoming disgust

In another part of the churchyard, meanwhile, a number of women had volunteered to cleanse suppurating wounds and boils by sucking them clean. The leg of a small girl was a festering mass of sores, some so deep that the bone was visible. The woman who had volunteered to treat her was one of those who had been miraculously cured and, apparently, God had now chosen her to demonstrate how easily human beings' disgust can be overcome. Yet even she

490

blenched as she saw and smelt the gangrened leg. She prayed silently for a moment, then bent her head and began to lap, swallowing the septic matter.

The behaviour of a 16-year-old girl named Gabrielle Moler, however, was even more bizarre. She removed her cloak and lay on the ground, her skirt modestly round her ankles. Four men, each holding a pointed iron bar, stood over her; and when the girl smiled at them, they lunged down at her, driving their rods into her stomach. Amazingly, there was no sign of blood and she remained serene. Next the bars were jammed under her chin, forcing her head back. It seemed inevitable that they would penetrate through to her mouth; yet when the points were removed, the flesh was unbroken.

The men then took up sharp-edged shovels, placed them against a breast, and pushed with all their might; but the girl went on smiling gently. The breast, trapped between shovels, should have been cut off but it seemed impervious to the assault. Next, the cutting edge of a shovel was placed against her throat, and the man wielding it did his best to cut off her head; but he did not seem to be able even to dent her neck.

The girl was now beaten with a great iron truncheon that was shaped like a pestle. A stone weighing half a hundredweight (25 kilograms) was raised above her body and dropped repeatedly from a height of several feet. Finally, she knelt in front of a blazing fire, and plunged her head into it: her hair and eyebrows were not even singed, and she procededed to eat.

A magistrate who witnessed these events went back repeatedly, until he had enough material for the first volume of an amazing book. It was presented to the King, Louis XV, who was so shocked and indignant that he had the magistrate thrown into prison.

The suppression of St Medard

The Paris authorities eventually decided that the scandal was becoming unbearable and closed down the churchyard. But these women had discovered that they could perform their miracles anywhere, and so continued for many years.

A hardened sceptic, the scientist La Condamine, was equally startled when, in 1759, he watched a girl being crucified on a wooden cross, nailed by the hands and feet over a period of several hours, and stabbed in the side with a spear. He noticed that all this obviously hurt the girl, and her wounds bled when the nails were removed; but she seemed none the worse for an ordeal that would have killed most people.

So what can we say of these miracles from the standpoint of the 20th century? Some writers believe that a kind of self-hypnosis was involved. But while this could explain the excrement-eater and the woman who sucked at festering wounds, it is less plausible in explaining other extreme feats of physical endurance.

These remind us rather of descriptions of the ceremonies of dervishes and fakirs. J.G. Bennett in his autobiography *Witness*, for example, describes watching a ritual in which a razor-sharp sword was placed across the belly of a naked man, and two heavy men jumped up and down on it – all without even marking the flesh. What seems to be at work here is some power of 'mind over matter', deeper than mere hypnosis, which is not yet understood but merits serious attention.

It would be absurd to stop looking for scientific explanations of the miracles of St Medard. But let us not, in the meantime, deceive ourselves by accepting superficial 'sceptical' explanations.

NATURAL OR SUPERNATURAL?

Nature produces a host of oddities that scientists cannot or do not try to explain. What is the origin of such mystifying phenomena?

The world abounds in phenomena that are observed by hundreds of people, but that lack scientific explanations or are simply ignored by scientists. Among them are such obvious anomalies as UFOs and apparitions. But there are many more that, although not embarrassing to the scientific community in the same way, are equally extraordinary. One conspicuous example is ball lightning which, despite consistent reports by reliable witnesses, was not accepted as a genuine phenomenon until the late 19th century.

In fact, the entire phenomenon of lightning is surrounded by mystery. Any school textbook will confirm that it is simply the rapid discharge of a large amount of electricity. Generally, the charge builds up in clouds, and the lightning takes the shortest possible path to the Earth's surface. Occasionally, however, something remarkable occurs and lightning is seen to strike *upwards*. Sometimes, too, lightning strikes *horizontally*. Horizontal lightning passing between clouds is not difficult to explain – the clouds merely hold different concentrations of electrical charge, and the lightning passes from the one with the higher potential to that with the lower potential. But what of *horizontal* lightning that will travel great distances, apparently to strike some particular object?

An extraordinary example of this occurred on 16 July 1873 in Hereford, England, and was reported by W. Clement Ley to Symons's *Monthly Meteorological Magazine*. After a showery morning, stormclouds began to appear. At around 10 a.m., a large cumulus stormcloud arose in the west-south-west and, in a clear blue sky, it travelled steadily north-eastwards. A bolt of lightning emerged and, in Ley's words: 'The electric fluid travelled near the earth over high ground covered with trees, buildings, avoided All Saints' and St Peter's spires, very near which it must have passed, and singled out a house in the more eastern part of the city'. To add to the unlikeliness of the event, this house was actually lower than the surrounding houses, and should therefore have been less vulnerable to being struck by lightning.

An instance of similarly bizarre selection by lightning was reported in a 1902 issue of *Nature*. When a house in Jefferson, Iowa, USA, was struck by lightning, it was found that every other plate in a pile of 12 plates in the house was broken. Could this have been because the intense electric field of the atmosphere was somehow intensified in every other plate, or was it the result of some purely mechanical action? The editors found themselves unable to comment on this odd occurrence, and were left wondering whether lightning can actually 'choose' what it will strike.

Strange tattoos

The subject of 'lightning pictures' – images allegedly 'photographed' on to living bodies or objects struck by lightning – was the cause of much scientific controversy during the 19th century. Indeed, the study of the subject was given its own name – *keranography*. The issue of the reality of such pictures is still undecided, however.

The first reliable report of the phenomenon was made by no less a person than the American diplomat and scientist Benjamin Franklin. In 1786, he wrote to the Meteorological Society of London about an incident that he remembered taking place some 20 years before.

A man who was standing close to a tree when it was struck by lightning was 'very much surprised to perceive on his breast a facsimile of that tree'. Similar incidents had also been reported much earlier: in 1596, for example, during a summer storm, lightning 'fell' into the cathedral at Wells, Somerset. An account of this appeared in *Adversaria,* a book by the scholar Isaac Casaubon, who died in 1614. 'The wonderful part was this, which afterwards was taken notice of by many, that the marks of a cross were found to be imprinted on the bodies of those then at divine service.'

The classic explanation of lightning pictures is that the images arise from the well-known dendritic – or branching – patterns that electrical discharges are known to produce on the surfaces of many materials. This may explain cases where the images are of trees, but does it explain the strange images of the cross in the Wells case? And can it apply to the following extraordinary story, told by James Shaw at a meeting of the Meteorological Society held on 24 March 1857?

'About 4 miles [7 kilometres] from the city of Bath, near the village of Coombe Hay, was ... an extensive wood of hazel and detached oak-trees. In the centre of this wood was a field of about 50 yards [45 metres] square, in which were six sheep, all of which were struck dead by lightning. When the skins were taken from the animals, a facsimile of a portion of the surrounding scenery was visible on the inner surface of each skin...

'I remember that it caused a great sensation at the time ... the small field and its surrounding wood were so familiar to me and my schoolfellows that when the skins were shown to us we, at once, identified the local scenery... '

Such 'pictures' sometimes occur in the sky, too. One day in 1801, Clement Hofbauer, later canonised by the Roman Catholic Church, was at prayer before the altar of St Joseph in a Warsaw church. As Zsolt Aradi relates in his *Book of Miracles*:

'Hundreds of people saw a cloud forming above the altar, then enveloping the figure of the saint, who disappeared from their sight. In his place, they saw a celestial vision. A woman of great beauty, with radiant features, appeared and smiled at the worshippers... '

Holy clouds?

There are many such cases. On 3 October 1843, Charles Cooper, labouring in a field near Warwick, England, heard a rumbling in the sky. He looked up to see a strange cloud, below which hovered three 'perfectly white' figures, calling to him with 'loud and mournful' noises. Cooper assumed they were angels. Other witnesses, working in a field some 6 miles (9 kilometres) away, agreed that they had also seen the remarkable cloud reported by Cooper, although not all of them saw the 'angels'.

Another report concerns a sighting of an odd cloud that is at least as remarkable as those already described, and considerably better substantiated. It shows that clouds may assume very strange shapes under entirely natural conditions.

On the evening of 22 March 1870, the barque *Lady of the Lake* was cruising in the mid-Atlantic close to the equator when a curiously-shaped cloud appeared towards the south-south-east. The sky was blue with patches of cirro-cumulus cloud. This particular cloud was circular and shaped like a wheel with four spokes, one much thicker than the rest. From the centre protruded a fifth spoke, broader and more distinct than the others, with a curved end. The cloud was light grey in colour and had a tail similar to that of a comet. It was in sight for around 45 minutes.

Reports of such ring-shaped clouds, often rotating, are not uncommon and could have a logical scientific explanation based on the action of atmospheric vortices, or whirlwind effects. Whatever its cause, the sight of one is a spectacular and disquieting experience.

The countenance divine

Simulacra is the term given to the shadowy likenesses of natural objects that can be seen in fire, water, clouds, or damp patches on walls, floors or other surfaces. Among the most common are likenesses of Christ's face. Some of these are sometimes said to be more a testimony to people's capacity to see what they wish to see rather than truly anomalous phenomena, however.

The *Houston Post* of 23 April 1977, for example, reported that a certain church in Shamokin, Pennsylvania, USA, had become a place of pilgrimage as the result of the appearance on the altar of an image of the face of Christ.

An even more bizarre example was recorded in the

International Herald Tribune of 25 July 1978. Maria Rubo, who lived in a farming hamlet in southern New Mexico, had been rolling out a tortilla – a kind of cornmeal flat bread – when she noticed that the dough contained a face. It looked like that of Christ. What made the event more remarkable was that this tortilla did not deteriorate after four or five days, as most do. Local people regarded the tortilla as a 'miracle' and their priest consented to give it his blessing, but the Archbishop of Santa Fe feared the start of a cult and advised extreme caution.

One of the best-known of the Christ simulacra is alleged to have appeared as shadows in the snow. It was once widely circulated by the media and is impressive, but of dubious provenance. The popular version of its origin is that someone took a photograph of the snow to use up a roll of film, and recognised the image of Christ only after the film was developed. Some stories say that the photograph was taken by a 12-year-old girl; others that it was made by some Californians who wanted to record an unusual snowfall. But perhaps the most poetic version has it that, in 1938, a Norwegian woman prayed to God to send her proof of his existence, that as a consequence she was divinely inspired to take an entirely random photograph in her garden, and that this picture resulted.

Another famous 'face of Christ' appeared as a cloud formation. A photograph of it was allegedly taken by a serviceman in the US Air Force during the Korean War. The photographer did not notice the image when he took the picture of American and Communist aeroplanes in action, however.

Meanwhile, other natural 'visual coincidences' include a camel-shaped rock near Santa Fe in New Mexico and the apparent image of a human face in a stalactite cave at Wiehl, near Cologne, Germany. Certain photographs even suggest that the surface of Mars bears huge effigies of human countenances. Stranger still, it is said that the marks on the tail of a butterfly fish from Zanzibar read in old Arabic: 'There is no God but Allah.'

Such images are so compelling to most people that any explanation in terms of purely natural, random phenomena is bound to seem inadequate.

THE CURSE OF THE BOY KING

Is it mere coincidence that so many people have either died or fallen ill after contact with Tutankhamun's tomb?

On 30 April 1923, a small group of people gathered for a funeral on Beacon Hill, high up on the ridge of downland running across north-west Hampshire, in Britain. They were there to bury George Edward Stanhope Molyneux Herbert, fifth Earl of Carnarvon, at a spot that looked out over his home, Highclere Castle, and the spreading estate that he had owned.

The Earl had died in what many came to regard as strange circumstances. Over the years, he had paid for excavations that had led, just five months previously, to the discovery of the tomb of Tutankhamun with all the treasures that had been stored up to guarantee the King's well-being in the afterlife. Carnarvon's death, coming so soon after the find and so inexplicably, stirred up fantasies of a dreadful link across the centuries, of the young King reaching out to his tomb's despoiler – of the curse of Tutankhamun.

Carnarvon's involvement with the royal tomb dated back some 15 or 20 years. In 1901, while driving in the German spa of Bad Schwalbach, he had overturned his car. As a result of this accident, which badly damaged his chest, he had difficulty in breathing, and his doctor suggested that he should spend the winters somewhere warm and dry. In those days, Egypt was a popular destination, with Luxor a particularly fashionable resort, offering hotels, antiquities and many exciting excursions to see the excavations taking place in the Valley of the Kings.

As a result, Carnarvon became interested in Egyptology, returning year after year, and even trying his hand at archaeology. Then, in 1907, he took on 33-year-old Harold Carter as his adviser. Carter had come to Egypt at the age of 17, working as a draughtsman for archaeologists. He subsequently took up a post in the Antiquities Service and supervised excavations in the Valley of the Kings. Then, after a dispute in which he felt he was in the right, he resigned. For the next four years, he supported himself by guiding tourists through the Valley of the Kings and by selling watercolour sketches of the scene. Carnarvon paid him £400 a year. Their aim was to find unrifled graves that would yield a reward in collectable antiquities.

During the next 15 years, and throughout the upheavals of the First World War, Carter delved on Carnarvon's behalf, discovering the occasional interesting tomb but hardly turning up sufficient collectables to justify the investment, which would eventually total about £40,000. By 1922, Carnarvon wanted to call things off. Carter visited him at Highclere, persuaded him to authorise one more season's digging and, perhaps in celebration, bought himself a canary.

Amazing discovery

When he arrived back in Luxor at the end of October, his Egyptian workers told him that the yellow singing bird would bring luck. On 1 November, they began digging in the last untouched area of the Valley, a 22-acre (1-hectare) triangle. On 4 November, they found a sunken stairway entrance; and by the 5th, they knew it marked a sealed tomb. Carter cabled Carnarvon, who came out from England with his daughter, Evelyn. On 26 November, after clearing away all the rubble, they broke through the blocked doorway.

Later, the whole world was to marvel at the shrines and tombs; life-size figures of the King, with gilded kilt and head-dress; the golden throne with its magnificent inlaid scene depicting the King and his wife; the jewellery that is a heady combination of beaten gold and semi-precious stones; the inner coffin made of solid gold so heavy that it took eight men to lift it up; and the burnished golden mask on the mummy itself which, with its eyes of lapis lazuli, obsidian and quartz, and its decorated head-dress and beard, symbolised the dead King as the god Osiris, ruler of the dead.

Carter and Carnarvon now knew exactly what they had found – the virtually undisturbed resting place of King Tutankhamun. In the days that followed, they staged an official opening of the outer chamber, began their preparations to move out the contents, and also proudly announced their discovery to the world. But in the midst of the excitement, however, the Egyptian workers found cause for worry. The 'lucky' canary, left in Carter's house near the entrance to the Valley of the Kings, had been gobbled up by a cobra that had found its way into the bird's cage. There would be further deaths, they said.

The first of hundreds of thousands of tourists soon came flocking to the Valley of the Kings to gaze at the entrance to the tomb and to pester the discoverers to let them enter.

Carnarvon returned to England for a while to make some arrangements of his own, including the sale to *The Times* of the exclusive right to report developments. By the middle of February, however, he was back in Luxor again.

By now, both men were suffering from stress, since their relationship with the Egyptian government had deteriorated into a quarrel over who owned the find and who should have access to the tomb. Carter was also working long hours in dreadful conditions to record and preserve the goods that they had taken from the tomb. One evening, Carnarvon called on Carter at his house. The two men argued fiercely, and

Carter told Carnarvon to leave. Although Carnarvon later wrote a conciliatory letter, it is possible that this was the last conversation they ever had.

The Pharaoh's revenge

By the end of February, Carnarvon was clearly in poor health. He looked pale and exhausted; his teeth chipped and fell out; and his temperature soared as he was shaken by a fever that came and went. Early in March, he moved to Cairo, and for a while his condition improved. Then it worsened once again. His wife, Lady Almina, set out from England, and his son, Lord Porchester, from India. On 26 March, his secretary wrote to Carter to inform him that Carnarvon had blood poisoning. Carter, too, travelled to Cairo. By 4 April, all had gathered in the Continental Savoy Hotel. Carnarvon had long since sunk into a coma; and his wife, son, daughter and colleague were waiting for the end.

Just before 2 a.m., the nurse came in to say that Carnarvon had died. He was 57. At that point, the lights in the hotel flickered and went out, and all of Cairo was plunged into darkness as the electricity was cut off. Five minutes later, it came back on. The Cairo electricity supply had always been erratic, but no one ever did produce an explanation for that particular breakdown.

Back in England, at that same moment, Carnarvon's fox terrier, Susan, began to howl and then died, to the consternation of the Scottish housekeeper at Highclere Castle.

The legend of the curse took root in fertile ground. Almost immediately, newspapers began printing reports of the hieroglyphics carved above the entrance to the tomb that threatened: 'Death shall come to him who touches the tomb.' Some added that further warnings came to light within the tomb, among them this one: 'Death will slay with wings whoever disturbeth the peace of the Pharaohs.'

Since then, a number of archaeologists and tourists who have visited the tomb either have been taken ill or died soon after, although it could be argued that they were old or ill already, or that the combination of travel, dusty heat and excitement was just too much. Professor James Henry Breasted, one of the gathering at the opening of the inner chamber, experienced a feverish illness, although he carried on working in the tomb itself and lived another 12 years before dying at the age of 70. But Professor La Fleur paid a visit to the tomb on his first day in Luxor and died that very night, in the hotel room next door to Breasted. An American multi-millionaire, George Jay Gould, also died suddenly after developing a fever on the day that he visited the tomb. A. C. Mace, one of Carter's assistants, gave up the job in 1924 after attacks of fever and died in 1928. Another assistant, Richard Bethell, died of circulatory failure at the age of 45.

All these deaths could, of course, be explained by natural causes. Maybe bacteria were lurking among the stirred-up dust. A forensic scientist, Alfred Lucas, had taken samples the day after the opening of the inner chamber; but although one showed positive, he pronounced the bacteria harmless. Maybe the fungus that covered the walls of the tomb triggered allergies or infestation. Maybe, as with Legionnaire's disease, infection of the respiratory ducts affected mainly those whose breathing was shallow and irregular, whether from age or from weakness (as was certainly the case with Carnarvon), or who had heavily indulged in alcohol. It was even suggested that the ancient Egyptians used their knowledge of poisons to protect the secrets of their King.

The legend lives on

Further tales of ill-fortune coalesced around the major exhibition of Tutankhamun's relics that was staged in London in 1972, and that then went on to the United States. One of these concerns the death of Dr Gamal ed-Din Mehrez, Director-General of the Egyptian government's Department of Antiquities. He said that he did not believe in the curse, although he acknowledged that all the mysterious deaths connected with the tomb undoubtedly gave cause for thought. 'Look at me,' he said. 'All my life I've been involved with tombs and mummies. I am surely the best proof that it is all coincidence.' Just four weeks later, however, as the exhibits were on their way to London, he died suddenly of a severe stroke, aged only 54.

It has been suggested, however, that Carter himself had started the rumour about the curse to keep tourists and thieves from trying to enter the tomb. Carter was certainly capable of such a trick. During the opening of the inner chamber, he sent out a number of conflicting descriptions of what was happening in order to mislead those waiting journalists who were hoping to break an exclusive story granted to *The Times*. A word to the gullible could well have seemed an easy way of keeping crowds and criminals at bay.

So perhaps public attention produced an artificially heightened awareness of every unfortunate incident that has apparently confirmed the existence of the curse. Or should Tutankhamun have been left undisturbed after all?